THE ATTAKAPAS COUNTRY

ILE COPAL ("Sweet Gum Grove"), the plantation home of Governor Alexandre Mouton, was built about 1850 of brick made by the slaves on the plantation. This is a reproduction of a painting by A. Persac in 1860. The persons in the picture are members of the Governor's family. The original is owned by Mrs. Paul R. Breaux, grand-daughter of Governor Mouton. This picture is copyrighted by Mrs. Breaux and is used here by special permission.

THE ATTAKAPAS COUNTRY

A History of Lafayette Parish, Louisiana

By

HARRY LEWIS GRIFFIN

Gretna 1999

Copyright © 1959
By Harry Lewis Griffin
All rights reserved
ISBN 1-56554-509-5
First printing: 1959
Second printing: 1974

Manufactured in the United States of America
Published by Pelican Publishing Company, Inc.
1000 Burmaster Street, Gretna, Louisiana 70053

CONTENTS

INTRODUCTION by Edith Garland Dupré................ ix

Chapter
I	Physical Setting	3
II	Original Inhabitants	5
III	First White Settlers.............................	12
IV	Early Life and Social Affairs.....................	18
V	Territorial and Political Evolution of the Parish....	21
VI	Founding and Naming a City.....................	27
VII	Vermilionville Incorporated	33
VIII	Lafayette, One Hundred Years Ago................	39
IX	From Village to City.............................	56
X	The White League in Lafayette Parish............	65
XI	The Towns of the Parish.........................	72
XII	The Founding of Churches.......................	76
XIII	Transportation and Travel.......................	85
XIV	The Schools of City and Parish...................	93
XV	Finance and Industry............................	105
XVI	Communications	115
XVII	Doctors, Dentists and Disease....................	122
XVIII	Law and the Courts.............................	130
XIX	Lafayette Parish in War.........................	142
XX	The Negro in Lafayette Parish...................	147
XXI	The Flood of 1927..............................	153
XXII	Social Organizations	168
	Biographies and Genealogies.....................	183
	Appendix — Old Records, Early Militia Lists, Cattle Brands, Lists of Officials, Censuses, Killed in Wars, Statistics, etc....................	211
	Bibliography and Sources........................	252

LIST OF ILLUSTRATIONS

"Ile Copal"—Plantation Home of Gov. Alexandre Mouton		Frontispiece
Map of Lafayette, Louisiana		Page 2
Swanton's Map Showing Areas Occupied by Attakapas and Other Gulf Coast Indians		" 6
An Attakapas Indian	Opposite	Page 16
Attakapas Indians, 1735	"	" 17
Dr. Antoine Bordat	"	" 24
Basil Crow	"	" 24
Governor Alexandre Mouton	"	" 25
Alexandre Mouton, Grandson of the Governor	"	" 25
Original Plan of Vermilionville, 1824		Page 29
Michel Eloi Girard	Opposite	Page 40
Mrs. Maxime Crow Girard	"	" 40
Dr. Matthew Creighton and his Wife	"	" 41
Cornelius Voorhies, Jr.	"	" 41
Albert Voorhies	"	" 41
Felix Voorhies	"	" 41
Vermilionville Environs		Page 41
Armajean Reon, Last of Attakapas to Speak the Language	"	" 48
Scene in the Attakapas Country	"	" 49
Oaks at "Beau Sejour"	"	" 49
Map of Vermilionville about 1800		Page 50
Home of Charles Homer Mouton	Opposite	Page 56
Latiolais House	Between Pgs.	56 and 57
Magnolia Plantation	"	" 56 " 57
Home of Dr. Thomas B. Hopkins	"	" 56 " 57
Dr. Michel Eloi Girard's Home	Opposite	Page 57
Long Plantation Home	"	" 57
Governor Mouton's Town House	"	" 72
Oakbourne Plantation Home	Between Pgs.	72 and 73
The Old Moss House	"	" 72 " 73
Myrtle Plantation Home	"	" 72 " 73
Percy Girard House	"	" 72 " 73
Arceneaux House	Opposite	Page 73
Plantation Home—Antoine Mouton	"	" 88
Richard Chargois House	"	" 88
Seller's House—Split into Two Houses, 1835	"	" 89
Residence of Jules Revillon	"	" 104
Couret House	"	" 104
Eastin Home	"	" 105
Residence of Charles Mouton	"	" 105
Pierre Gerac's Residence	"	" 116
Home of Edward Mouton, Jr.	"	" 117

An Old Acadian House	Opposite	Page	132
Scene on Bayou Teche	"	"	132
School of Mrs. Homer Bailey	"	"	133
Store of Joachem Revillon	"	"	133
Group of Confederate Veterans, 1885	"	"	144
Class at Public School, 1896	"	"	145
Picnic Group at Chargois Springs, 1898	"	"	160
Jefferson Caffery	"	"	161
Most Rev. Jules Jeanmard, Bishop of Lafayette	"	"	161
Rev. Charles Burton Mouton	"	"	161
Lombard's Hotel and Bar	"	"	176
"Little Willie's" Bus	"	"	176
Parish Jail, 1869	Between	Pgs. 176 and	177
Recorder's Office, 1860	"	" 176 "	177
City Hotel, 1845	"	" 176 "	177
Orleans Hotel, 1880	"	" 176 "	177
Cottage Hotel, 1890	Opposite	Page	177
Begnaud's Saloon, 1855	"	"	177
Constantin's Livery Stable	"	"	192
Office of the Justice of the Peace, 1880	Between	Pgs. 192 and	193
The "Kill" from a Deer Hunt, 1925	"	" 192 "	193
Store of John O. Mouton, 1868	"	" 192 "	193
Store of Benjamin Falk, 1865	"	" 192 "	193
Office of "Lafayette Gazette", 1895	Opposite	Page	193
The Bakery, 1885	"	"	193
Lafayette Court House Built in 1859	"	"	208
First Episcopal Church, 1901	Between	Pgs. 208 and	209
Statue Honoring Gov. Mouton	"	" 208 "	209
Mausoleum of Governor Jacques Dupre and Wife at Opelousas, 1830	"	" 208 "	209
Statue of General Alfred Mouton at Lafayette	Opposite	Page	209
Section of Confederate Battle Flag	"	"	209
Map of Early Survey of a Land Grant		Page	217
Mardi Gras Scenes at Lafayette	Opposite	"	224
Mardi Gras Proclamation, Lafayette, 1877	Between	Pgs. 224 and	225
Dr. Edwin L. Stephens	"	" 224 "	225
Catholic Churches of Lafayette	"	" 224 "	225
Sacred Heart Academy at Grand Coteau	Opposite	Page	225
Mt. Carmel Convent, 1873	"	"	225
Scene on Southwestern Louisiana Institute Campus	"	"	240
Members of First Faculty of Southwestern Louisiana Institute	Opposite	Page	241
Southwestern L. I. Cadet Corp, 1906	"	"	241
Brands of Cattlemen	Pages 241, 242, 243		
Members of Cast at Performance of "Monsieur Beaucaire"—S. L. I., 1902	Opposite	Page	256
First Football Team of S. L. I., 1903	"	"	256
Flood of 1927	"	"	257

INTRODUCTION

Harry Lewis Griffin, Dean Emeritus of the College of Liberal Arts at Southwestern Louisiana Institute, was born near Clarksburg, West Virginia, of distinguished Virginia ancestry.

After graduating from the University of West Virginia, he studied at the University of Chicago where in due time he received the degree of Doctor of Jurisprudence. While he was in Chicago, he made the acquaintance of Messrs. H. C. Bond and A. W. Bittle, who as members of the Southwestern Faculty, spoke so highly of him to Dr. Stephens that his appointment as Professor of History and Political Science followed immediately.

From the start he devoted himself whole-heartedly to building up his department and to contributing to the rising standards of the college.

In 1921, he was named the first dean of the newly organized College of Liberal Arts which at that time included the departments of Agriculture and Engineering, each of these destined to become later a college in its own right.

One of his finest achievements was his wise and zealous work that led to Southwestern's being accredited by the Southern Association of Colleges.

This is what Dr. Stephens had to say in appreciation of his work. "I must especially mention the able management of Dean Harry L. Griffin in the presentation of Southwestern's case before the various committees of the Association of Southern Colleges."

To try further to do him complete justice, I shall borrow from an unknown author a paragraph which expresses forcefully what he has meant to Southwestern.

"As Dean of Southwestern's College of Liberal Arts his influence for good has been far-reaching. Not only has he worked valiantly to make it a highly respected institution; but as a counsellor to students, he has exercised a profound and benevolent influence in the lives of thousands of students who have enjoyed and appreciated his guidance."

He has always devoted himself to building up the Department of Foreign Languages. He has unceasingly urged upon his students the study of foreign languages especially French.

In both the Parish and the City of Lafayette he has always played a vital part. It was he who wrote the history of Lafayette Parish from which were taken the episodes for the pageant "The Attakapas Trail" that was staged in 1923 to celebrate the hundredth anniversary of the Parish of Lafayette. For the City of Lafayette Centennial pageant, he wrote a history of the city from which scenes were selected and dramatized. He directed all phases of the pageant.

He is a charter member of France Amérique de la Louisiane Acadienne. He has always been deeply absorbed in the Acadians and their history. Besides having the interest of an historian, his feelings for them are deeper because of family ties. The crowning event of his association with the Acadians was his marriage to Lucile Meredith Mouton, the generous and charming great-granddaughter of the first Democratic Governor of Louisiana, Alexandre Mouton.

In closing, let my last word be an appreciation of Dean Griffin the man, who stands out because of his high principles and integrity and whose example should long be remembered by all who put their faith in Justice and in Truth.

Edith Garland Dupre

THE ATTAKAPAS COUNTRY

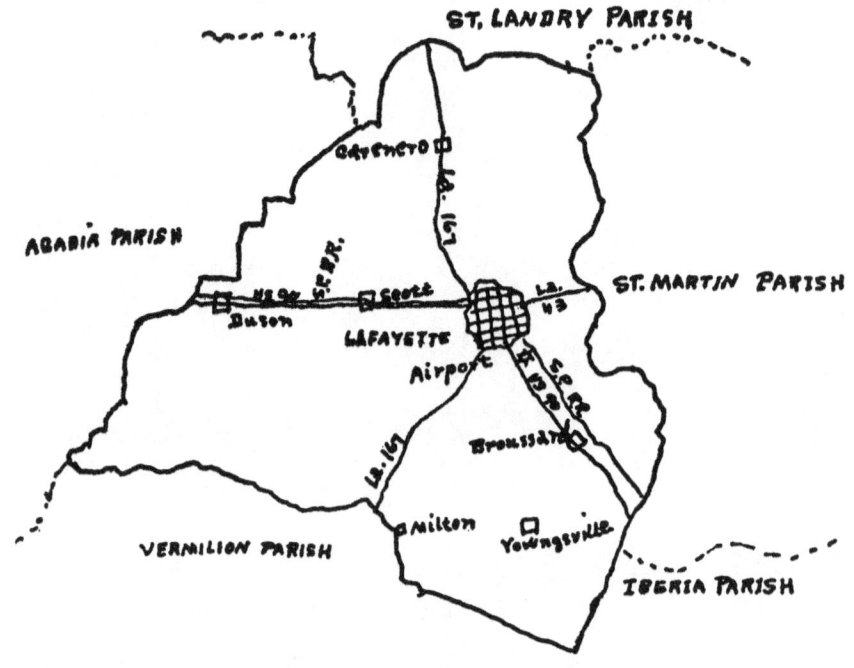

CHAPTER I

PHYSICAL SETTING

The Parish of Lafayette, of which the City of Lafayette is the administrative seat, is situated in the center of a vast region commonly referred to as Southwest Louisiana. This region, designated in the early records of Louisiana as the Attakapas and Opelousas Districts, includes all that territory that presently comprises the Parishes of Acadia, Evangeline, Iberia, St. Landry, St. Martin, St. Mary, Vermilion and Lafayette. It is bounded on the north by the Avoyelles District, on the east by the swirling waters of the Atchafalaya River, on the south by Bays of Atchafalaya, Côte Blanche, Weeks and Vermilion, all of which merge into the blue waters of the Gulf of Mexico; and on the west by the slow-moving Mermentau River.

Running from north to south through St. Landry, St. Martin, Lafayette Parishes and into Vermilion Parish, is a range of gently undulating hills which form a kind of backbone to the region. From this range of hills the land slopes gently into the bottoms and swamps of the Atchafalaya River on the east, into the sea marshes on the south, into the wide flat prairie on the west, and into the palmetto flats and alluvial bottoms of the Avoyelles district on the north. The entire region is drained by the Rivers Atchafalaya and Mermentau and the Bayous* Vermilion and Têche, all of which flow generally from north to south and find their outlets in the Gulf of Mexico.

The elevation of this territory ranges from thirteen feet above sea level in St. Mary Parish to thirty-nine at Lafayette and fifty-nine in St. Landry. The rainfall varies from three inches in January to thirteen inches in July; and the mean temperature from forty-nine in January to eighty-two degrees in July.

This region is the richest in the state and by Longfellow was

---

*Local residents call these smaller streams a "bayou" instead of a creek or river.

appropriately named the Eden of Louisiana. The fertile soil in this rich area is suitable for many varieties of crops. On the central ridge cotton is the principal crop; to the east sugar cane prevails; and to the west rice is produced in tremendous quantities. Over the whole area cattle, corn, sweet potatoes and hay thrive as important crops. Fruits, pecans, and vegetables are grown in abundance.

The eight parishes whose history, traditions and people have so many elements in common, and of which Lafayette is the center, contained in 1950 an industrious, thriving population of 354,087. The earliest settlers in these parishes were for the most part Acadians exiled from Nova Scotia in 1755 by their English conquerors. The basic population is composed, therefore, of the descendants of this sturdy race, whose speech, religion and customs still reflect the influence of the mother country, France. The cotton industry in the eighteen-thirties brought in English speaking planters from the South Atlantic states; the rise of the rice industry in the eighteen-nineties brought many settlers from the wheat farms of the midwest, and the rise of the oil industry in the nineteen-thirties and forties has added from all over the United States many industrial minded citizens to the ever expanding population. Add to these racial elements a sprinkling of persons of Spanish, German, Italian, Jewish and Assyrian origin one finds in Southwest Louisiana representatives of the principal races and cultures of the Western world living in unity and cooperation.

Lafayette Parish proper has all the climatic and soil characteristics common to the entire region. Practically all the crops and products described above are produced in this parish. It is cut into nearly two equal parts by the Vermilion Bayou which flows from north to south and empties into Vermilion Bay, thirty-five miles south of Lafayette. East of the bayou the territory is rolling and is known as the Cote Geleé or frozen hills. That part of the parish that lies to the north between Bayous Vermilion and Carencro is known as Beau Bassin. West of Bayou Vermilion the country stretches to the west and southwest in the form of a wide prairie. To the eye of the tourist the Cote Geleé hills, the bottoms of Beau Bassin and the rolling prairies of the west present a view of ever changing beauty.

CHAPTER II

ORIGINAL INHABITANTS

The earliest known inhabitants of the part of Louisiana which is the subject of this history were the Attakapas Indians. As their name indicates they were supposed to eat their prisoners of war. At one time they were very powerful and made themselves feared by all the surrounding tribes of Indians. Tradition has it that neighboring tribes formed a league for the purpose of resisting their aggressions. There followed then a war of extermination. After a few preliminary fights, according to Indian tradition, the forces of the two enemies met in a great battle on a hill about three miles west of the present town of St. Martinville. There the hated Attakapas were completely overwhelmed and nearly annihilated. The remnants of the once powerful tribe, now reduced to a harmless condition, were either incorporated into the victorious tribes or allowed to remain unmolested in the land of their former greatness. A few of their degenerate descendants may still be seen in the swamps around Grand Lake near Franklin. This decisive battle occurred a short time before this region was first visited by the white man.

There have been handed down to us a number of interesting Indian legends. One of them tells us how Bayou Teche got its name. It was told that in early Indian days a huge snake was seen on the banks of the bayou. Its great size, poisonous breath and the lashing of its tail when infuriated struck terror into the hearts of all Indians in the surrounding country. Finally a great body of warriors assembled for the purpose of killing it, but it was some time before they could summon sufficient courage to approach the terrifying reptile. At last, however, the snake was dispatched with clubs, after the warriors had fatally wounded it by piercing its body with many arrows. To commemorate their victory the Indians gave to the stream the name Tenche or Têche, meaning snake.

To the Indians the lake near St. Martinville, which we now know by the name, Catahoula, was a sacred body of water. In their

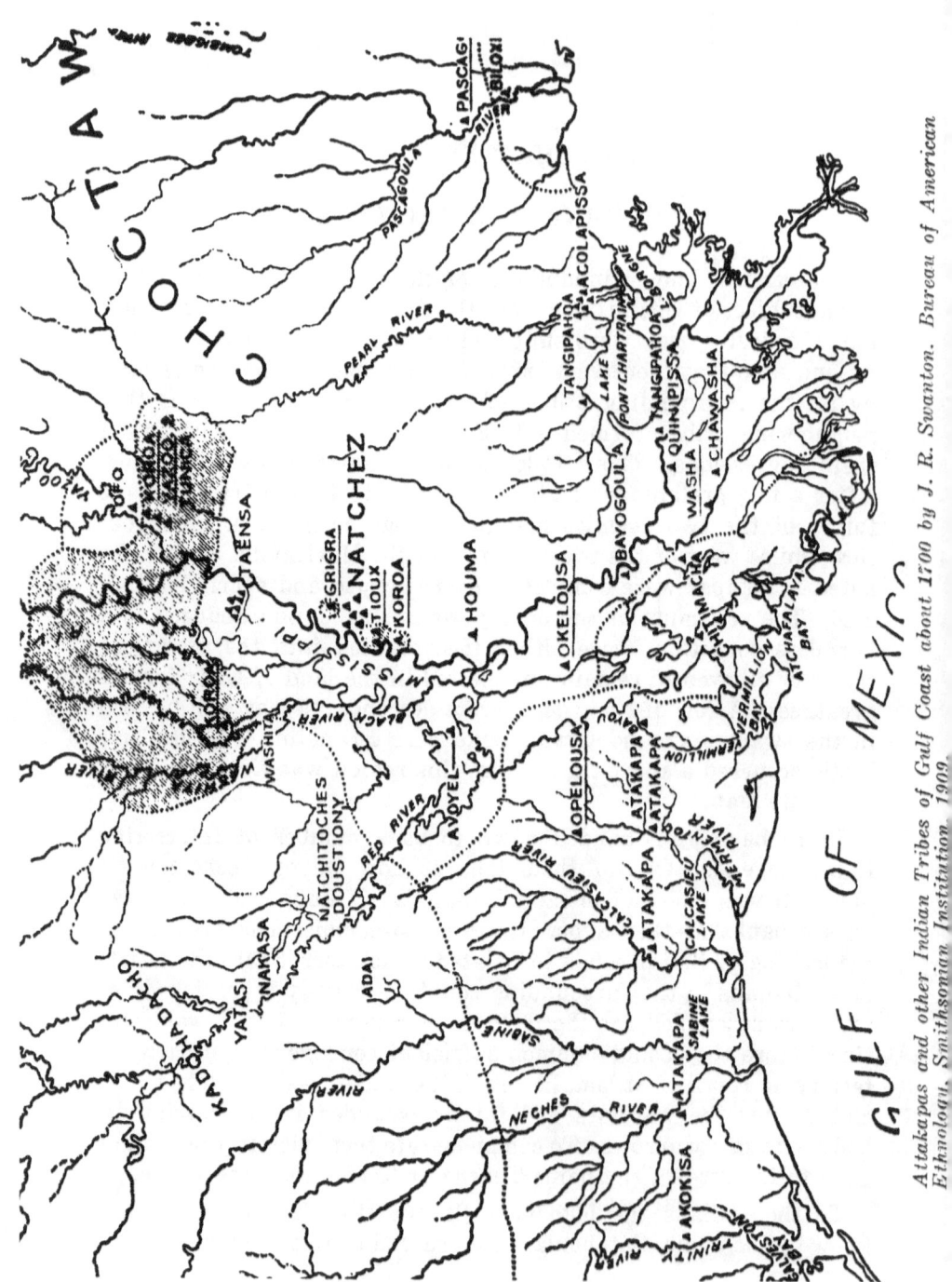

Attakapas and other Indian Tribes of Gulf Coast about 1700 by J. R. Swanton. Bureau of American Ethnology, Smithsonian Institution, 1909.

language the name Catahoula meant sacrifice. Under the mighty live-oaks standing on the high banks of this beautiful clear lake the Indians gathered to offer up to the Great Spirit their sacrifice in propitiation of their sins. Beneath its pure waters they plunged their bodies to be cleansed of moral and physical impurities. Into its sacred waves they dipped their amulets and arrows to make them effective against their enemies. If by chance one of their number were drowned while performing these sacred rites, it was a sign of the displeasure of the great Manitou, and was regarded as a punishment for some crime committed by the unhappy victim. Every Indian regarded it a sacred duty to make a pilgrimage to this holy lake and was unhappy if it were not his privilege to do so.

These Indians, like most of their kinsmen, were not civilized. Their culture was that of the rough stone age, as their weapons and implements were made of roughly shaped pieces of flint, stone or bone. They lived usually in crude huts, huddled together in miserable villages. The men spent most of their time hunting, fishing or fighting while the women remained at home to do the work of house and field. The men were, however, skilled hunters and the women acquired the art of making pottery and baskets. Their religion consisted in worshipping objects of nature, such as the moon and sun, and the spirits of departed ancestors. Their dead were often buried in large mounds in which were placed the weapons and trinkets of the deceased warriors. The remains of some of these mounds may still be seen along the high banks of the Bayous Têche and Vermilion.

The following description of the Attakapas Indians and their history is taken from Swanton's "Indian Tribes of the Lower Mississippi Valley."

> The name of this tribe is Choctaw, signifying "man-eater," and indicates the unsavory reputation which the tribe had acquired among Mississippi river people. Many of the early maps designate southwestern Louisiana and the entire Texas coast as a country occupied by "wandering cannibal tribes," and Atakapa itself is often thought to have been employed in a general, indefinite sense. As a matter of fact, however, it is never known to have been applied to any Indians except those between Vermilion and Galveston bays, i.e., to those constituting what is now called the Atakapan linguistic stock. In a political sense it came to designate a district embracing the present parishes of St. Mary, Iberia, St. Martin, Lafayette, and Vermilion. From this it might seem as if the Atakapa had once occupied the entire region, but according to the best

evidence St. Mary and the eastern parts of Iberia and St. Martin were in Chitimacha territory. On the other hand, the Atakapa extended very much beyond these limits to the westward over what are now the parishes of Calcasieu, Cameron, Acadia, and parts of St. Landry, then included in the district of Opelousas.

As the Atakapa country lay at some distance from the first centers of colonization, it was not encroached upon to any great extent until late in the eighteenth century. At that time there appear to have been three main bands of Atakapa in Louisiana occupying the same number of principal river valleys. The easternmost were on Vermilion river and bay. Their chief village seems to have been above Abbeville, but there is said to have been a smaller one lower down. The head chief of this division in the latter part of the eighteenth century is called Kinemo, Kanimo, Skunnemoke, or Escanimon. Ashnoya and his son Bernard also appear frequently as parties to the sale of lands in the same neighborhood and probably belonged to the same division, though they may have had a separate village.* In November, 1760, it is recorded that a Mr. Fusilier de la Clair purchased from Rinemo [Kinemo], chief of the Atakapa village, called in French "Lamonier," the said village and land depending thereon of 2 leagues in front from north to south, limited on the west by the river Vermilion and on the east by the river Teche. About the same time three or four other purchases were made from the Atakapa Indians, by which a very large proportion of the land of that district and nearly or quite all of the valuable lands on the river Teche were embraced. The Spanish governor, O'Reilly, however, passed regulations or ordinances by which no grant of land in Opelousas, Atakapas, or Natchitoches, could exceed 1 league square, and this ordinance appears to have been applied to a certain degree to purchases already made. Many tracts of land were purchased from the Atakapa Indians about the time Louisiana was transferred to the United States, and some subsequent to that change at a time when it was known on good information that those Indians were reduced to a single village, the inhabitants of which were short of one hundred. In some instances six or eight distinct tracts were sold by the same individual Indian.

In spite of the sales above alluded to, the Vermilion village was not abandoned until early in the last century. In 1779 this band furnished 60 men to Galvez's expedition against the British forts on the Mississippi.

The next important band of Atakapa toward the west lived on Mermentou river and its branches. They furnished 120 men to Galvez's expedition. In 1787 we are informed that the

---
*According to the Chitimacha there was once an Atakapa village on the site of Loreauville.

principal Atakapa village in that district was at the "Island of Woods," later known as "the Island of Lacasine," from an Indian reputed to be its chief. It extended the entire length of this island, but the principal settlement was at the upper end. About 1799 it was abandoned and the people moved to a village on the Nementou (Mermentou). It was probably shortly after this that Lacasine was succeeded by Célestine la Tortue. The latter appears to have been before that time chief of a village "on the prairie of Nezpique." His father, who had been chief before him, was named La Tortue, whence the son's last name. Mention is also made of a chief Nementou, but it is uncertain whether this was the native name of Célestine, a title derived from the name of his village, or another person altogether. It is stated plainly that this was the last Atakapa village among the eastern Atakapa, and Indians are cited as living here down to 1836.* Later a few at least went west to reside with the Calcasieu band, but most appear to have scattered. At Washington, La., is a woman whose father belonged to the Vermilion band, and somewhere in Oklahoma is another eastern Atakapa named Felix Wartell.

The Calcasieu band lived along the river of that name and the lakes through which it flows. A characteristic scene in the old Atakapa country is shown. Nearly all of the surviving Atakapa belong to this band. The survivors were interviewed by Doctor Gatschet in 1885 and a considerable vocabulary of their language collected, besides several texts. In 1907 and 1908 the writer visited them and found that there are still nine who remember something of the language. Almost all of these are living apart, however, and they use it so seldom that old grammatical distinctions are being lost or confused. It will not be long, therefore, before it sinks to the level of a vocabulary and finally disappears. The following are the names of those who still speak Atakapa: Teet Verdine and Eliza Verdine, his sister, who lives near Westlake, La.; Armojean Reon and Mrs. Delia Morse, who are in Lake Charles, but in different parts of the city; Delphine Williams, wife of J. R. Williams, Beaumont, Tex., and Ellen Sclovon or Esclovon, sisters of Armojean Reon's mother; Eugene Reon, brother of Armojean, a Sanctification preacher, last reported from Wichita, Kans.; Mary Jones, *née* Cameron, Armojean's cousin, wife of a preacher of the same sect; and Felix Wartell, already referred to, whose mother, Victorine, belonged to the eastern Atakapa, and who at one time took up land in Oklahoma.

From the statements of various writers it appears that there were representatives of this stock on the Sabine. On the Neches and lower Trinity, as well as the country between, was a small tribe called Orcoquisac by the Spaniards. A mis-

---

*Most of the information in what goes before has been obtained from the Amer. State Papers Relating to Public Lands, III, 96, 114, 1834.

sion was founded among them, but lasted only a short time. This tribe became noted as that among which M. de Belle-Isle was abandoned and among whom he lived for a number of years. Unfortunately he has not left a record of any of the words of their language, and we are unable to affirm their relationship positively, but there is good reason to believe that it was with the Atakapa of Louisiana. There can be little question that it differed from that of any of their other neighbors. In 1805, according to Sibley, the Atakapa numbered about 80 men, including 30 Tunica and Houma who had settled among them. They seem to have lived on by themselves in the same region until gradually reduced and exterminated by the advance of the white settlements.

From mission records recently examined by Professor Bolton, of the University of Texas, it appears probable that the Bidai, hitherto supposed to be of Caddoan stock, were affiliated with the Atakapa, and that the Deadoses and other tribes, of which little more than the names survive, were also connected with them.

All that we know of the ethnology of the Atakapa is contained in Duralde's letter cited already in connection with the Chitimacha. The Atakapa section is as follows:

> The Atacapas pretend that they are come out of the sea, that a prophet or man inspired by God laid down the rules of conduct to their first ancestors (*pères*), which consisted in not doing any evil. They believe in an author of all things: that those who do well go above, and that those who do evil descend under the earth in the shades. They speak of a deluge which swallowed up men, animals, and the land, and it was only those who resided along a high land or mountain (that of San Antonio, if we may judge) who escaped this calamity.
>
> According to their law a man ceases to bear his own name as soon as he has a child born, and he is then called 'the father of such a boy,' giving the name of the child. If the child dies the father again assumes his own name. The women alone are charged with the labors of the field and of the household.
>
> The mounds according to them were intended to elevate and distinguish the dwellings of the chiefs, and were thrown up under their supervision by the women. * * *
>
> Many years before the discovery of the elephant in the bayou called Carancro an Atakapas savage had informed a man who is at present in my service in the capacity of cow-herd that the ancestors of his nation transmitted [the story] to their descendants that a beast of enormous size had perished either in this bayou or in one of the two water courses a short distance from it without their being able to indicate the true place, the antiquity of the event having without doubt made them forget it. The fact has realized the tradition.

This was written at Atakapas (now Franklin), April 23, 1802, and therefore applies particularly to the eastern Atakapa, or Hiye'kiti, as the Lake Charles people called them. Whether the beliefs of the western Atakapa were the same we shall probably never know, but as some of the Chitimacha stories collected by the writers were known to them, it is probable that there was comparatively little difference. Dialectically, however, there was some divergence, judging by a comparison of Duralde's vocabulary with that obtained by Gatschet.

CHAPTER III

FIRST WHITE SETTLERS

It is not known definitely who were the first white settlers in what is now Lafayette Parish. Prior to the cession of Louisiana by France to Spain in 1762 there were scattered over the Attakapas region a few trappers, ranchmen and smugglers. In 1769 the population of the entire district was only 409, according to a census taken in that year by acting Governor O'Reilly. These probably consisted of French Canadians, English traders from the Carolinas, and French trappers from the settlements around New Orleans. The first considerable influx of population began soon after 1763.

In 1755 the Acadians had been cruelly exiled from their native homes in Nova Scotia* by their English governors, and scattered among the English colonies on the Atlantic coast from Maine to Georgia. These exiles were not content to be absorbed into the then hated English populations of the colonies, and naturally turned their faces toward Louisiana, where lived their kinsmen, speaking their language and worshipping according to their own beloved religion. Just when the first Acadians reached Louisiana cannot be definitely stated. There is a tradition in the Mouton family that Salvador Mouton settled in St. James Parish in 1756. Gayarre, the Louisiana historian, wrote that Acadians from the American colonies settled on the left bank of the Mississippi River as early as 1758. It is entirely possible that a few hardy Acadians did escape from the colonies, cross the Allegheny Mountains, and follow trappers and traders to Louisiana. Some of the refugees in Canada may have done the same. According to Judge Voorhies, the party, with which came the character known to the literary world as Evangeline, left Maryland and crossed the Allegheny Mountains to the waters of the Cumberland River. There they felled trees in the forest, built barges, and, embarking on them with their scanty possessions, floated down the Cumberland to the Ohio, thence to

---
*Known originally as Acadia.

the Mississippi and down the swift waters of that stream to a point near the present town of Plaquemine, Louisiana. From there they wound their way through swamps and tortuous bayous until they came to the Têche. On the placid waters of this bayou they soon reached the Poste des Attakapas, now St. Martinville.* There they were cared for by officials of the Spanish government until they could be assigned lands in the surrounding region.

There was no heavy influx of Acadian exiles into this section of Louisiana, however, until after the close of the French and Indian War in 1763.† After that they came from the American Colonies, Canada, Nova Scotia, San Domingo, and France in a steady stream, which reached its crest during the period of 1780 to 1787, when the French government gave up its attempts to keep in France the 4500 Acadian refugees who had found their way back to the mother country, and decreed that they might go wherever they desired. This movement continued despite the fact that, by the Treaty of Fontainbleau, signed November 2, 1762, France had ceded to Spain all of Louisiana including the so-called Isle of Orleans. The news of the transfer did not reach Louisiana until some time in 1764. One can only imagine the chagrin and disappointment of the newly arrived Acadians when they learned that they were to become subjects of Spain and not of their beloved France.

It was not until April 4, 1764 that we find any official announcement of the coming of the Acadians to Louisiana. On that date, according to the journal of d'Abadie, there arrived on a ship from New York several Acadian families numbering twenty persons. A few months later Foucault announced the arrival of a ship from San Domingo with one hundred ninety-three on board. He described them as pitiful and poor. He said he looked after their needs until he could send them to the Attakapas and Opelousas regions; and one finds others arriving with increasing frequency. On April 24, 1765 the military commander at New Orleans reported the arrival of several Acadian families, and that more were expected every day. He had planned to settle them along the Mississippi River, but, because the land there overflowed he decided to send them to the Opelousas and Attakapas prairies, where cattle raising promised to be profitable. Aubry, acting governor between the French and Spanish regimes, stated that the Attakapas District was sixty or eighty leagues from New Orleans by way of the

*Often misspelled St. Martinsville.
†Known in Europe as the Seven Years War.

Mississippi River and Bayou Plaquemines, and the trip required six days. On April 20, another group of Acadians arrived and, after supplying their needs in the amount of 15,000 pounds he sent them to the Attakapas District. With this last group was sent an engineer to assign to the newcomers appropriate lands along navigable streams in such a way that they could be of help to each other in the clearing of land, building of homes and opening up of roads. Some of these Acadians brought card money issued to them by such governors of Canada as Bigot, Vergor, and Niverville, and bearing dates from 1752 5o 1760. While this had no value in Louisiana, it is interesting to note that it bore as payees such names as Broussard, Trahan, Braud, Bernard, Boudrot, Poirier, Bourgeois, Roy, LeBlanc, Thibaudeau, Arceneau, Guilbeau, Cormier and Doucet.

In his correspondence of 1765 Aubry, having just received sixty Acadian families from San Domingo, and having heard that three hundred men, women and children were on their way up the river to New Orleans, and that four thousand more Acadians might be expected, said it appeared that Louisiana was about to become a new Acadia. The prospect of so many at that time worried him and Foucault because they were not prepared to take care of so many, since provisions were low and it was reported that some of them had smallpox. However Aubry described them as brave, hard working, and faithful to their county and religion. He expressed the idea also that they will accomplish marvels if given assistance. His worries did not end there, however, because in February 1765, 230 more arrived. They were followed by 80 others on May 4 and a day later by 48 families, all of whom were sent to the Opelousas district. Thus were founded the thriving Acadian centers of St. Martinville in St. Martin Parish, and Opelousas in St. Landry Parish.

It should be noted here that, though Louisiana became Spanish territory in 1762, Spain did not take firm possession of the territory until 1768 when Spain sent Governor O'Reilly to crush the growing opposition to Spanish authority and establish securely Spanish power in the territory. In the interim French governors d'Abadie and Aubry administered the colony under Spanish supervision. Spain was anxious to build up her newly acquired possession and from the beginning encouraged new settlers, including the Acadians, to establish homes in her territory. To these she granted land without cost and in many instances furnished the pioneers with livestock and farm implements.

During the French Revolution of 1789 many of the French Royalists fled the revolution and sought safety and new homes in Louisiana. Among them one finds in this area such names as St. Julien, de la Houssaye, deClouet, de St. Clair and deBlanc. During this period also, and thereafter, as the fame of Louisiana spread in France, there came to this district Frenchmen with such names as Beraud, Gerac, Lacoste, Estilette, Francez, Girard, Rousseau, Trahan, Verot and Vigneaux. These early settlers came direct from France and not from Acadia. Names typical of the Acadians were Breaux, Guidry, LeBlanc, Broussard, Martin, Arceneaux, Mouton, Doucet, Robichaux, Landry and Richard. After the purchase of Louisiana by the United States in 1803, early settlers in this parish from Kentucky, South Carolina, Georgia and Mississippi gave us the names Creighton, Clegg, Cade, Smedes, Wallace, Webb and Hutchinson.

An interesting sidelight on the beginning of the cattle industry in this area is found in a contract made in New Orleans on April 3, 1765 between a certain Captain Dauterive and a group of Acadian chieftains, namely, Joseph Broussard, dit Beausoleil, Alexandre Broussard, Joseph Guilbeau, Jean Duga, Oliver Thibaudau, Pierre Arcenaud, and Victor Broussard. In this contract Dauterive engaged to furnish each Acadian family with five cows and one bull for six consecutive years, and replace all losses during the first year, on the following conditions: the contract may be rescinded after three years with the increase being equally divided; proceeds of the sale of cattle before the expiration of the contract shall be equally divided; after six years Captain Dauterive is to receive back the same number of cattle given, with one half the increase. How many Acadian families took advantage of this contract is not known but it is certain that some of the signers did move into the Attakapas district.

From the foregoing discussion it seems clear that many of the first permanent white settlers in Lafayette Parish were Acadians. The French and Spanish officials granted lands freely along the bayous Carencro and Vermilion, and soon Acadians originally sent to the Poste des Attakapas and Opelousas began to settle along these streams and their tributaries. The average size of the land grants was six or eight arpents* front on a stream with a depth of 40

---

*Arpent — a French land unit slightly less than an acre.

arpents; but in the Opelousas and Attakapas districts, where cattle raising was popular, grants of a square league were authorized. Where the land was less than a league in depth, however, then a grant of two leagues front with a depth of half a league might be made; but no grant of forty-two arpents front and depth would be made to any person who was not the owner of one hundred head of horned cattle, a few horses and sheep, and two slaves.

One of the first settlers to make a permanent home in Lafayette was Andrew Martin, who took up lands in the third ward, probably along what is now known as Moss Street Extension. He was an exiled Acadian and soon engaged in raising cattle. Many of his descendants still live in this parish, some in the area where he settled. His pastures were the boundless grass covered prairies, and he used Indians as herders. Soon his cattle were numbered by the thousands. It was said that he could speak the language of the Indians, was their equal in the chase, and when occasion demanded, dared to slay them. Nor was his good wife less fearless than he in the face of danger from the Indians. On one occasion, it was related, her husband lay sick and helpless in bed. An Indian came to their house and demanded taffia (whisky) which Mrs. Martin refused to give him. Drawing a long knife the savage swore by the "graves of his fathers" that he would have taffia or kill the sick man who lay there helpless in bed. But the "pale face squaw" was equal to the occasion, and, grabbing a pestle from a heavy mortar, she struck him such a blow on the head that his skull was crushed and he died instantly.

About the same time that Andrew Martin came to this community Jean and Marin Mouton settled on Bayou Carencro. The site of Jean Mouton's home on Bayou Carencro is a few miles north of the main highway from Carencro to Sunset. On it is a part of the original dwelling, surrounded with magnificent live oaks. They were the sons of Salvador Mouton who had settled in St. James Parish in 1756. Jean Mouton soon became possessed of vast lands in Lafayette Parish, including much of the area on which the city of Lafayette now stands. He traded with the Indians who liked him for his fair dealings. He wore a chapeau or hat while his brother Marin wore a homespun capuchon or cap. To this day the descendants of Jean Mouton are called Chapeau Moutons. It is said that Jean Mouton was big both of body and heart being good natured and kind to all. It was recorded that he treated his slaves so kindly that he made a practice of buying other slaves

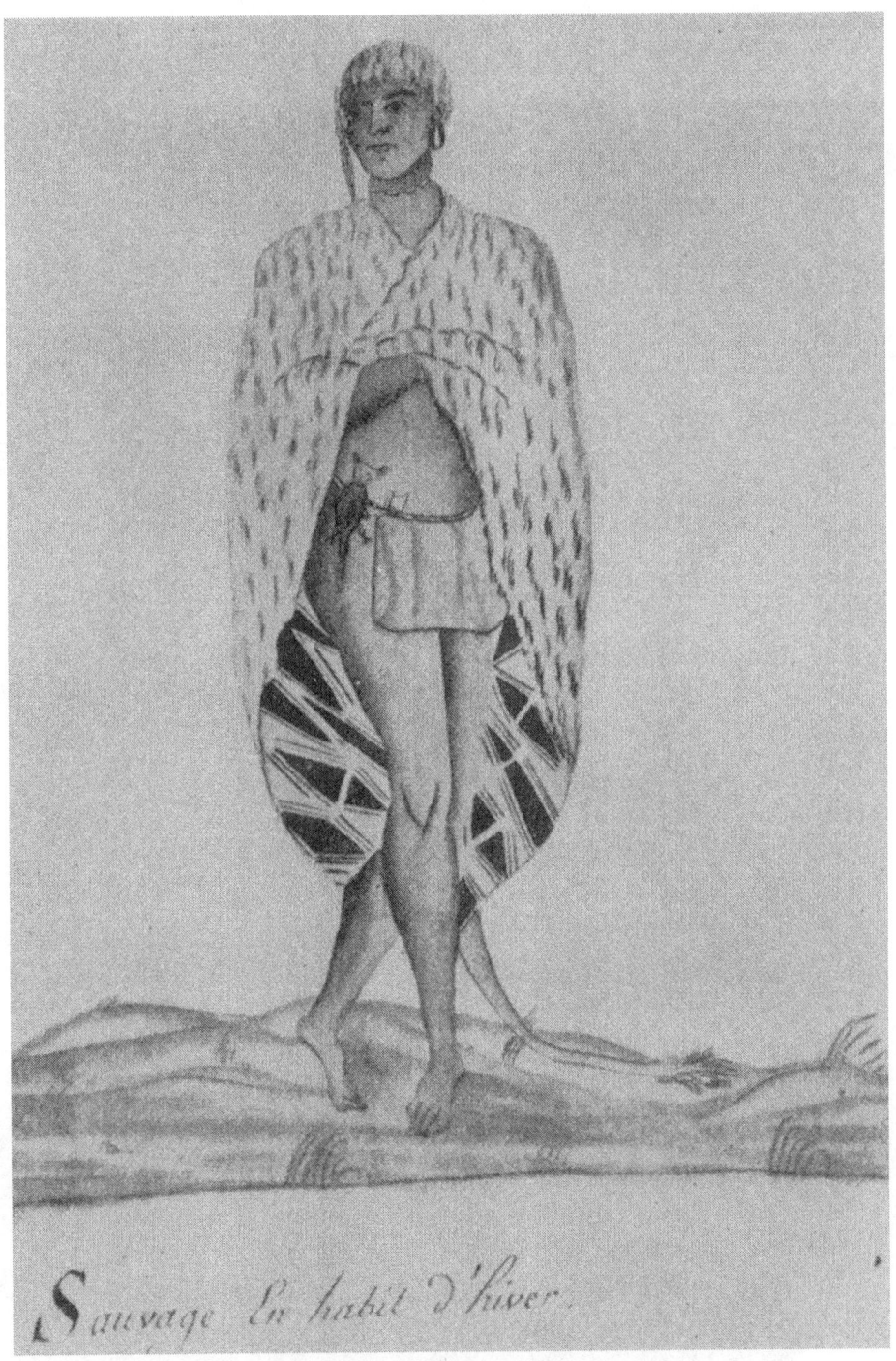

AN ATTAKAPAS INDIAN — 1735

Bushnell theorizes that this may be an Attakapas Indian on the basis that he or his costume resembles the man labelled "Atakapas" in the group picture on next page. The Indian above is a man of Lower Louisiana in winter dress. Buffalo skins, dressed and becoming soft and pliable without removing the hair, were used throughout the Mississippi Valley in winter. The sketch shows a robe decorated with a simple design in red and black. From a drawing by A. DeBatz in Peabody Museum, Harvard. (Courtesy of Smithsonian Institution)

"During the year. 1735 the French took many Illinois Indians to lower Louisiana to assist in the war against the Chickasaw. From the drawing it is evident that not only warriors but women and children made the long journey down the Mississippi. In the sketch the chief, on the extreme left, is shown with his right hand resting on the head of a Whooping Crane (Grus Americana) which may indicate that the bird has been domesticated. This would agree with Lawson's statement about the Congaree of North Carolina: 'They take storks and cranes before they can fly and breed them as tame and familiar as dung-hill fowls.'

The Atakapas is represented holding a calumet in his right hand and a small pipe in the left, with a quiver filled with arrows on his back, but no bow. The scene is probably the bank of Mississippi. (From D. I. Bushnell, "Drawings by A. DeBatz in Louisiana, 1732-1735." Courtesy Smithsonian Institution.)

who had escaped from their masters to the swamps, knowing that they would come voluntarily to him when they learned he was to be their new master.

The Breaux were the earliest settlers where they city of Lafayette now stands. The Babineaux were early settlers in the vicinity of Carencro and the Thibodeaux and Broussards first settled on Cote Geleé near Broussard. The ancestor of the Broussard family was Gourhept Broussard who was called "Beausoliel" because of his smiling countenance. He was commissioned Captain of Militia in the Attakapas District by the French acting governor in 1765.

Toward the end of the eighteenth century there settled in the parish a most interesting character, one Leon Latiolais who became a large stock raiser. It is said that he knew well the entire region from Vermilion to New Orleans and could direct his course across the prairies by the stars, and through the dark forests by the bark on the trees. He served under Jackson in the War of 1812 and won the praise of his general at the Battle of New Orleans. It was in planning the battle that the general called for some one to carry a message through the dense swamps to one of his officers. The comrades of Latiolais recommended him to Jackson and he was accordingly summoned to appear before the general. At his appearance Jackson scrutinized him from head to foot and asked him if he could carry the papers bearing the message. On his giving an affirmative answer Jackson then asked him: "If the enemy catch you will you give him the message?"

The immediate answer of Latiolais was: "If they get it they will have to take it out of my belly." It is needless to say that he was entrusted with the message which he delivered safely to the American officer. Such was the character of the pioneers who first braved the dangers of the Indians and the unknown forces of nature in what was still a wilderness.

CHAPTER IV

EARLY LIFE AND SOCIAL AFFAIRS

The early inhabitants of Lafayette and the surrounding countryside were an honest industrious people who were content to live in peace and security. Their first houses were made of cypress logs with the chinks filled in with clay mixed with moss. In some cases the outer walls were made of heavy studs resting on heavy hand hewn sills. Cross pieces were wedged between the studs, and the intervening spaces filled with clay mixed with moss and smoothed to a plaster-like surface on the inside. The outside of the walls were covered with clapboards. When the logs were in place or the cross pieces put in position with the assistance of neighbors, all joined in to mix the clay and moss to be used as plaster which was prepared in the following manner. First a pit was dug and filled with loose clay. This in turn was well sprinkled with water from the nearby bayou. Into this pit was next scattered quantities of moss. Then, having removed their shoes, the men tramped the moss until it was well mixed with the clay. The resultant mixture was then spread between the logs or the studs, as the case might be, and allowed to dry. When a roof of hand split shingles and a floor of roughly hewn boards had been laid, and a crib like chimney of sticks plastered with clay had been built, the house was then ready to be occupied.

However uninviting such a house might seem it soon became the center of a comfortable domestic scene. The good wife picked cotton from the field from which she separated the seeds with her own hands. This done she spun the fibre into yarn on her own spinning wheel. The yarn she wove into cloth, dyed into pleasing colors with peach tree leaves and indigo. From the cloth she made clothes for her family, blankets for her beds, curtains for her windows, and a carpet for her floor. The cows she milked herself, and from the cream made an occasional pat of butter by shaking it in a gourd or bottle.

Nor did the building of the house bring to an end the tasks of the husband. He busied himself with the small crops necessary to furnish subsistence to his numerous family. His small farm he planted in cotton, cane, corn, rice and tobacco; and for meal he pounded his corn in a wooden mortar. From the mane of his horses he cut hair which he braided into ropes, horse collars, and harness. To get wood for fuel and lumber he had only to go to the swamp that flanked his farm, where he found it in abundance and free for the taking. Occasionally he visited the nearest store where he exchanged a few eggs for coffee and other small necessities. Otherwise he was independent of the world, having few wants that his own domain did not supply. As for music, the mocking bird in his fig tree sang for him daily. Pictures he saw in the sky and in the bayou at his feet. So long as his children kept well and his crops prospered there was nothing else that he desired. The knowledge to be had in books did not trouble him and the news that the visitor told him over a demi-tasse of black coffee left him content.

Not all the settlers and their descendants, however, were satisfied with their humble stations. Gradually there was kindled in their hearts the flame of ambition for better things. The wealth that came from cattle, cane, and cotton enabled them to expand their holdings, build better homes and assume positions of influence. The first improvement in their homes came with the development of sawmills, such as those operated by Honoré Beraud and John Creighton. With lumber from these mills they could build the neat Acadian cottages with the steep roof projecting over a gallery in front, from which rose a steep stairway to the garçonnier in the attic. Some became large planters, who with the help of slaves, built large two-storied houses of brick and wood with double galleries in front and rear, such as that constructed by Charles Homer Mouton, and still standing on Sterling Avenue in Lafayette; or the high-ceiling mansion of Senator Mouton with its tall columns and lookout on the roof, Isle Copal.

During his lifetime the home of Senator Mouton became the center of business, culture and social activities. In his library were found books of fiction, history and biography in both French and English — often rare — including an autographed set of Audubon's *Birds of America*. The dignified and liberal character of the hospitality offered in his stately mansion was in noticeable contrast to that given in the modest home of the pioneer. To his home came statesmen and men of letters or financiers who wanted his cooperation in building the first railroad to Vermilionville, or in opening up Bayou Vermilion to navigation by steamboats. There the visitors discussed with him grave matters of business and state, or repeated the latest news of the theatres in New Orleans and the newest gossip from Washington. Between times the women regaled themselves with discussions of the coming social season in New Orleans, the French opera, or with gossip concerning the season's debutantes; the men with hunting and fishing expeditions. In fact, the life in the mansion was an indication that a new era in the social life of Lafayette Parish was about to dawn.

George W. Cable visited Governor Mouton in this mansion on Bayou Vermilion. After describing the countryside around Vermilionville with its small Acadian homesteads in his *Bonaventure* Cable wrote:

> Here is one on a smooth green billow of land, just without the town. It is not like the rest — a large brick house, its Greek porch half hid in a grove of oaks. On that dreadful day more than a century ago, when the British in far-off Acadie shut into the chapel the villagers of Grand Pré, a certain widow fled with her children to the woods, and there subsisted for ten days on roots and berries, until finally, the standing crops as well as the houses being destroyed, she was compelled to accept exile, and in time found her way with others to these prairies. Her son founded Vermilionville. Her grandson rose to power, — sat in the Senate of the United States. From early manhood to hale gray age, the people of his state were pleased to hold him, now in one capacity, now in another, in their honored service. They made him Senator, Governor, President of the Secession Conventon, what you will. I have seen the portrait for which he sat in early manhood to a noted English court painter: dark waving locks; strong well-chiseled features; fine clear eyes; an air of warm steady, glowing intellectual energy. It hangs in the home of which I speak. And I have seen an old ambrotype of him, taken in the days of this story: hair short cropped, gray; eyes thoughtful, courageous, mouth firm, kind and ready to smile.

CHAPTER V

TERRITORIAL AND POLITICAL EVOLUTION OF THE PARISH

UNDER FRANCE AND SPAIN

The process by which Lafayette Parish emerged as a separate unit from the vast territory of old French Louisiana forms an interesting story. When Louisiana comprised all that vast territory which extended from Canada to the Gulf of Mexico and from the Allegheny Mountains on the east to the Rockies on the west, it had been divided by its French rulers, in 1721, into nine great administrative districts. Over each of these districts was placed a commandant and a judge. When Bienville in 1723 moved the capital from Mobile to New Orleans the Attakapas region, of which Lafayette Parish was then a part, was included in the New Orleans District from which it was governed. The New Orleans officials seldom visited the district as it was then populated principally by Indians, trappers and smugglers.

When O'Reilly took possession of Louisiana for Spain in 1768, he divided Louisiana into eleven districts with a commandant over each with the Attakapas region still in the New Orleans District. About the same time Louisiana was divided into twenty-one ecclesiastical parishes for religious administration. In 1792 Governor Carondelet provided for the appointment of syndics, officers similar to justices of the peace, to be stationed about nine miles apart with jurisdiction over an area about equal to the present parish ward.* In these divisions we have an indication of how the political subdivisions, now known as the parish and ward, had their origin in Louisiana.

It was not until the Spanish Regime began in 1768 that any special attention was paid to this part of Louisiana. Under the Spanish policy of encouraging agriculture and maintaining a

---
*Parish is the equivalent of county. Ward is a political subdivision of the parish similar to the *beat* in Mississippi or *district* in West Virginia.

strong government in all parts of the territory, the small settlement at St. Martinville was converted into a permanent military post, and a resident commander was appointed in order to enforce Spanish law and keep the peace. This station became known as "Postes des Attakapas" and henceforth all civil and military affairs of the Attakapas region were administered from this post by the commandant. In addition to being the leader of the militia, this official also exercised powers similar to those now possessed by a justice of the peace. He had jurisdiction over all disputes between citizens involving amounts up to $20. If this amount was exceeded he took in writing the petitions of the parties, which, with the written evidence, he forwarded to the royal officials in New Orleans for final adjudication. The commandant was the executive officer of the district, enforcing all judgments, also serving as notary and judge in the settlement of estates. As a military officer he examined the passports of strangers and allowed no one to settle in his district without a permit from the governor. In certain cases the commandant was authorized to celebrate marriages. Such marriages, in the absence of a priest, were called marriages "per verba de presenti,"* being permitted only on condition that they would be subsequently validated in a religious ceremony; although failure to do so did not necessarily invalidate the original one.

UNDER THE UNITED STATES

It was under the system described above that the territory including the present parish was governed from 1769 to 1803 when Louisiana became a possession of the United States, with William C. C. Claiborne as its first governor. In 1804 the Congress divided the Louisiana Territory into two parts and designated that portion south of thirty-three degrees latitude as the Territory of Orleans which, with certain changes and additions, became the present state of Louisiana. In 1805 Governor Claiborne's legislative council divided the territory of Orleans into twelve counties; one was Attakapas County which included the present parishes of St. Martin, St. Mary, Iberia, Lafayette and Vermilion. This division, having became unsatisfactory to the native inhabitants because of such innovations as jury trial, English language, and the common law,† the legislative council in 1807 discarded the county set up,

---

*By word of those present.
†The English system of law based on custom.

except as a unit for levying territorial taxes and electing territorial representatives. At the same time the state was divided into nineteen civil parishes. Thus the County of Attakapas became St. Martin Parish, of which the present Lafayette Parish was still a part.

Under this new set up the parish judge, appointed by the governor, was endowed with all the powers of county judge, county clerk, sheriff, coroner and treasurer. He with the justices of the peace and a jury of twelve inhabitants constituted a Parish Assembly which functioned as a policy-making and administrative body in matters of police, taxation, and internal improvements. Between 1807 and 1824 however the justices of the peace were eliminated from the assembly or police jury,* as it came to be called, and by 1845 the parish judge had been shorn of all his excessive powers.

In 1811, one year before Louisiana became a state, the territorial council decreed, "The County of Attakapas shall be divided into two parishes to be called the Parish of St. Martin and the Parish of St. Mary." Here the council refers to the Parish of St. Martin by its old county name of Attakapas.

FORMATION OF LAFAYETTE PARISH

By act of January 17, 1823 the Louisiana legislature directed: "The parish of St. Martin is and shall be, by the present act, divided; and a new parish be formed out of the western part of the said parish, which shall be called and known by the name of the Parish of Lafayette." The boundary lines as set in the act showed that the new parish embraced the territory that presently includes both Lafayette and Vermilion Parishes. An act of 1844 cut off the southwestern part of Lafayette Parish and formed it into Vermilion Parish. Iberia Parish was formed in 1868 from territory taken from both St. Martin and St. Mary Parishes. Thus did Lafayette Parish evolve from the county Attakapas and assume, with a few subsequent boundary adjustments, the size and shape as we know it today. As the act creating the parish was consummated during the enthusiasm attending the expected visit of General Lafayette to the United States, it was quite natural that the name chosen for the new parish should be Lafayette.

---
*Police jury is the equivalent of the county commission or county court in other states.

Parish Government

The methods by which the new parish was first governed have gone through many changes. When the first parish government was organized on June 2, 1823, the staff of parish officers consisted of a sheriff and ex-officio tax collector, a parish judge and ex-officio recorder, and a police jury of nine members. These officers, together with justices of the peace, the coroner were all appointed by the governor. The police jury was empowered to elect a constable, a parish treasurer, five school administrators and three tax assessors. The parish judge was president of the police jury and presided over its sessions. Serving this parish along with several others, there were a district judge, a district attorney and a recorder of marks and brands, all appointed by the governor. These officers continued to be appointed by him until 1846 when the new constitution of 1845 went into effect.

A glance at this first meeting of the police jury in this infant parish is indeed interesting. At this meeting, which was held in the home of Judge Thomas B. Brashear, there were present Judge Thomas B. Brashear, who presided, and the following police jurors: Jean Guilbeau, André Martin, William Hathorne, Charles Hebert, John Wilbourn, Joseph Bernard, Thomas Beraud, Shadrach Porter and John Meriman, representing wards one to nine in the order named. The first matter of business was the election of a parish constable. To this highly important office was elected Hubert Chargois, who accepted the honor and took the oath of office on the spot. For clerk, William Reeves was elected; for treasurer, Francis Carmouche; and for assessors, John Wilbourne, Charles Mouton and André Martin.

At this and subsequent meetings we find the jurors passing ordinances, making provision for the laying out of roads and the building of the first bridges. Other ordinances set up regulations concerning the coming and going of slaves and imposed penalties for violations of these rules. A novel provision concerning fines to be levided on law violators was that one half of the fine assessed was to go to the informer. In order to maintain peace and protect life and property there was appointed for each ward a chief of patrol. This officer was authorized to prepare a roll of all able-bodied men in his ward between the ages of sixteen and forty-five. These men, armed with guns and pistols, were required to do guard duty and patrol in turns a regular beat, either night or day, as ordered by

Dr. Antoine Bordat, an ex-surgeon of the French army, in New Orleans about 1765. The father of Marthe Bordat, the wife of Jean Mouton, founder of Vermilionville.

Basil Crow, Pioneer Lawyer

Governor Alexandre Mouton

Alexandre Mouton, Grandson of Governor Mouton, Author of unpublished memoirs quoted here.

the chief of patrol. A heavy fine faced those who refused to perform such duty when ordered to do so. This elaborate system of policing the wards seems to have been inspired by the fear of an uprising of slaves against their masters.

Probably the most significant change in the parish government, from the democratic standpoint, came when the constitution of 1845, inspired by Governor Alexandre Mouton, provided that most parish offices, including the police jury, should be filled by popular election rather than appointment by the governor. As the parish expanded in population and wealth and in its services to the people, its governmental machinery became necessarily more elaborate, as shown in the next paragraphs.

Under the Constitution of 1921 now in effect the voters of the parish, in conjunction with the voters of Acadia and Vermilion parishes, elect three district judges and a district attorney; in conjunction with those in Iberia and St. Martin Parishes the voters elect two state senators and from Lafayette Parish they elect three representatives to the state legislature. Elected by the voters of this parish only are a sheriff and ex-officio tax collector; a clerk of court and ex-officio recorder; a tax assessor; a coroner and ex-officio parish physician; a police jury of fourteen members; and a parish school board of fourteen members. The police jury in turn appoints a secretary, a treasurer, a registrar of voters, a home demonstration agent and assistants, an agricultural agent and assistants, five members of a department of public welfare, a five member board of health, which in turn appoints a health unit of five persons. The school board appoints a parish school superintendent, assistant superintendents and supervisors, a secretary and treasurer as well as all school principals, teachers, janitors and bus drivers. A jury commission of five citizens and the clerk of court is appointed by the district court.

Thus is seen that the work of governing the parish was for many years comparatively simple and inexpensive. The taxes levied for the first year amounted to only $2000.00, compared with $231,838.38 in 1922 and $290,479.54 in 1952. The first police jurors received a per diem of only two dollars, whereas today they receive thirty dollars. These more recent tax receipts represent the taxes collected for the general parish government and do not include special levies for schools, roads and drainage. Nor do they include the thousands of dollars contributed by state and federal governments for education, health and welfare.

Concerning the Municipal Ticket of 1899

The following report published in the Lafayette Gazette, March 25, 1899, of a Democratic mass meeting held for the purpose of nominating candidates for municipal office in the city of Lafayette.

MUNICIPAL TICKET

Nominated by a Democratic Mass Meeting Held Monday Night in the Court House

Pursuant to a call signed by Judge C. Debaillon, Messrs. William Campbell, E. G. Voorhies, A. M. Martin, and Judge Julian Mouton, the Democrats of the town of Lafayette met at the court house last Monday to nominate candidates for mayor and councilmen to be voted for at the election which will be held next May.

The meeting was called to order by Hon. William Campbell, who requested Judge Debaillon to preside. Mr. Ed. G. Voorhies was elected secretary of the meeting. Judge Julian Mouton moved that a committee of five be appointed to form a ticket to be submitted to the assembly. Sheriff (Issac) Broussard seconded the motion.

The chair appointed the following gentlemen to serve on the committee: Judge Julian Mouton, Sheriff I. A. Broussard, A. M. Martin, A. E. Mouton, and Horace Broussard.

The committee retired; about half an hour later returned to the court room. Judge Julian Mouton read the report. It read as follows:

For Mayor: William Campbell

For Councilmen: Charles O. Mouton   John O. Mouton
Dr. F. E. Girard   J. E. Martin
H. H. Hohorst   George A. deBlanc
Felix Demanade

CHAPTER VI

FOUNDING AND NAMING A CITY

It is a well known law that wherever occurs a break in transportation there will grow a city. The fact that Lafayette stands where it is today is due to the working of that law. The present location of the bridge at Pin Hook marks the end of navigation on Vermilion Bayou and the beginning of transportation on land. The early English traders who smuggled their wares up the Vermilion, contrary to French and Spanish law, found their progress blocked at that point due to the failure of deep water. Consequently they tied up their boats there and waited for the Indians, scattered trappers, and ranchers to come to purchase their merchandise. Little Manchac was the name given by the traders to this place. In the course of time, however, the name Little Manchac gradually gave way to the more familiar name of Pin Hook. How this name originated is not definitely known. Reed, in his work, "Place Names of Indian Origin" suggests it may have come from the Choctaw Indian name of "pinashuk," which means linden or basswood tree. Local residents, however, prefer to rely on the explanation based on a popular legend. According to this story there was in the early days an old Frenchman who kept a restaurant near the bridge which became famous for the delicious fried chicken served to its patrons. Some one became curious to know where the proprietor got the fine chickens and decided to watch the place. While he was thus keeping his vigils early one morning, he was astonished to see the owner at a window fasten a grain of corn on a bent pin which he in turn tied to a long string. Holding one end of the string in his hand he tossed the grain of corn out the window into his yard, which was being invaded by chickens belonging to neighboring families. One of the chickens soon swallowed the grain of corn and for its trouble was quickly hauled flapping into the kitchen. This procedure was kept up until the day's supply of chickens was obtained. According to tradition, therefore, it was from this incident that the place was given the name, Pin Hook.

By the year 1800 the priests from the Poste des Attakapas who visited the settlements on the bayou had begun to refer to the place as "au Vermilion" and soon this name came into current usage; though there is evidence that the settlement was subsequently referred to as the village of St. Jean, after the name given to the Catholic chapel which had been built prior to 1821 on land owned by Jean Mouton, and dedicated as "L'eglise St. Jean du Vermilion." In fact transfers of property recorded in the courthouse in St. Martinville frequently described the property as located in the "Village of St. Jean au Vermilion." The final selection of a name and location for the future city had to wait on the events recorded below.

The legislative act which, on January 17, 1823, brought into being the Parish of Lafayette, provided for the appointment of a commission to choose a site on which were to be erected the necessary public buildings in which the activities of the new parish government were to be carried on. This commission was appointed on April 18, 1823, and consisted of the following five persons: Francois Carmouche, Arnan Dugas, Joseph Bernard, Louis Hebert and Shadrach Porter.

Soon after the appointment of this commission John and William Reeves, who were anxious to develop the lands which they owned near the Pin Hook bridge and near what is now the Bendel Gardens subdivision, offered severally to donate to the parish two superficial arpents of this land, provided the parish courthouse and other public buildings be located thereon. The commissioners were to have the privilege of selecting the site, and, after having done so, deeds to the designated tracts were to be made out to the parish by the donors. In pursuance to this written offer by John and William Reeves the Commissioners met on April 19, 1823, formally accepted the offer and by ballot selected a site near the Vermilion bridge as a convenient place where the courts of the parish were to be held, all public affairs transacted, and a court house and other public buildings erected. Thereupon John and William Reeves, together with their sureties, John Bronson and J. D. Nixon, executed two deeds each of which transferred to the parish two arpents of land. Both were executed on November 26, 1823 and recorded as entries 158 and 159, in the "Old Series" of parish records.

Soon after the parish had accepted and taken possession of these two tracts the police jury built a jail on them at a cost of $2500.00, but did not build a courthouse there as expected. A rented room in the vicinity of Vermilion bridge was used for court meetings on at least three separate occasions. The failure of the parish to build a courthouse immediately on the site donated was a disappointment to the Reeves family and its partisans for obvious reasons.

Meantime, as stated above, there had been built a Catholic chapel, at the place where St. John's Cathedral now stands, on the land of Jean Mouton. In 1821 Jean Mouton donated this site containing five and one half arpents to the trustees of the Catholic congregation and in the same year Vermilionville with the surrounding territory was separated from Grand Coteau and erected into a separate parish with its own pastor. With this development the church

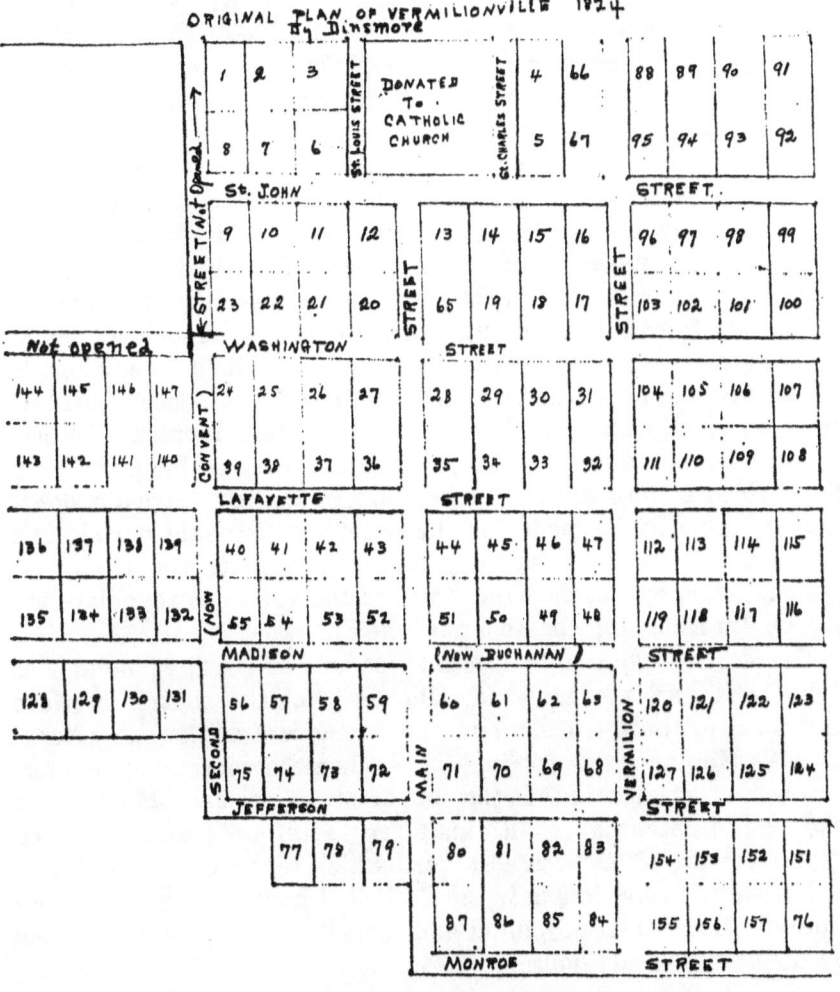

with its resident priest soon became a magnet to draw homeseekers and various activities within its orbit.

As Jean Mouton saw his church become the center of religious and social activities for the surrounding area, he soon conceived the idea of laying out a town on his lands which surrounded it. At the same time he observed that the newly created parish was without a definitely established seat of justice. He accordingly conceived and executed designs for recognition of the village which he saw spontaneously springing up around the parish church. He thereupon, with the aid of his friends, sought and received from the legislature authority to lay out a town on his land situated near Bayou Vermilion in the Parish of Lafayette, which "shall be called Vermilionville and the plan thereof shall be deposited in the office of the judge of the aforesaid parish." This act also required the police jury of the parish to adopt such by-laws as might be proper for the policing of the new town.

Having laid out his town in lots and streets in accordance with the legislative authority described above, Jean Mouton, his family and friends, in spite of the fact that a location for the parish seat had already been legally chosen, succeeded in having the legislature of Louisiana, on April 7, 1824, pass an act directing the judge of the parish to call an election in order that the freeholders might choose a place where the court of justice might hold its sessions in the future, either at the then accepted site or at a newly offered one near the Roman Catholic Church which Jean Mouton now proposed to donate to the parish. This act also directed the police jury to provide for the erection of a court house and to receive any donations which may be made for the benefit of the said parish, and declared that all laws contrary to the provisions are hereby repealed. Thus was opened the way for the voters to repudiate the site at Pin Hook and choose a new one.

The election required by this act was held on the first Monday of July, 1824. All the evidence indicates that the contest between advocates of the Pin Hook site and supporters of the site offered by Jean Mouton was a spirited one. When the votes were counted, however, it was found that the supporters of the Jean Mouton site had won. In accordance with his offer, therefore, Jean Mouton, on September 20, 1824 executed a deed which conveyed to the Parish of Lafayette twelve lots near the Catholic Church and lying on both sides of Main Street adjoining and including the grounds occupied by the present court house.

As already indicated this change in the location of the seat of justice from the Vermilion bridge to the present site was not accomplished without considerable controversy. Soon after the election just described had been held, Joseph Reeves, representing the Reeves family, seized the four arpents which had been donated by John and William Reeves, and by force excluded the parish from using either the land or the jail which had been erected thereon, alleging that the donation had been voided by the selection of another site for a seat of justice. As a result of this action the police jury on May 12, 1824 filed suit against Joseph Reeves in the District Court, praying that the parish be restored to the peaceful possession of the said lots and jail and that it be quieted in its title to the same.

In defending his right to take back the four arpents on which the jail had been erected, Joseph Reeves urged that the act under which a new location near the church had been selected was unconstitutional and therefore void. He further alleged that more than fifty persons, none of whom were authorized by law to vote, were admitted to vote in the said election and that all did vote to change the seat of justice from Pin Hook to the site offered by Jean Mouton. He alleged further that if this vote, improperly permitted in the election, had been rejected, a large legal majority would have been in favor of the seat of justice remaining at the place fixed upon by the commissioners appointed originally.

The defendant, Joseph Reeves, said further that many individuals who voted at the election in favor of the change were hired and bribed to vote in the manner they did, and that the election is therefore wholly illegal and void; thus the pretended majority mentioned in the petition was obtained by bribery and corruption.

The judgment rendered by the District Court on April 20, 1827 confirmed the title to the Parish of Lafayette, and enjoined the defendant Joseph Reeves from interfering with the free use and enjoyment of the property. The decree did provide, though, that should the police jury remove the jail from the land then the title to the property would revert to the defendant.

Joseph Reeves, however, was not satisfied with this decision and appealed his case. The appeal was heard before the Supreme Court in the Western District at Opelousas. In its decision it held that the lower court had erred, and further decreed that, since the donation had been made on condition that the court house should be placed on the land given, the removal of the seat of justice to another place dissolved the contract. In restoring the property to its former owner the court wryly remarked:

"It is not to be supposed that any man in his senses would make a donation for the purpose of having a jail placed at his door."

The outcome of this litigation cleared the way for locating the courthouse and other parish buildings on the land donated by Jean Mouton. The most significant result, however, was that the future town and parish seat was to grow up around Jean Mouton's church and not on the banks of Bayou Vermilion at Pin Hook as the Reeves family and its partisans had hoped.

CHAPTER VII

VERMILIONVILLE INCORPORATED

The village of Vermilionville, as laid out for Jean Mouton by his surveyor, John Dinsmore, Jr. contained no crooked streets. All streets ran north to south and east to west. They remained that way until the railroad was completed by and around the town in 1881. As new streets were opened up or existing ones extended they were curved either to parallel the railroad or to cross it at right angles. Roughly speaking the town was bounded on the east by what is now Polk Street, on the south by Convent Street, on the west by the Coulee back of the Catholic Church and on the north by a line running east and west drawn through the present Home Building and Loan office, 523 Jefferson Street, and the Southern Bell Telephone Building. Marked off on the town plot were 156 lots, each having a frontage of 96 feet and a depth of 140 feet. With the exception of St. John Street the streets running north and south were named after the presidents of the United States.

Between 1823 and 1830 Jean Mouton disposed of his lots rather rapidly. To the Parish of Lafayette he donated twelve lots numbered as follows on his town plot: lots 43 and 52 with the buildings on the south side of Main Street; also lots 72, 79, 88, 95, 104, 71, 80, 87, 96 and 103. For most lots sold Jean Mouton received for each a note for $150.00 payable in two years with interest at ten per cent. Many names of the first purchasers of these lots have long been forgotten in Lafayette. However, some of them are still familiar. For instance: On October 4, 1823 lots 45 and 50 on which is located the Dan Chevrolet garage were sold to Thomas B. Brashear; on October 1, 1823, lots 3 and 6, on which now stands the Bishop's residence was sold to Sieur A. Droz; on November 6, 1823 lot 42, on which stands Beadle's Feed Store, was sold to Louis Julien Forguet; on December 7, 1825 lots 60 and 61, now occupied by the rear of the Lafayette Motors building, were sold to William Hathorne; on September 23, 1824, lot 13, now occupied by the home of Clayton Martin was sold to Jaques F. Ribetty; on December 4,

1824, lot 57, on which stands the home of the late Judge Paul Debaillon, was sold to John Crow; on September 23, 1824, lot 140, now occupied by the home of Thad and Elizabeth Montgomery, was sold to Olidon Broussard. Some others to whom Jean sold lots during this time were: John B. Prass, lot 3; Judiah Nixon, lot 135; Francois St. Juste, lots 136, 137; Hubert Chargois, lots 29 to 34; B. Castillon, lot 40; Josiah Martin, lot 54; Joseph Rouly, lot 141; and Francois Lefevre, lots 46 and 49.

The main business section centered around the court house and on West Main Street between the Church and court house. It was not long before boutiques (stores) began to spring up along Main Street and on St. John Street across from the church. The great live oak which stands on the church grounds was already there and customers coming to shop parked their horses and buggies under its shade while they shopped or stood around and gossiped.

By 1836 the town had grown to the extent that its citizens thought it should be incorporated. By legislative act of March 11, 1836 the limits of the town were fixed and Vermilionville was formally incorporated and a charter issued. By the terms of this charter the town was to be governed by five councilmen. That the problems of government were few and simple may be seen by reading the Charter, a copy of which follows:

An Act
To Incorporate the Town of Vermilionville in the Parish of Lafayette

Section 1. Be it enacted by the Senate and House of Representatives of the State of Louisiana, in general assembly convened, that all the free white male citizens of the United States, and of the State of Louisiana, who shall have attained the age of twenty-one years, shall have resided in the Parish of Lafayette one year next preceding the passage of this act, and who at the period of its passage shall reside within the limits hereafter described, be and they are hereby authorized to meet on the first Monday of May next, and on the first Monday of May in each succeeding year, and to elect five persons who shall constitute a body politic or corporation, under the name and style of the "City Council of the town of Vermilionville" and no one shall be eligible who is not a citizen of the United States, and of the State of Louisiana, and a resident within the limits of said town; and besides the owner and possessor of real estate within said limits of the value of three hundred dollars, and over the age of twenty-one years.

Section 2. Be it further enacted, etc., that the limits of the said town of Vermilionville shall be included in the following boundaries, to wit: on the east by East Street on the south by Third Street; on the north by a street one square north of Vermilion Street to run east and west; and on the west by a line to be run due north and south, intersecting the last mentioned street to be run, and Third Street, so as to include the Roman Catholic Church, and the grounds belonging to the same, the whole in conformity with a plan made by John Dinsmore, Jr., and now deposited in the office of the Parish Judge of the Parish of Lafayette.

Section 3. Be it further enacted, etc., that the aforesaid elections shall be held at the Court House in said town, and shall be by ballot, and the ballot box shall be kept open from ten o'clock A.M., until five o'clock P.M., under the superintendence of the clerk of the District Court and the Sheriff of the Parish of Lafayette, whose duty it shall be to give at least ten days previous notice of the day, place and hour of such elections, by papers posted up at the Court House and church doors in English and French. And the five persons who have obtained the greatest number of votes shall be declared duly elected members of the City Council of the Town of Vermilionville, and shall hold their offices for one year from the said first Monday of May in each year, and until their successors shall be duly elected.

Section 4. Be it further enacted, etc., that before entering in office the members thus elected shall take and subscribe before a Justice of the Peace of said Parish, an oath faithfully and impartially to fulfill the duties imposed upon them by this act, which oath shall be certified by said Justice of the Peace on the certificate of their election, which shall be filed in the office of the clerk of said town.

Section 5. Be it further enacted, etc., that the said City Council shall meet annually on the Monday next after their election or as soon thereafter as may be, and elect one of their number as President of said Council by a majority of the vote of all said members, whose duty it shall be to preside at all their sittings; to sign all ordinances and resolutions passed by said council; to call special meetings of said council, whenever he shall deem such meetings expedient, and to grant commissions to such officers as may lawfully be appointed by said City Council.

Section 6. Be it further enacted, etc., that in case of any vacancy occurring in said council, it shall be the duty of the President to give ten days notice, in a manner hereinbefore provided, of the time and place of holding an election to fill such vacancy; and such election shall be presided by any two members of said council, who shall have power to grant a certificate of election to the person elected to supply such vacancy.

Section 7. Be it further enacted, etc., that the said City Council, or a majority of them, shall have power to pass and establish such by-laws and ordinances for the good order, maintenance and government of the town of Vermilionville as they may deem necessary, not being contrary to the constitution and laws of the state. To pass ordinances for the police of slaves, grog-shops, billiard houses or tables, public and market houses; to lay a tax thereon; and to apply the funds thus raised to the use and benefit of said town, as they may deem advisable. Also to levy an annual tax on all property situated or owned within said town, and liable to a State tax, and to collect the same; provided, that the said tax shall in no case exceed twenty-five cents a year on every hundred dollars of the value of the property taxed; and provided, that the said City Council shall never levy on any stores, shops, public houses, retailers of good, any annual tax to a greater amount than shall be levied by the state for the same year; but they may levy an annual tax on grog shops and billiard tables to any extent they may think proper.

Section 8. Be it further enacted, etc., that said City Council shall have power to ordain and pass any ordinance which they may deem expedient for keeping in good order the streets and market houses, and for the general police of said town, and to impose fines and penalties on any persons violating or neglecting to observe their ordinances; provided that no fine to be thus imposed shall exceed twenty-five dollars; to be sued for and recovered in the name of said City Council before any Justice of Peace of the Parish of Lafayette.

Section 9. Be it further enacted, etc., that said City Council shall appoint a town clerk for said town who shall hold his office during the will of said council; he shall keep a bound book in which shall be recorded all the laws and ordinances passed by said council, signed by the President and countersigned by the clerk; he shall also keep a book in which shall be recorded proceedings of said City Council; and shall do such other duties as the said City Council may require of him; and may receive such a salary as they shall allow him.

Section 10. Be it further enacted, etc., that said Council shall also appoint a town constable, whose duty it shall be to attend all the sittings of the Council and execute all their legal orders. He shall also be collector of all taxes levied by said Council and shall furnish such bond and security as they may require of him for the faithful execution of his duties as such. He shall hold his office for one year and shall receive such salary as the said council may allow him.

Section 11. Be it further enacted, etc., that the said town clerk shall act as assessor of the taxable property in said town.

Section 12. Be it further enacted, etc., that said City Council shall appoint a Treasurer who shall give bond as security in such amount as said Council shall determine. He shall hold his office for one year, and shall do such duties as said Council shall require of him, and may receive such salary as they shall allow him.

Section 13. And be it further enacted, etc., that the Police Jury of the Parish of Lafayette shall no longer have or exercise any jurisdiction within the aforesaid limits except it be over the court-house of jail of said Parish; provided that whenever it shall be necessary to lay a tax for the purpose of building or repairing court-house or jail of said Parish, the property within said town shall be equally taxed with the property of the Parish generally.

>(Signed) Alcee Labranche
>Speaker of the House of Representatives
>
>(Signed) C. Derbigny
>President of the Senate
>
>Approved March 11, 1836
>(Signed) E. D. White
>Governor of the State of Louisiana

The provisions of this charter remained in effect until 1869, when the town was reincorporated by act of the legislature. Under this charter the boundaries of the town were extended, and a new government by a mayor and seven Councilmen provided for. The first mayor under this charter was Alphonse Neveu. Some other mayors elected to office under this charter were William Brandt, 1871; August Monnier, 1873; John O. Mouton, 1875; G. C. Salles, 1876; John Clegg, 1879; and W. B. Bailey, 1884. In 1884 the Charter of 1869 was amended to change the name of Vermilionville to Lafayette. The reason why this change had not been made earlier, as many had desired, was that the name Lafayette had already been given to a suburb of New Orleans. Just prior to 1884, however, this suburb had been included in the city limits of New Orleans, and, with its post office, ceased to exist. Thus was Vermilionville free to take a new name.

The provisions of the amended charter remained in effect until 1914, when, in an election, the citizens of Lafayette voted to discard the mayor-council government and to replace it with the commission form. Under this plan Lafayette is now governed by three commissioners elected at large from the city: a commissioner of public safety who is ex-officio mayor; a second as commissioner of finance; and a third as commissioner of public property. Elected with them is a chief of police. The three commissioners as a body enact all ordinances and appoint all city employees. Each is expected to devote full time to the duties of his office. The first commissioners under this new charter were F. E. Girard, **trustee of public safety and ex-officio mayor**; J. C. Herpin, trustee of public property, and J. P. Colomb, trustee of finance.

CHAPTER VIII

LAFAYETTE, ONE HUNDRED YEARS AGO

GENERAL VIEW

From the unpublished memoirs of the late Alexander Mouton, grandson and namesake of Governor Mouton, one gets an authentic view of Vermilionville and its environs on the eve of the Civil War. He writes: "At the beginning of the fifth decade of the nineteenth century I was born on the banks of the Vermilion River at Walnut Grove plantation. It got its name from the large number of walnut trees that grew on the property, which was a wedding gift to my mother from her father, Governor Alexandre Mouton. The boundary lines of the plantation ran as follows: east by the Vermilion River, west by Coulee Mine and north by the properties of John Baumgartner and Jim Higginbotham. Jim Higginbotham's property was on the river bank, touching Baumgartner's and the main road." The plantation included most of what is now Bendel Gardens Subdivision.

Alexander's father was Jean Sosthene Mouton and his mother was Charlotte Odéide Mouton, daughter of Governor Mouton. As a young girl living with her father in Washington, while he served as senator from Louisiana, Charlotte Odéide had attended the Visitation Convent from which she was graduated.

The home stood on the high bank of the Vermilion River a few hundred yards below the Pin Hook Bridge. From the front gallery young Alexander had a beautiful view of the river and the rolling countryside beyond. From this vantage point he gives us an interesting description of the surrounding country. Directly across the river from his home was the plantation of Izidor Broussard whose house stood at the top of the hill. On his plantation Mr. Broussard, with his slaves, cultivated cotton and raised cattle, horses, and sheep. He describes Broussard as a man with a loud voice which could be heard morning and night calling his mules and giving orders to his slaves. Down the bayou about three miles on the same side was the large plantation and stately home of Honoré Beraud, who also operated a saw mill. Up the bayou about a mile, where the Wallis home now stands, was the property of John Republican Creighton, son of the Doctor Creighton mentioned elsewhere in this book. John was married to Euphemie Mouton, a niece of Governor Mouton. Besides cultivating cotton on his place he had near the bayou a saw mill, which sawed into lumber logs floated down the stream from the swamp of Governor Mouton. Attached to the engine of the saw mill Creighton had a grits mill in which every two weeks he ground into grits and meal the corn which his neighbors brought. A short distance from the rear of Creighton's property was the plantation of Pierre Meaux.

Mr. Mouton also gives an interesting description of the neighbors who lived near the bridge on the highway leading into Vermilionville. The bridge across the bayou is described as a low wooden structure with a draw which could be opened to permit the passage of boats. Facing the bayou, between Walnut Grove and the highway was the home of Jim Higgingotham. By the road at the bridge he had a large warehouse used to store merchandise delivered by occasional steam boats or stored there for shipping. Close by was his shop where, as an expert wheelwright, he made hickory chairs with rawhide seats, spinning wheels, and other similar articles. Adjoining this he also operated a lumber yard. Along the highway near the bridge were several houses one of which was the restaurant of Louis Grangé, famous for its chicken pies. Another prominent place in this little community was the saloon and billiard parlor of William Butcher. People coming into Vermilionville from the east usually stopped at the bridge to water their horses; then, after crossing, sought refreshment either at Butcher's saloon or Grange's restaurant.

From the bridge Mr. Mouton takes us down the Pin Hook road into the village of Vermilionville. On the left next to Higginbotham's place was the house and shop of John Baumgartner. In his shop Baumgartner made cypress cisterns, hogsheads, and molasses barrels which he sold to the planters. He was an elderly man with no family except a housekeeper, old Mammy Barah, who was kind-hearted and loved by all who knew her. Besides keeping house she always cultivated a fine vegetable garden and a peach orchard bearing large, juicy clingstone peaches. The habitations along the road into the village were few. First on the left was the home of Henry Monnier, who kept a store in the village. Then on

Michel Eloi Girard, charter member of the Lafayette Masonic Lodge and prominent attorney during the early days of Lafayette. Husband of Maxime Crow. (Courtesy of M. Eloi Girard.)

Mrs. Maxime Crow Girard, who with her son, Crow, donated the twenty-five acres on which the first buildings of Southwestern were constructed. (Courtesy of M. Eloi Girard.)

Dr. Matthew Creighton, and his wife, the former Polly Turpin Jacobs
(Below) Three Distinguished Members of the Voorhies Family

CORNELIUS VOORHIES, Jr.
Justice of Supreme Court

ALBERT VOORHIES
Justice of Supreme Court

FELIX VOORHIES
Judge of 19th Judicial District Ct.

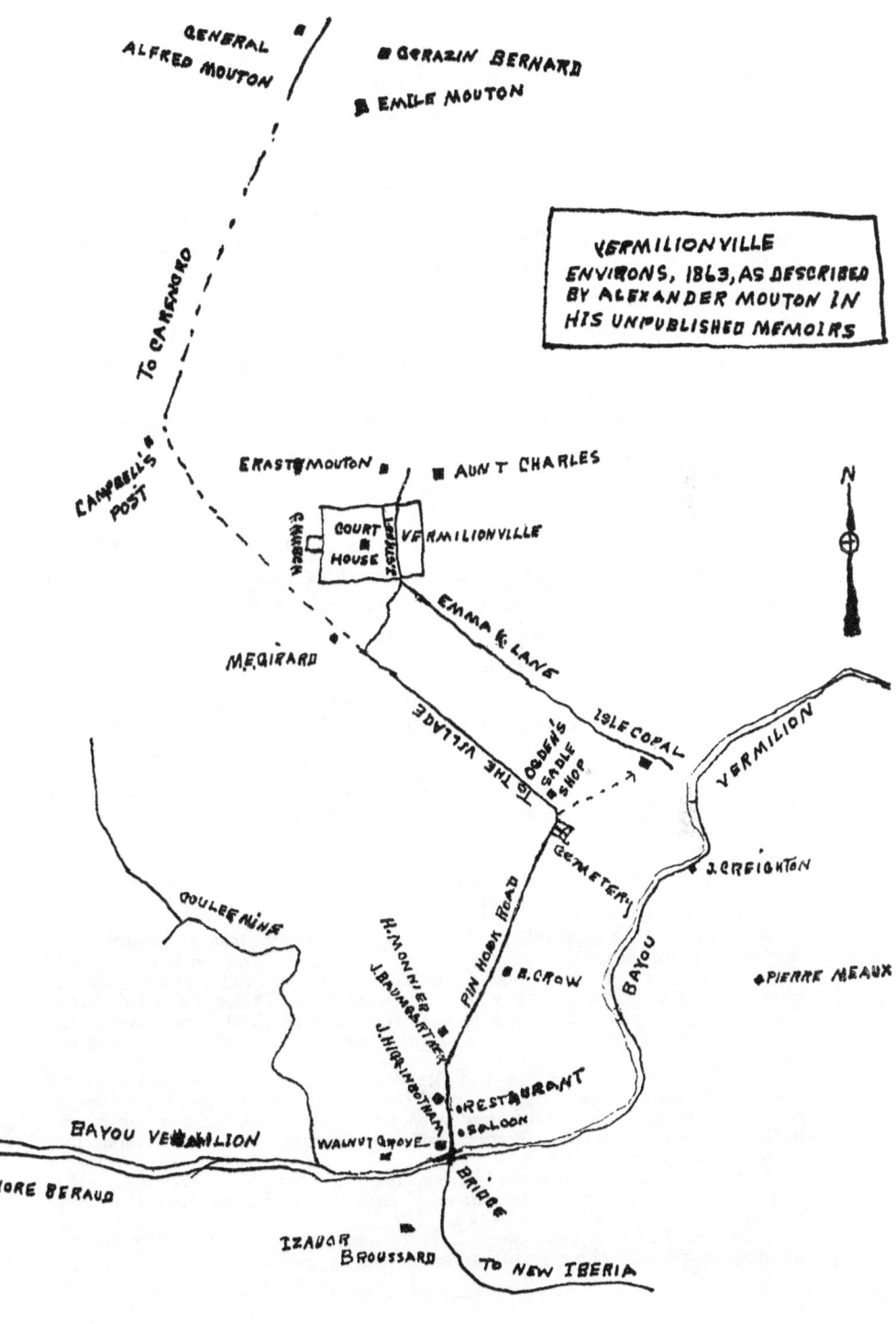

the right about midway was the home and Porter plantation of Mr. Basil Crow. At the turn of the road, at the graveyard, was the saddle shop of Mr. Ogden. The frontage of this road was owned mostly by Basil Crow who had planted pecan trees on both sides.

At the graveyard (now the Protestant Cemetery) should one continue straight a few hundred yards, instead of turning left into the village, he would find himself in the yard of Governor Alexandre Mouton's colonial mansion, Ile Copal,* which stood on the spot now occupied by the LeRosen School. At this time Governor Mouton had retired from active politics and was devoting his time to his sugar plantation and the manufacture of sugar, which he carried on with the help of over sixty slaves. Several hundred yards from his home was his brick sugar mill and between the two a long row of neat cabins occupied by his slaves. Mr. Mouton writes that the governor treated his slaves with great kindness, having provided them with a hall for their dances, a hospital, a church and a consecrated graveyard. He assigned to each a garden plot and allowed them to gather moss and raise chickens to sell in the village. The governor was a large landowner, and at the time he presided over the secession convention, was the possessor of over nineteen thousand acres of land. His plantation began at the present city hall and extended up Oak Avenue to his home and thence across the Bayou Vermilion far into the swamps toward Lake Martin. The lane leading from his home into the village was long known as the Emma K. Lane, after his second wife Emma Kitchell Gardner, who had the slaves plant oak trees along both

---

*Ile Copal, a grove of sweet gum trees. The explorer LaSalle is said to have been the first to use Copal as the designation of the Sweet Gum Tree (Liquidambar stryciflua L.)

Joutel writes in March 1687: "We found the country pleasant enough about that river (probably the Trinity in Texas) though the land did not seem to be any of the best; but still it was delightful to the eye, well planted with fine trees of several sorts, among which is one that M. De La Salle has named Copal, being very beautiful, the leaves of it between those of the maple and the lime trees in resemblance, and from it comes a gum of a very agreeable scent."

Spanish Copal, from which the Standard French took the word in the seventeenth century is a derivative of Aztec *Copalli*, the generic name for resin, yielded by various trees and used by the Mexican Indians for incense in their temples. Louisiana French, so far as I know, has no other name than *Copal* for the sweet gum tree.

B. F. French, *Historical Collections*, 1846, p. 145; cf. Margry, III, 335.

Reed, William A., Ph.D., *Louisiana French*, Baton Rouge, Louisiana State University Press, 1931. pp. 139-140.

Along the Gulf Coast trappers, hunters and fishermen frequently refer to a clump of trees in the marshes as an island.

sides of it in order to create a shaded driveway to town. The lane is now Oak Avenue, but the trees unfortunately have succumbed to the pitiless demands of progress.

BEAU SEJOUR

Directly across the bayou from Ile Copal was Beau Sejour, the plantation of Jean Sosthene and Odéide Mouton. After the burning of their home in Walnut Grove by the Federals in the Civil War, the home was built about 1865. In 1942 it was dismantled to make way for the Lafayette air port. The famous park and its beautiful picnic grounds are gone; only the magnificent live oaks still stand, as if "In Memoriam." The old home, built of magnolia wood cut by Jean Sosthene, was bought by George Voorhies who used it in the construction of his home on Lamar Street.

With respect to the village of Vermilionville Mr. Mouton had this to say: The residences and stores were comparatively few. The stores sold that which was needed in a rural way: ploughs, hoes, nails, iron braces needed to hitch mules to the plough; and of course, coffee, sugar, pins, needles, fish hooks, spurs, spinning wheels to spin cotton and wool to make clothes to put on their backs. The principal ones were Aristide Chiax, Revillon, and Harris Monquis. Within close proximity to the village was the home of Aunt Charles, my grandaunt, for she was the widow of Charles Mouton, Governor Mouton's brother. Her home, with its garden of roses and flowers of all kinds was a beautiful spot. On her plantation back of her residence she planted cotton; but she took great pride in her vegetable garden, which was quite extensive. This garden was handled by Antoine, a mulatto, a fine specimen of a man, who was honest and anything but lazy. The demand for the output of the garden was great, yet, according to custom, it was gladly given.

Near Aunt Charles' habitation there was another house, the former residence of Governor Alexander Mouton. The building is still to be seen. It is now a two story structure made of cypress wood. Every child of his first marriage was born in it except the first one, born in Opelousas; this one later became General Alfred Mouton. Not far from the residence of Aunt Charles lived Eraste Mouton, lawyer, district judge, and owner and editor of one of the first papers published in Vermilionville: one sheet, French on one side and English on the other. Eraste was a very charitable man, his left hand never knowing what the right hand was doing. He was very fond of hunting, and, since game of all kinds was very plentiful, his chances of giving vent to this great pleasure were not little. He was a very good shot especially on the wing, forever bagging woodcock and snipe. I know this to be true for we often went gunning together.

In the village not far from the home of Eraste lived William Mouton, son of Césaire Mouton, brother of the governor. Both Césaire and son William were graduates of Yale College. Césaire was a very bright and intelligent young man but his career of great promise had been cut short by his death at the age of thirty-three. William had a wonderful memory and could quote the British poets, including Shakespeare and Byron, off hand without previous preparation. He was considered by all a born orator; and so great and effective was his eloquence that he devoted his talents to prosecuting and defending criminal cases.

Near the village were the residences of Eloi Girard, one of the prominent lawyers of that time, Basil Crow, a cotton cultivator, and Jeff Caffery, also a planter. The courthouse was a one story brick structure covered with slate. The floor was on the ground paved with brick. The jail was also brick. In 1859 another courthouse replaced this one. It was two stories made of cypress lumber brought from the adjoining swamps. The Catholic Church, built by Jean Mouton with his slaves of cypress lumber, still stood in its original location.

The easy and sumptuous manner in which many planters of this prosperous era lived is best demonstrated in Mr. Mouton's account of his visits to the sugar plantation home and ranch of his uncle, Antoine Emile Mouton, the brother of Governor Mouton. Uncle Emile's sugar plantation and home was located about half way between Vermilionville and Carencro on what today would be an extension of Pierce Street. The house, the neglected remains of which are still standing, was a two story structure of brick surrounded with kitchen in the rear and other buildings. To the rear was a large pond or lake, a sugar house and, nearby, a race track and a vast enclosure in which were kept a herd of many deer. There were numerous slaves who served as house servants, coachmen and field hands. All around were many live oak trees to shade the grounds. Near this plantation were the cotton plantations of Mr. Gerazin Bernard and Mr. Horace Voorhies. Across the highway to Carencro was the plantation of Alfred Mouton who later became General.

In addition to his sugar plantation home, Emile also owned, where the town of Rayne now stands, an extensive cattle and horse ranch. On this he branded each year as many as three thousand calves and fifteen hundred colts. Being a lover of sports and the outdoor life he considered this ranch his favorite possession. On it was a large ranch house which he kept supplied all the year round with provisions and staffed with house servants, stable boys and other ranch personnel; and when he was not occupying it, it was his delight to turn it over fully provisioned and staffed to his friends and relatives for week long hunting parties. Doves, quail and grouse were so plentiful that they frequently came into the barnyard and mingled with the numerous chickens there. On these occasions when the men were not hunting or feasting they amused themselves by playing a card game called "Moroc", using chips to record their wagers.

A Few Surviving Landmarks

On a high hill overlooking the road to Pont a Mouton, under a grove of majestic live oaks, stood the home of Jean Sosthene Mouton, son of Jean and grandfather of Alexander mentioned above. Along what is now Moss Street Extension are still standing some of the homes of the pioneer Martin and Latiolais families. Among the homes that have withstood the ravages of time may be mentioned the Honoré Beraud home on Bayou Vermilion, which is now rapidly falling into a state of decay; and the handsome Gerazin Bernard home now owned and occupied by Mrs. William Couret. This is in a perfect state of preservation,

Another of these homes, now within the limits of Lafayette at 338 Sterling Avenue is presently owned by Dr. Nugier Des Ormeaux. This handsome house was built in 1848 by Charles Homer Mouton, a prominent local jurist who later served as lieutenant governor of Louisiana. The home stood originally in the midst of a large plantation then on the outskirts of Vermilionville. The two-story structure is typical of the better homes of its time. The lower portion is of brick and the upper of wood. Square columns in front rise to meet the projecting roof which forms galleries across the front both below and above. In the roof are set three dormer windows. In the rear were galleries similar to those in front, but which have been recently enclosed. Though restored, renovated, and changed many times the main structure has retained its original distinctive features. The kitchen was placed slightly to the rear of the house.

The magnificent live oak trees extending today along Sterling and Mudd avenues once formed part of a large grove around the Mouton home.

On Saturday nights the slaves were allowed to hold jamborees in the grove, the distinctive feature of which was the playing of the

"Bamboula" by an old slave named Basil. Dressed ceremoniously in a black suit with white collar and cuffs, Basil thumped out the "Bamboula" on a piece of cowhide stretched tightly across a hollow stump, while the other slaves danced joyously around. His skill was so well known throughout this area that on these nights there was always an interested crowd of spectators looking on.

The Mouton property was later acquired by Dr. F. S. Mudd who sold all but the house and grounds to the late John Cameron Nickerson and Leo Judice, who laid it out in building lots which now form the Mudd and Sterling Grove subdivisions. Many of the streets were named for the members of the Mudd family: Mudd Avenue, Clye Avenue, Elizabeth Avenue, Dudley Avenue, Sterling Avenue, Greig Street. Since Dr. Mudd's death the home has been owned and occupied successively by Louis Domengeaux, Leufroy Burguieres, L. E. White, Maxime Roy and the present occupant.

The house now occupied by the Lafayette Museum has an interesting history. For many years it was known as Governor Mouton's town house. Having been built about 1800 by Jean Mouton on land owned by him, it consisted of one large room with a kitchen at the rear. In 1820 Jean's son, Alexandre, the future senator and governor, added three rooms to it and occupied it with his first wife, the former Zilia Rousseau, a granddaughter of Ex-Governor Jean Jaques Dupré and a reputed beauty. In his "Stories of Dixie" James W. Nicholson said this of her: "While residing in Washington with her husband, Senator Mouton, the celebrated sculptor, Powers, carved the 'Greek Slave.' In selecting a model hand for his famous statue he is said to have chosen the hand of Mrs. Mouton who was noted alike for the beauty of her face and the symmetry of her form." It was also said by Mrs. Mouton's grandson, Alexander, that her hand was used as a model for the hand of Pocahontas in the painting of that Indian princess which hangs in the rotunda of the capitol in Washington.

Three of the four children of this union were born in this house. The reason that the first and oldest, Alfred, the future general, was not born there was that he arrived while the family was visiting relatives in Opelousas. The three born there were Mathilde, who married General Frank Gardner, Odéide, who married Major Jean Sosthene Mouton, and Cecilia who died of a fever in 1863.

Alexander with his family continued to reside in the house until 1836. Meanwhile on March 5, 1834, in an exchange of property with his brothers, Césaire and Antoine Emile, he became sole owner of the house and lots 142, 143, 144 and 145 on which it stood as shown on the original plan of Vermilionville. Two years later Alexandre sold the house and four lots to Cornelius Voorhies, who after a brief residence therein sold it, on November 27, 1836, to Messrs. Samuel M. and Benjamin P. Paxton. On July 5, 1849 the Paxtons sold the same to Dr. W. G. Mills, "except one small dwelling house estimated separately, being the same where the Messrs. Paxton formerly resided." It was Dr. Mills who added the second and third floors and the lookout tower on the roof. Circulated currently among the patients of the good doctor was the saying that he would have to double his fees in order to pay the cost of the lookout tower. Ten years later, at the succession sale of Dr. Mills the house with the four lots was acquired by Mr. William B. Erwin who in turn left it to his four daughters: Henrietta B. Erwin, wife of W. D. Beraud; Roberta T. Erwin, wife of Theodore E. Mumme; Maxime M. Erwin; and Eva L. Erwin, wife of Isaac H. Satterfield. For some time the house was occupied by the Satterfield family. On December 16, 1896, in the final settlement of the Erwin estate, the heirs sold the property to Dr. Percy M. Girard for $3000.000 plus the assumption of a note for $850.

Mr. Girard did not occupy the house immediately but rented it to Mr. John Ramsey who lived in it while he cultivated sugar cane in what is now Elmhurst Subdivision. In 1913 Mr. and Mrs. Ramsey were conducting a boarding house there.

At 514 Buchanan Street stands a good example of the modest but comfortable homes built in Vermilionville around 1850. In 1851 Richard Chargois purchased from Governor Alexandre Mouton the lot on which he built this house. With few changes it still stands as originally constructed. The cypress lumber used in the building of this house was taken from the swamps around Lake Charlotte back of the present airport. The bricks were made at the Paxton brickyard by Richard Chargois himself. As was usual in those days bricks to form the walls were laid between the studs after the framework of the house was up. They were plastered on the inside and covered with weather boards on the outside. This construction made the house warm in winter and cool in summer. The ceilings are supported by hand hewn beams. Differing from those in the early homes of the Acadians the stairway is on the inside rather than rising to the attic from the front porch. Aged double wooden storm doors, when open on each side, expose the then popular double doors with upper sectional panes of glass. The attic windows still possess the original wooden shutters, with the characteristic hand forged hinges; the downstairs windows are covered with the old batten shutters. A faded red metal roof now covers the original hand-split cypress shingles.

Originally there stood back from the rear of the main structure a two-room cypress building which included a kitchen and dining room; for in those days the kitchen was separated from the main house to give the slaves more freedom and to keep from the living quarters the tantalizing fragrance arising from the food being cooked in the kitchen. The only other change in the original house consists of the addition of a kitchen and bathroom.

At the time of his death Richard Chargois was constable, jailer, saloon keeper and brick maker. His brother Hubert became the first constable of Lafayette parish in 1823. A daughter of Richard Chargois married Charles Camille Salles; and a daughter of this marriage, Miss Josette Salles, now owns and occupies this interesting house. It has thus, from the time of its construction, always been in the possession of some one of the family. Though it is now within the expanding central commercial district of the city, the modest owner steadfastly refuses to sell it at present day high prices, preferring to live out her days in the midst of her cherished heirlooms, brightened by the soft mellow light of candles and oil lamps.

The two-story house on the Pin Hook road, presently occupied by Horace Rickey, has an interesting history. It was built long before the Civil War and was at one time used as a kind of hotel frequented by traveling men who made it their headquarters while in this area. At the time of the Civil War it was the home of Henry Monnier. It later came into the possession of the late Dr. Percy Girard who lived in it for many years. While it has been modernized it still retains its original features.

Forgotten Landmarks

The property adjoining the cathedral on which is located the buildings of the cathedral high school has seen many changes since the first settlers came to what became Vermilionville and Lafayette. Near the spot where stands the modern home of the Christian Brothers was one of the first stores in what is now Lafayette. It was owned and operated by a Mr. Castigo even before the first chapel was built on Jean Mouton's land. In 1814 Castigo suddenly and mysteriously closed his store and disappeared from the com-

Above — Armojean Reon with Group

ARMOJEAN REON — 1907
AMONG THE LAST OF THE ATTAKAPAS INDIANS

(One of the few remaining speakers of the language). Photographs on this page by J. R. Swanton. Courtesy of Bureau of American Ethnology, Smithsonian Institution.

Above, left —
Armojean Reon

Below, left —
Armojean with logs

Below, right —
Home of Armojean Reon, Lake Charles, La.

Typical scene in the Attakapas country. Photograph by J. R. Swanton about 1907. (Courtesy Bureau of American Ethnology, Smithsonian Institution)

The Oaks of Beau Sejour

munity, much to the puzzlement of the settlers. It was later learned that, as a member of Lafitte's pirate gang, he had gone to join Lafitte's contingent in the defense of New Orleans, and thus participated in the famous battle of January 8, 1815. After the battle he returned to the small settlement, reopened his store, and lived a peaceful and orderly life thereafter. He no doubt had been included in the proclamation of pardon which General Jackson issued in 1815 to Lafitte and his followers as a reward for their aid in the defeat of the British.

On the land occupied by the Cathedral High School once stood the private bank operated by William Clegg. It is believed that prior to Clegg's banking activities the branch office of discount and deposit of the Union Bank of Louisiana was located in the same building.

On the lot now occupied by the modern home of the Christian Brothers there stood, years ago, the home of two brothers named Taylor, who conducted a drug store in an adjoining building. The home was acquired by the Eastin family from whom it descended to Elia Martin, the wife of the late Judge O. C. Mouton. Judge Mouton occupied it as his home for many years. In 1920 he sold it to the Christian Brothers who made their home in it until the construction of their present modern one.

Not long after the founding of Vermilionville we find that Dr. Michel Girard purchased two lots at the rear of the present bishop's residence and on them built his home. At that time a small lane separated them from the cemetery. Long before the Civil War there stood on the corner of the bishop's property the store of Charles Homer Mouton. Later on this corner was the site of the Gerac home which was known as the "Old Gerac House" until removed to erect the Bishop's residence. The original plot plan of Vermilionville showed a street on each side of the church property. It was facing this street that stood St. John's College founded by Father Forge soon after he took charge of the Parish in 1881, but soon abandoned.

At the corner of Congress and Buchanan Streets on land now occupied by a filling station and the home of the late Joseph E. Mouton once stood the home of Eraste Mouton, the father of Joseph and the French editor of "L'Echo de Vermilionville." Standing in front of his home along what is now Congress Street was a row of towering white cypress trees interspersed with lovely crepe myrtles. In the rear were large live oak trees. Between the house and

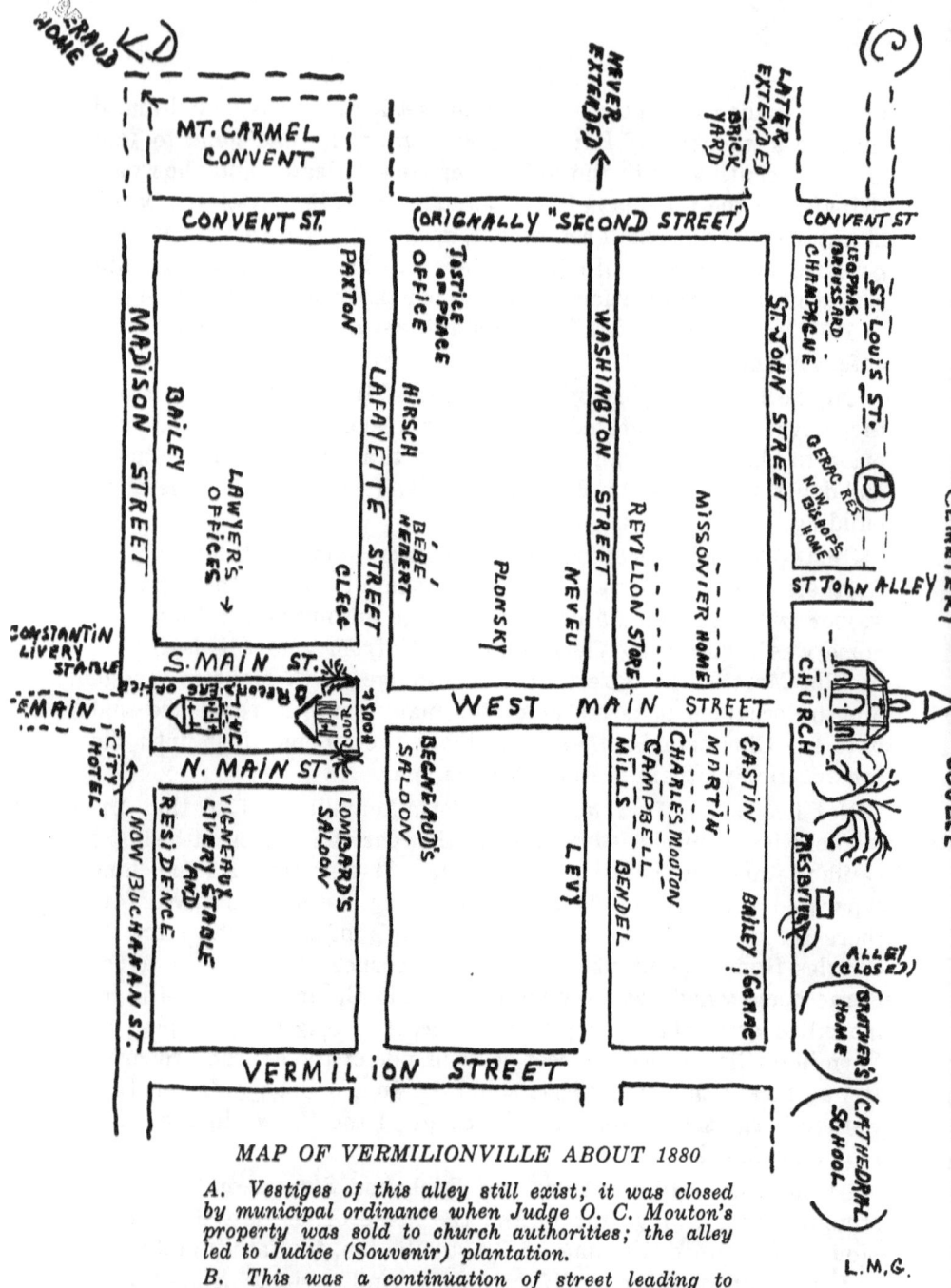

MAP OF VERMILIONVILLE ABOUT 1880

A. Vestiges of this alley still exist; it was closed by municipal ordinance when Judge O. C. Mouton's property was sold to church authorities; the alley led to Judice (Souvenir) plantation.

B. This was a continuation of street leading to church from Convent Street. Former proprietors (Geracs — now Bishop's home) and Cleophas Broussard (later Labbe and now Champagne property) enclosed same and obliterated it.

C. Old road to Hohorst, Mrs. Hazard Eastin and elsewhere.

D. Old road to Lee Avenue, finally to Tin Can Alley (now College Avenue in front of Southwestern) and then to Pin Hook Road, leading to Cote Gelee and points east.

the oaks there was once a beautiful, old fashioned French designed garden teeming with beautiful and exotic flowers tended by a French gardener. Today the cypress and myrtle trees are gone and a filling station occupies the site of the old home. However, between it and the present home, shaded by one of the remaining live oaks, Mrs. Mouton has recreated the garden, brightened all the year round with flaming azaleas, rare camellias, amaryllis and gladiolas.

Across Garfield Street at its intersection with Polk Street once stood the plantation home of Madam Charles Mouton, the former Julie Latiolais, whose husband was the son of Jean Mouton and father of Charles Homer Mouton and Eraste mentioned above. This was long before the railroad came to Vermilionville and her plantation facing Garfield Street stretched far back across the present railroad tracks. At that time the land between Madame Charles' home and the home of Eraste was still vacant so that, when the voices in one home were raised, they could be heard at the other.

When the railroad came into Vermilionville in the early eighties Madame Charles sold her home and much of her plantation to the railroad company which located its tracks, station and offices on it. To Judge J. G. Parkerson, who negotiated the sale for the company, it gave the home of Madame Charles with the adjoining grounds as a reward for his services. From the judge the property descended to his daughter, Mrs. Eppie Mills; and from her to the late William P. Mills, whose children now operate a portion of it as a parking lot.

On the property now occupied by the First National Funeral Home there stood, prior to 1846, the store of Mr. Jules Revillon, the grandfather of the late Mrs. Paul Krauss. He had come to Vermilionville directly from France, where he had known Napoleon Bonaparte intimately, about whom some of the later members of his family have handed down the stories he related about Bonaparte.

At 201 West Vermilion Street once stood the Lafayette House operated by Richard Chargois, prior to the building of his home at 514 Buchanan Street. An interesting advertisement by the new proprietor of this house appeared in the English side of the *Impartial* on September 4, 1847.

Lafayette House
Vermilionville, La.

The travelling and resident public are respectfully informed that the subscriber has just taken possession of the above house, lately occupied by Mr. R. Chargois. He intends keeping the house upon such a plan that persons can be accommodated at all hours with anything the country affords. His table will be amply provided; his bar will be supplied with good liquors; and his bedrooms will also be furnished with good and comfortable bedding. He requests the attention of the travelling public, especially as he intends to spare no pains in making all those who may favor him with their patronage as comfortable as possible. His charges will be moderate; and, as every exertion will be made to give satisfaction, he hopes to be liberally patronized.

W. B. Bailey

Just after the turn of the nineteenth century there came from London to Vermilionville three brothers, Richard, Hubert and Sebastian Chargois. Having been brickmakers in London, they soon established the first brick making plant in the infant village. Their plant was located on the east side of St. John Street between Convent Street and College Avenue. The bricks made here were used in the construction of many of Vermilionville's early homes. On March 7, 1837 Sebastian Chargois sold the plant to Samuel W. Paxton, together with some eighty thousand bricks. Paxton continued to operate it for several years before it was abandoned. The excavation from which the clay for the bricks had been taken soon filled with water and thereafter was known to the older residents as the old swimming hole. However, after two young cousins, sons of prominent families, had drowned in it, the city authorities ordered it filled. One cousin was Labat Judice, son of Numa J. Judice; the other was Scranton, son of Albert Judice. Nevertheless there remained for many years a depression there until further filling took place in order that homes could be built on the site of the old swimming hole.

On the grounds now occupied by the Azalea Motor Court and facing Vermilion Street stood the boyhood home of Vermilionville's first graduate dentist, Doctor H. C. Salles. The home, known for over fifty years as the "Old Moss House," was built by the father of Doctor Salles in 1851. There, during the war between the states, the French flag was raised when it was learned that the Union army, led by General Banks, was marching through. Many neighboring women and children rushed to this home for protection. Dr. H. C. Salles was then a small boy, but to his wife and son, Paul, he often related the vivid impression made upon all taking refuge in the home who heard the soldiers, as they marched by, repeat with the cadence of their marching: "French flag, French flag, French flag."

Across the street from the home of the late Judge Paul Debaillon at 721 Buchanan Street, once stood the shop in which was printed *L'Echo de Vermilionville*, a weekly newspaper published in both English and French. The French editor was Eraste Mouton and the English editor Abijah Bailey. During the Civil War both men were in the Confederate army, but the paper continued to be published as late as 1863 by Columbus C. Bailey, a younger brother of Abijah Bailey.

On West Main Street directly across from the First National Funeral Home there stood until recently the old Béraud Home, built in 1851 in about the same manner as the Josette Salles home, with inner walls of plastered brick and covered on the outside with cypress weather boards. In a building next door the Béraud brothers for many years conducted a general store.

On the corner where is presently located the Lafayette Sanitarium once stood the St. Joseph Academy, built and donated by Father Etienne Jules Foltier April 27, 1859. The late Mr. Joseph Albert Chargois, who was ninety-one years old in 1937 and a resident of Lafayette, attended this college in the fist years of its existence and after its close attended Vermilionville Academy which was located on the corner of East Vermilion and Jefferson Streets, across from the Gordon Hotel.

On the north corner of College Avenue and Cherry Street, now occupied by the home of the late Mrs. Ralph Voorhies, was the home of Michel Eloi Girard, surrounded by his plantation. After his death his widow, the former Maxime Crow, lived there. Later one portion of the plantation descended to a son, Dr. Felix E. Girard, who from it developed Elmhurst Subdivision. Another part descended to another son, Crow Girard, who created from it the Girard Subdivision.

Of the old homes that have disappeared perhaps the one best entitled to be called a mansion was that of Governor Alexandre Mouton. This house stood on the plot now occupied by the LeRosen public school. It was an imposing two-story structure of brick and was built by the governor a few years prior to the Civil War. It stood on an elevation which sloped gradually to the bayou which it faced. After the governor's death it was inherited by his daughter, Marie, who was married to Dr. Homer D. Guidry. After her death it was purchased by the Lafayette Parish School Board to be used as a school. It had been occupied for this purpose only a short time when it caught fire and burned to the ground. While it was still standing and occupied by the Guidry family it was visited by a young Southwestern student, Marjorie Bouvier, whose description of it was published in Southwestern's student paper, *The Vermilion*, on November 20, 1920. Her description in part follows.

The old home, as it stands today, is in a state of delapidation and almost ruin. It fills one with a certain amount of sadness to stand and gaze upon the beauties of long ago which are fast passing out of reach. The home, as it looks today, is not beautiful, but the thought of what it has been makes it a structure grand and good to look upon.

As one approaches the house, he is impressed, not with the grandeur or the magnificence, but with the dignity and hospitality so suggestive of real southern people.

The house is built of brick and simply as a square, the plainness of which is relieved by the treatment of the porch. The porch does not extend across the width of the front, only so far as to include two of the four large front windows and the entrance door. Four large, square columns extend from the ground to the roof of the second floor. There is no second floor gallery so the loftiness and stateliness of the porch is increased. The entrance has a wide sill and above it is a transom with three panels of glass; to the sides of the door are small panels with insets of glass. The ceiling of the gallery roof is artistically paneled in white wainscoting. Four half-columns protrude from the wall of the front to give support to the immense beams that are required to hold up the gable. This gable is ornamented with many designs cut out of wood. In the center of the triangle is a crescent window of colored glass. The door of entrance is massive and of four panels; the old locks and bolts tell of the many hands that have pushed them to shut out friend and foe.

The hall, though not as spacious as many of the old houses, is, nevertheless, quite large. The ceilings are high, the walls of plaster. The moulding is also made of plaster and is in plain, conventional design. At the back of the hall are the stairs, which are steep and narrow. As you gaze upon them you can almost see the wife of Alexandre Mouton, in her dress crinoline, ascend them to prepare for bed.

Four doors enter the hall from the different rooms, two on each side. On the left side the doors are close together, and each is the entrance to a bedroom. Both of these rooms are large and have immense windows and casements. Between the rooms is a pair of sliding doors. In the front room is an entrance to a closet under the stairs where perhaps Governor Mouton kept his fire arms or his choice wines. On the other side of the hall the doors are far apart. One enters the living room and the other the dining room. Both of these rooms have large windows which were once draped in the finest of velvets and upon the walls are many fine old pictures. The mantelpieces are both of black marble splashed with white. The base boards appear to be of the same material, but, upon closer view, one finds that they are only of wood well painted to represent marble.

The back porch extends across the width of the house and is supported by six square columns. Above there is also a second gallery whose balustrades are of hand hewn wood. The lawn at the back is very large and contains many old pecan and live oak trees laden with the gray moss peculiar to this section of the country. As one leaves the house from the back he is able to obtain a full view of the top of the house. Four large chimneys protrude from the roof and in the center is the belfry. The bell is gone, but it was the custom to ring this bell to summon the slaves from all over the plantation. The belfry, which is made of wood, is weather beaten and worn.

In 1860 Governor Mouton had a French artist, A. Persac, execute a painting of his home showing the house, slave quarters, and sugar mill. This painting shows a wing projecting from each side at the rear of the house, one the kitchen and the other the governor's office. The two rooms described above as bedrooms were originally the parlor and drawing room. The bedrooms were upstairs. A large reproduction of this painting may be seen in the Maison Francais-Acadienne on the Southwestern Louisiana Institute campus. The original is in the possession of a granddaughter of Governor Mouton, Mrs. Paul Breaux of Rayne, Louisiana.

CHAPTER IX

FROM VILLAGE TO CITY

Jean Mouton's village of a dozen or so blocks grew very slowly and it was many years before the development of new subdivisions forced an extension of its boundaries. After Jean's death in 1831 much of his property in and around the village was inherited by three of his sons, Alexander, Césaire, and Antoine Emile. Evidently they expected the town to expand because soon after their father's death they entered into a written agreement by which each bound himself to contribute his proportionate share of lots for the future development of the village. That Césaire intended to keep his part of the agreement is confirmed in a sale of land he made to Cornelius Voorhies on June 9, 1834. On that date he sold to Voorhies for twenty-five hundred dollars a tract of land facing five arpents on Vermilion Bayou and extending forty arpents back toward the village. In the deed was stipulated the condition that Voorhies would furnish toward the extension of the town the same number of lots that he, Césaire, was obligated to contribute. Whether Voorhies was ever called upon to carry out that part of the agreement is not known. In 1847, however, Alexander kept his part of the agreement by laying out additional lots between what is now Congress Street and the Home Building and Loan office, 523 Jefferson, thus extending Jefferson Street a short distance.

The village, however, did not grow as rapidly as expected; in fact there was little real extension until the completion of the railroad to Vermilionville in 1880. One of the first major additions came with the opening of the Mills subdivision in 1856. Washington Street was extended to the north in 1870. Next came the Mouton addition along extensions of Vermilion and Main Streets to the east. By the time the trains were running the first McComb subdivision had been opened and Jefferson Street extended to the railroad. This extension was first given the name Pierce Street but later changed to Jefferson. In 1880 the second McComb subdivision was opened north of the railroad. The present Jefferson Boulevard

The Charles Homer Mouton Home as it appears on Sterling Avenue. Built about 1845.

LATIOLAIS HOUSE

On the Pont de Mouton Road, built by Alexandre, called "Cocquelin," Latiolais about 1820. Alexandre was the son of Joseph Latiolais, of the War of 1812 fame, and Marie Francoise Nezatte. The Joseph Latiolais home was near Breaux Bridge, in St. Martin's Parish. Near the house grew the famous Arnaud Robert live oak, the "Vice-President" of Dr. E. L. Stephens' Live Oak Society. "Cocquelin" was married to Emelie, daughter of Joseph, second son of Jean Mouton and Cidalise Arceneaux.

MAGNOLIA PLANTATION — HOUSE BUILT ABOUT 1840.

(Below) The Home of Dr. Thomas B. Hopkins was situated at the north corner of Pierce and West Simcoe Street, being built about 1850. Dr. and Mrs. Hopkins are on the porch with members of their family.

(Above) Dr. Michel Eloi Girard's Home — built in 1840 — in the rear of the late Mrs. Ralph Voorhies's home at 403 West College and Cherry Street. Elmhurst addition had not been opened at this period; the house was in a yard of beautiful trees.

(Below) Long Plantation Home. In his memoirs Mr. Alexander Mouton (1853-1938) said, "Down the Vermilion River south of Walnut Grove (now Bendel Gardens) about three miles on the East Bank lived Honore Beraud the owner of considerable land — there were many ponds and at the closing of the day about sundown large numbers of ducks would light." Mr. Beraud died of yellow fever during the epidemic in 1858.

was then called Lincoln Avenue. It was not until near the turn of the century that Mudd and Sterling Grove Subdivisions were developed. The same was true of the Girard and Elmhurst additions.

The first extension of the town limits took place in 1869 when the charter was amended to set up the mayor-council type of government. By 1900 the boundaries were approximately as follows: Beginning at a point where College Avenue crosses the coulee at the rear of the Catholic cemetery, the boundary followed the coulee to Cameron Street, then along Cameron Street to the railroad; thence along Mudd Avenue to Moss Street; from Moss Street to Simcoe to Twelfth Street; following Twelfth Street to the railroad the boundary crossed the railroad tracks to Lamar; thence along Lamar to College and north on College to the point of beginning. At that time, therefore, such places as Southwestern, Sears Roebuck, the Junior High School, the municipal golf course and swimming pool, the Nona Theatre, the Memorial Health Center, the Charity and Lady of Lourdes Hospitals were all outside the corporate boundaries. The area between Southwestern and Vermilion Bayou was still a series of cane, cotton and corn fields. Only a few houses dotted the landscape. West of the coulee at the rear of the Catholic cemetery and the Lafayette Sanitarium lay the Souvenir Plantation of Mrs. Alix Judice and the plantations of Eraste Landry and Demas Comeaux.

Prior to the Civil War Vermilionville was a much more prosperous town than in the eighteen seventies. Surrounded with cattle ranches, sugar and cotton plantations it was the center of much wealth. There was much buying and selling of land and slaves were in ready demand. After the war came hard times. With their slaves gone and their plantations ravaged, the planters knew not where to turn. Land became a drug on the market with no labor to cultivate it. Because of the heavy taxes and penalties levied by the carpetbag government many were forced to dispose of their lands. Consequently many of the younger sons turned to other occupations. The village progress was slowed up by these conditions. It was George W. Cable who, in his novel, *Bonaventure*, published in 1888, referred to the village as "the sorry little town of Vermilionville." Cable had visited this section before the publication of his book and had been entertained by Governor Mouton at his home at Ile Copal. While his descriptions of the countryside are excellent, yet he ridiculed the people, their names, customs, and manners in his book. This response to the hospitality shown him by all during his visit here so incensed the citizens of St. Martinville that they burned him in effigy on the main street of the town. Because of his distortions, dislike for Cable and his works became a tradition in South Louisiana.

It was the completion of the railroad, the location of its shops here, and the location of Southwestern Louisiana Institute in its midst that furnished the first real impetus to the town's growth. The early location of business establishments near the courthouse and church has already been referred to. The coming of railroads, however, soon changed the direction of the town's development. With the extension of Jefferson Street to the railroad it was not long until new business establishments opened on that thoroughfare, rather than in the older section of the town. This was true especially after the year 1900.

The rapidity with which this change took place becomes clear after reading an interview with Mr. Charles Debaillon published in the *Lafayette Progress* on July 12, 1958. Mr. Debaillon took the census of Lafayette in 1900 under a commission issued to him by Mr. William Clegg, Supervisor of the United States census for the Third District of Louisiana. He holds vivid memories of Lafayette at that time.

Mr. Debaillon remarks that Lafayette, with a population of 3314, had already become the hub city of the area and, for a town its size, boasted many clothing and general merchandise stores, livery stables, hotels, saloons, a volunteer fire brigade, blacksmith shops, an opera house, and drug stores. He is the only living charter member of the Hobo Fire Company which was organized in 1897. He said this early fire fighting company had a two-wheeled hose truck with about five hundred feet of hose. It had to be pulled by hand, the firemen running to the fire. At that time there was sufficient pressure to throw water above any building then in existence.

In speaking of the Falk Opera House, located on Washington Street between West Vermilion and Main Streets, Mr. Debaillon states that this was the chief gathering place for entertainment, recalling that the Emma Warren Company played there. Traveling opera troupes and minstrels performed there frequently, having come in private railroad cars. This was also the scene of frequent public dances. When the Jefferson Theatre was built in 1904, however, the Falk Opera House, now outmoded, closed its doors. The building for some time thereafter was occupied by a furniture store until it was destroyed by fire some thirty years ago.

In 1900 most of the principal stores and business establishments were still in the older part of town. Mentioned by Mr. Debaillon in this area were the Leon Plonsky Store on Lafayette Street, Constantine's livery stable where Joe Boulanger presently has a service station at 801 South Buchanan Street, the John Vigneaux livery stable near the present Pittsburg Plate Glass store at 222 West Main Street. Coffins could also be bought at this livery stable as there were no undertaking establishments as we know them today. Other stores in this area were Mrs. W. C. Martin's store on West Main near the present D. H. Castille's appliance store; the Joe Plonsky store and the L. Levy store on Washington street between West Main and Vermilion; and across from it the B. Falk Store. On the corner of Vermilion and South Washington was the Gardebled drug store; and Mrs. John O. Mouton conducted on the corner of Vermilion and Washington a store specializing in ladies wear. Other establishments were: William Clegg's drug store on the corner of Main and Lafayette, now occupied by Beadle's feed store; the old Revillon store on the site of the National Funeral home; the Leopold LaCoste blacksmith shop on Buchanan Street at the rear of the present McCrory building; and the Gus La Coste Hardware Store on the corner of Vermilion and South Buchanan Streets.

On Jefferson Street, which today is considered the main business thoroughfare, there were in 1900 comparatively few business houses. Mentioned by Mr. Debaillon were the First National Bank at its present location; the Moss Brothers and Company drug store across from the present Gordon Hotel; the Gus Schmulen dry goods store on the site of the Guaranty Bank and Trust Company; the Mouton Brothers general store where Heymann's Department Store now is; the George Doucet Drug Store across the street from the Mouton Brothers store; the Sidney Veazey livery stable where the Evangeline Hotel now stands; and the John O. Mouton store near the present shop of Lighting Cleaners. North of the railroad on what is now Jefferson Boulevard was the Racca Hotel and next to it the store of Morris Rosenfield.

In 1900 there were no garages or filling stations, no hospitals; no large school buildings, steam laundries, gas mains, or a sewerage system. Many families still depended on wells and cisterns for their water supply. The unpaved streets were narrow, dusty, and sometimes impassable in rainy weather. A few board sidewalks spewed water on the pedestrian when he stepped on them in wet weather. In 1904 the business men in the newly developing section realized that, unless some of the streets were widened, business would go elsewhere. The two streets in question were Jefferson from the present city hall to Garfield Street and Vermilion from Lee to St. John. The mayor at that time was Mr. Charles D. Caffery. The problem was finally solved when merchants on one side of the street donated the land and moved their buildings back fifteen feet while the merchants on the other side paid the expense of moving.

By 1915, only fifteen years after Mr. Debaillon's census, Jefferson Street was well on its way to becoming the main business thoroughfare it is today. The Gordon Hotel and Jefferson Theatre had been completed and were in full operation. On the corner of Jefferson and East Main, now occupied by the Lafayette Motor Company, Moore Biossat had opened Lafayette's first garage and was selling Overland automobiles. Moss Pharmacy and Moss Hardware had occupied their new two-story building across from the Gordon Hotel. The Century Club had built its two-story club at 534 Jefferson Street, now occupied by the Woodmen of the World and Bell's Shoe Store. Across the street was Mose Levy's large store popularly called the Blue Front Store. Two doors from the Century Club was Biossat's Jewelry Store. In the two-story building at 509 Jefferson, now occupied by Stein's men's wear and McCann's shoe stores Sig Kahn conducted a men's clothing store. On the corner of Congress and Jefferson Vic and Willie Levy had erected a large two-story brick building in which they conducted a dry goods store known as the White Front Store. On the corner across the street had arisen the new home of the Bank of Lafayette and Trust Company. Near the present Krauss Jewelry Store stood a large two-story frame building in which Mrs. Charles Jeanmard conducted a dressmaking establishment. This building was later moved to 1037 Johnston Street and converted into a residence, now the home of Mr. and Mrs. Herbert E. Schilling. On the corner of Jefferson and Garfield now occupied by Montgomery Ward's Store was Daigre's Variety Store. Two doors from it was Yandle's soda fountain and candy shop. On the corner across Garfield from Daigre's stores was the small, handsome Episcopal Church. Across Jefferson from the Variety store was a Chinese laundry, McFadden's Grocery Store and Joe Bienvenue's Tailor Shop. Two doors from the tailor shop was the large residence of Judge G. A. (Bedon) Martin. A livery stable still occupied the site of the

Evangeline Hotel. Toward the railroad on the corner of Jefferson and Cypress Streets Morris Rosenfield had erected the large brick building, now occupied by the Richard Furniture Company, in which he conducted a dry goods store. With his family he occupied an apartment on the second floor. Across Jefferson Street was the large hardware store of Denbo and Nicholson.

Between these major business houses were frequent vacant lots and an occasional small office or shop. Except in the hotels there were few eating places. At the railroad station there was the Brown News Restaurant in the Southern Pacific office building. Near by in what is now the Carroll Hotel was Marion's Restaurant noted for good food. Near the present Lightning Cleaners was a Chinese restaurant catering to small groups, mostly men. Near Biossat's Jewelry Store was a restaurant that often served game in season.

The growth of Lafayette can best be visualized by a look at the census records. The census of 1870 showed a population of 777 of which 454 were white and 323 colored. Ten years later the number was only 815. With the coming of the railroad with its divisional offices and shops, the number of inhabitants increased more rapidly. By 1890 the population had reached 2100. By 1900, 3000; by 1910, 6000; by 1920, 9000; and by 1930, 15,000. After the oil companies began to move their offices into Lafayette, the city grew by leaps and bounds. In 1940 the population was 19,210; in 1950, 33,541; and in 1958 it was estimated to be 50,000 within the city limits with another eight or ten thousand in the outlying subdivisions.

As time went on the city acquired by slow degrees all the facilities that furnish the comforts of a modern city. In 1897 were voted bonds in the amount of $30,000.00 for the installation of the first water works and electric light plant. Six years later were built the first cement sidewalks in the business section. In the same year the city officials authorized the purchase of new equipment for the volunteer fire department. In 1902 the citizens voted bonds for the first modern high school, located where the new post office is now being built; for a public market; and for extending the water and light service. In 1915 an ordinance provided for the sprinkling of the streets. In the same year a bond issue of $75,000.00 made possible the gravelling of the two main streets in the business section and the same treatment of two or three roads leading out of town. Three years later another bond issue of the same amount was authorized for the construction of sanitary sewers. In 1919 came the climax when the citizens voted $425,000.00 in bonds for the paving of Jefferson Street; the gravelling of other important streets; the laying of storm sewers; the extension of water mains, and the improvement of the water works. In 1928 another bond issue of $211,000.00 made possible the installation of the first sewage disposal plant, the extension of storm sewers, and the building of a municipal swmiming pool and golf course. In October of the same year the proceeds of a bond issue of $25,000.00 was used to purchase one hundred sixty acres of land east of the city as the beginning of the present airport. A third bond issue of $125,000.00 provided for the further extension of water mains and the installation of the first water filtration system. In 1929 the proceeds of a three mill tax, to run for ten years, were to be used for the paving of additional streets, a portion of this levy being anticipated immediately for the paving of several miles of streets in the central business section of the city. With the proceeds of this tax and very substantial assistance of the Works Progress Administration the city was able, in 1936, to black top many miles of streets in the residential districts. This paving program has been continued at the expense of the property owners so that today there are within the city over sixty miles of paved streets and an equal number of miles surfaced with gravel.

To meet the pressing demands of a rapidly growing population the citizens, in 1949, voted a record breaking bond issue of eight million dollars: seven millions of revenue bonds and one million of public improvement bonds. The proceeds of these issues were used for the construction of a new and enlarged electric light plant; the extension of electric wires; the installation of a larger sewage disposal plant and extension of the sewerage system; the enlargement and improvement of the water works and extension of water mains; and the development of additional public parks and recreation facilities. These improvements were designed to meet the needs of a population of sixty thousand; a goal that, at the present rate of growth, will soon become a reality.

One utility the citizens of Lafayette had long hoped for was gas for domestic and industrial use. To meet this long felt need the Louisiana Public Utility Company, in 1926, erected a plant for the manufacture of artificial gas and laid distribution pipe lines through the main sections of the city. The cost of the gas was so high, however, that many were precluded from its use. The only hope of reduced cost seemed to lie in the bringing of natural gas from the numerous producing wells of North Louisiana. Accordingly, in November 1931, the United Gas Company installed a high pressure line bearing this much needed commodity to the limits of Lafayette. From this company the Louisiana Public Utilities bought the gas which it distributed to its customers through its own existing lines. With this plentiful supply the company was able to reduce the price so that a greater number could use gas for domestic and industrial purposes. Whereas artificial gas had cost the average consumer one dollar seventy-five cents per thousand cubic feet, the natural gas cost him only ninety cents. For large consumers the cost was as low as thirty cents. As a consequence of this facility the ease and comfort of living were greatly enhanced and the industrial potentialities of the city considerably enlarged.

The hotel facilities demanded by a growing city have in recent years been greatly expanded. In 1928 the Down Town Realty Company of Shreveport acquired the ground on Jefferson Street that had long been occupied by a livery stable and on it constructed Lafayette's first modern, fireproof hotel, the Evangeline, at a cost of $300,000. About the same time the owners of the Gordon Hotel added a fourth story to it, completely modernized it, and thus converted it into an attractive, up-to-date hostelry. Today the traveller will find in the city five hotels with three hundred and thirty-five rooms and a dozen tourist courts with about two hundred units. The two or three restaurants of 1900 have multiplied into a dozen or more, some of which are famous for fine food.

March 29, 1953 was a red letter day in the history of the City and Parish of Lafayette. On that date was dedicated the Lafayette Public Library. This event marked the culmination of the pioneering efforts of the Women's Club, Les Vingt Quatre, and a citizens library committee. Both the Women's Club and Les Vingt Quatre had sponsored lending libraries in the past. Following them came the Municipal Library which first occupied the old city hall facing the courthouse square and later the basement of the old Southside School. The new library, built at a cost of $134,000.00 on grounds donated by the Parish School Board, was financed by a parish-wide bond issue of $100,000.00 and the proceeds of a city tax. The library is the central unit of a parish-wide system with a branch in each town of the parish and a bookmobile to serve rural areas. The library is administered by a city-parish board consisting of five members appointed in turn by the city trustees and police jury. During the period of construction and at the time of the dedication the chairman of the board was Miss Edith Dupré, a life-long worker in the cause of education and intellectual advancement. In her closing remarks at the dedication ceremonies she made the significant statement: "No institution is as vital to the preservation of a democracy as a library."

It is not possible here to trace all the steps by which the village of Vermilionville has been transformed into the City of Lafayette. In closing this chapter the writer might point out that the village which had no public parks now can boast of over three hundred acres in parks and playgrounds, several swimming pools, a municipal stadium, baseball park and a recreation center building. The one theatre has increased to five. The volunteer fire department, with its one two-wheeled hose cart, has grown into five modern fire stations with nine motorized pieces of fire fighting equipment, manned by fifty-four full time trained firemen. Instead of the one constable of Jean Mouton's time there is a police force of over forty including two policewomen. The one original Church of St. John the Evangelist has expanded to thirty-two representing fifteen different denominations. Southwestern Louisiana Institute, opened in 1901 on a campus of twenty-five acres with a few students, now occupies over five hundred acres with an annual enrollment of five thousand. Beyond the expanded city limits on every road leading out of town are residential subdivisions, schools and market centers, all waiting to be incorporated into an ever growing Lafayette.

CHAPTER X

THE WHITE LEAGUE IN LAFAYETTE PARISH

During the trying days of Reconstruction in Louisiana the citizens of Vermilionville and Lafayette Parish actively opposed the corrupt carpet bag government in state and parish. In the election of 1872 Governor Henry C. Warmoth, the radical governor of Louisiana, had switched his support from the radical Republican Party to the Conservative Democratic Party. The Radical Republican candidate for governor was W. P. Kellogg; the Conservative Democratic candidate was John McEnery. Since Governor Warmoth controlled the election machinery, his returning board declared McEnery elected by a majority of ten thousand votes. The Radical Republican returning board, however, counted Kellogg in and with the aid of federal troops installed him in office.

After this defeat Conservative Democrats began to prepare for the next election four years hence, determined to restore white rule in the state. To that end they formed a quasi-secret armed organization known as the White League. Headed by Murphy J. Foster, a rising young statesman from Franklin, Louisiana, the leaders encouraged the forming of other chapters of this league throughout the state.

As evidence that the people of Lafayette Parish joined wholeheartedly in these efforts to throw off the yoke of radical rule, there appeared in the Lafayette Advertiser the following call:
"To the people of the Parish of Lafayette:

In response to the requests of the Democratic State Central Committee that delegates be elected to a state convention to assemble in Baton Rouge on the fourth Monday of August next to select a state treasurer and members of Congress for the several congressional districts, the undersigned respectfully invite all democratic voters, who desire substantial and thorough reform in all our public affairs, to meet at the courthouse on Saturday the 15th day of August for the purpose of selecting delegates to the said convention and also of electing a parish Central Committee."

The above call was signed by the following:

W. B. Bailey, member State Central Committee, Vermilionville, July 25, 1874.
S. J. Montgomery
H. Jamison, Jr.
W. H. Cunningham, M. D.
Arthur Greig
J. D. Trahan, M. D.
John S. Whittington
Alex M. Guidry
N. Breaux
M. L. Lyons, M. D.
Joseph Louviere
L. P. Revillon
H. M. Bailey
C. T. Patin
Camille Sellers
F. S. Mudd, M. D.
Ed. Eug. Mouton
M. F. Rigues
Jean Bernard
Paulin Arceneaux
R. C. Landry
Nathan Foreman
M. T. Martin
John Clegg

The people met at the courthouse of the Parish of Lafayette on Saturday, August 15, 1874, and, on motion of Mr. W. B. Bailey, Col. John R. Creighton was unanimously elected president and L. P. Revillon and F. P. Parent secretaries.

Resolutions offered by C. H. Mouton, Esq. and seconded by E. E. Mouton, Esq. were unanimously adopted. Briefly stated they were:

1. That this Parish Convention endorse the address of the Democratic State Central Committee and the address of the Committee of Seventy.

2. That the members of this Parish Convention are hopeful that the state convention, which is to assemble at Baton Rouge on the 24th instant, will present the people of this state a platform or declaration of principles that will unite them in one solid and compact opposition to radical rule and Negro supremacy.

3. That on William Pitt Kellogg we look as a usurper of the state government of Louisiana, and that we do unreservedly denounce him as such, and his government as illegal, unjust, and oppressive.

4. That this convention elect five delegates to represent this parish in the State Convention to assemble at Baton Rouge on the 24th instant; that they shall cast the vote of this parish as a unit on all questions that may come before said convention.

5. On motion of C. T. Patin the following persons were elected by acclamation delegates to the Baton Rouge Convention: Victor Martin, Gustave St. Julien, Alexandre Del Homme, C. H. Mouton, and John Clegg.

6. On motion of E. E. Mouton, Esq., resolved that the thanks of this meeting be tendered to the president of the meeting for the able and dignified manner with which he presided over it.

7. On motion of E. E. Mouton, Esq., resolved that the thanks of this meeting be tendered to R. H. Marr, Esq., of New Orleans, Chairman of the Committee of Seventy, for his noble and disinterested conduct in defending the rights of the people of Louisiana.

8. On motion of E. E. Mouton, Esq., Resolved that the proceedings of this meeting be published in the New Orleans *Bee and Bulletin* and the *Lafayette Advertiser*.

On motion of C. H. Mouton the meeting then adjourned.

L. Philibert Revillon	John Creighton
F. P. Parent	President
Secretaries	

Meantime there had been organized in Lafayette Parish fourteen White League Clubs. Immediately after the Baton Rouge Convention the Vermilionville White League Club met and passed in effect the following resolutions:

1. That the Vermilion White League Club, numbering eighty-three members, ratify the resolutions of the White Peoples Convention held in Baton Rouge on the 24th and 25th of August, 1874.

2. That the members of the club do hereby pledge themselves to support the nominees of said convention and to use all honorable means to ensure their election.

3. That while claiming for ourselves the right to organize under a name of our own choice, we emphatically declare that we shall continue as White Leaguers to labor for the Baton Rouge nominees; and we feel that we shall be preponderent in electing them all under our present organization, which we are determined to keep up until after the November election.

4. That copies of these Resolutions be transmitted immediately to all White League Clubs of the Parish of Lafayette with respectful request to adopt similar ratifying resolutions and transmit them to the Parish Committee of the White League in order to have the same published.

Copies of the above resolutions were transmitted to all the White League Clubs of the Parish. Below is the date each club ratified them, the name of the club, the number of members, and names of the officers:

Date	Club Name	Number of Members	Officers
Sept. 2, 1874	Isle de Canes	27	M. G. Broussard, President
Sept. 1, 1874	John Caruthers Club	57	John Caruthers, President Esteve Guidry, Secretary
Sept. 1, 1874	Carencro Central Club	78	N. Broussard, President A. Broussard, Secretary
Aug. 31, 1874	Lafayette White League Club	51	J. Edmond Mouton, President Vic Martin, Secretary
Aug. 30, 1874	Begnaud's Club	46	A. D. Boudreaux, President Alexandre DelHomme, Secretary
Sept. 1, 1874	Beau Bassin Club	73	P. D. Guilbeau, President V. E. Dupuis, Secretary
Sept. 2, 1874	St. Julien Club	50	J. G. St. Julien, President J. S. Bernard, Secretary
Sept. 6, 1874	Dugas Club	29	Joachim Dugas, President P. O. Richard, Secretary
Sept. 5, 1874	Old Cote Gelee Club	58	Norbert Landry, President R. C. Landry, Secretary
Sept. 15, 1874	Charles Hebert's Club	18	D. C. Hebert, President E. Vincent, Secretary
	Royville Club		P. B. Roy, President F. P. Parent, Secretary
	White Man's Club		C. T. Patin, President A. D. Verot, Secretary

Since the White League Clubs were armed and operated in secret it is difficult to learn the methods employed by them in carrying out their professed purposes. Some light, however, is thrown on their plans in a series of resolutions passed by the Club Begnaud, No. 2, on September 2, 1874. The record of this action was written in French, which, translated, reads as follows:

Club Begnaud, No. 2, of the White League of the Parish of Lafayette,

September 2, 1874

Resolved that,

We propose to the different clubs of the parish the following manner for the choice of candidates at the next election for the vacant places in and for the Parish of Lafayette.

Article I. The clubs of each district will assemble as a deliberating body and will choose the candidates for the places in the parish which will be filled at the next election, and will send a copy of the ticket which they have thus formed to the parish committee.

Article II. The committee, after having received returns of each district, will send them in their entirety to the president of each club to be submitted to the votes of the members of these clubs.

Article III. The president of each club and two commissioners chosen by him will count the votes and will send, the day after the election, by the president, a return signed by them to be remitted to the committee of the parish, who, with the presidents of the clubs, will form a board of return.

Article IV. The board of returns, after having taken note of the returns presented to it, and, having been assured of the names which command a majority, will proclaim the parish ticket which all the members of the White League of the parish are obliged to uphold.

Article V. The clubs of each district will choose also a candidate for the member of the police jury, justice of the peace, and constable for that district. These candidates will also be proclaimed by the board of returns in order that they be upheld by all the White Leagues of the parish.

Article VI. The parish committee will set the day that the districts will assemble to propose the candidates for the offices of the parish; also the day for the different clubs to form the ticket of the parish.

A. D. Boudreaux, President
J. Ozeme LeBlanc
Chas. A. Boudreaux, Assistant Secretary
Toledano Begnaud

A citizen of Broussard, now long gone, dictated to Mrs. Sarah Bernard a description of the methods used in that village to restore white supremacy. The author is obligated to Mr. John J. Reaux for it. It reads as follows:

> Politics in Broussard were rather dark and drastic during the reconstruction period. All the governing was done by self-appointed men. They formed a committee, headed by Marcel Fabre, Lucien St. Julien and Adrian Labbe. The order was run something like the Ku Klux Klan. They took the law in their own hands. They whipped those who stole and even chased them out of town. They killed those who opposed their opinions or spoke in public against their order. It was rather hard to exist or even speak because you never knew who was friend or foe. It was known that some Negroes were frequently found hanging from a tree by their necks and left to be eaten by mosquitoes and other insects.
>
> After a certain time the order grew very large. Anyone could join who wanted to be ruled by the leaders. These men patrolled the street and roads at night on horseback. No children were allowed on the street after eight o'clock at night. This was done particularly because of the Negroes. The governor of the state at that time was very lenient toward the Negroes and let them vote. Every time there was a race for an office the Negro candidate would win.
>
> There was one man who did something to stamp out Negro voting. That was Mr. Aurelien Olivier. The people voted on tables lit with candles. Mr. Olivier put out the candles and mixed all the votes together and counted most of the votes for the white people's candidates.
>
> This street patrolling with guns at night succeeded in blotting out Negro voting in Broussard.

As the election of 1876 approached many thought the reconstruction struggle was reaching a climax. The activities of the White League, especially after its failure to overthrow the corrupt government of Kellogg in the famous Battle of New Orleans on September 14, 1874, had attracted the sympathetic attention of the whole country. Meantime the Republicans had nominated G. B. Packard and C. C. Antoine for governor and lieutenant governor. The Democrats had nominated Francis T. Nicholls and Louis A. Wiltz. Prior to the election Governor Kellogg had appointed Republican registrars who registered most Negroes and few whites.

Despite these efforts, however, the Democrats claimed for their candidates, including presidential electors, a majority of nearly ten thousand. The election of president of the United States was also in dispute between Republican Rutherford B. Hayes and

Democrat Samuel J. Tilden. Governor Kellogg, in control of the state returning board, certified the Republican electors. The supporters of Nicholls declared him elected and certified Democratic electors for Tilden. Candidate Hayes hinted that if the electoral votes in dispute were counted for him he would withdraw federal troops from the South. In January 1877 an Electoral Commission declared Hayes elected. Soon after his inauguration in March, he ordered federal troops withdrawn from Louisiana and the entire South. The effect of this was that Packard, who had installed himself and associates in office, could not hold on without the support of federal troops. The consequence was that he and his whole gang had to step down and let the Nicholls and Wiltz administration take over. Thus ended the struggle for white supremacy in Louisiana and the Parish of Lafayette. The task of the White League had at last been accomplished.

CHAPTER XI

THE TOWNS OF THE PARISH

The coming of settlers to the vicinity of Carencro probably occurred before that of Lafayette. There are two theories as to the origin of the name Carencro, both having their origin in the same phenomenon. There is a legend that in Indian days a mastodon died in the vicinity. Thousands of buzzards fed for weeks on the dead animal, leaving the bare and whitened bones lying in the midst of the prairie. One explanation would have the bayou and town receive the name from the English "Carrion Crow," meaning buzzard. The other would have the name derived from the Spanish "Carnero" meaning bone pile, a word which in French usage soon became Carencro. This name prevailed until 1874, when Mr. Pierre Cormier gave the land for a new church on condition that the church be named St. Pierre. This condition was agreed to and for some years after the completion of the church the embryo town was called St. Pierre. When Mr. Francez moved to town he revived the name Carencro, with the result that this name has become permanently attached to the town. There are, however, citizens of Carencro who would like to see the name St. Pierre revived and many suggestions to that effect have been made in recent years, but to no avail.

As stated elsewhere herein, the first settlers in the vicinity of Carencro were Jean and Marin Mouton, who came from St. James Parish about 1770 and took up lands on nearby Bayou Carencro. They were soon joined by Charles Peck, Traville Bernard, Rosamond Breaux and Ovnac Arceneaux. These men first engaged in stock raising using some of the remaining Indians as herders. The last of these Indians was an old woman of the Opelousas tribe named Celina, who died at the age of one hundred and five years in 1878 on the farm of Roche Mouton.

For many years Carencro was only a mere village. In 1880, however, when the building of Morgan's Louisiana Railroad through the town was assured, the town was formally laid out and incor-

Governor Mouton's Town House, built originally by his father, Jean Mouton, about 1800, was occupied by the Governor and his family from 1820 until 1836. It is now owned and occupied by the Lafayette Museum.

(Above) Oakbourne Plantation Home of Colonel Gustave Breaux as it appears today

(Below) The old Moss House was the boyhood home of Lafayette's first graduate dentist, Doctor H. C. Salles. The house was built by the father of Doctor Salles in 1851.

Myrtle Plantation home and office of Dr. Matthew Creighton. Built in 1811.

(Below) The Percy Girard House — circa 1820. On the southside of Pin Hook Road, 1320 Pin Hook Road, it is about one quarter mile from the bridge over Bayou Vermilion. Before the founding of Vermilionville this home was occupied by a Mr. Monnier, a Belgian. Farther down the Pin Hook Road lived the Demanade brothers, Felix and Paul, from St. John the Baptiste Parish. Felix was a leader in the community. On the Demanade place was the old home lived in by Paul, once the postmaster. It was destroyed by fire. In this area were the lands of the Cafferys and the Brashears. "Les Jardins de Mouton" occupy a portion of this land today.

ARCENEAUX HOUSE

Just off the Carencro highway, approximately five miles north of Lafayette, the former home of Louis Joseph Arceneaux and the present home of his daughters, Misses Josette and Mathilde Arceneaux and their niece, Miss Beatrix Breaux, is one of the few remaining early Acadian houses of the area. This sturdy house was built in 1832 (approximately) by Pierre Bienvenu (b. 1812, d. 1855), grandson of Louis Pierre Arceneaux, b. 1731, Nova Scotia, the reputed "Gabriel" of Longfellow's Evangeline, who in 1787 established his home and large cattle ranch on the west ridge of Vermilion Bayou in the Beau Bassin area, designated as "Settlement of the Arceneaux Family," on W. Darby's map of Louisiana, 1816. The site of Louis Pierre Arceneaux's old homestead, destroyed during a storm several years ago, is marked by beautiful live oak trees, the veritable Gabriel Oaks.

porated. For some reason the government provided for in this charter was allowed to lapse, and the town was not re-incorporated until 1905. The first mayor under this charter was Dr. R. J. Francez. With the railroad at its door, running from Lafayette to Alexandria, and a branch line running east to Huron plantation, it soon became a thriving center with several large stores, a bank, a parochial school, a public high school and a sugar factory. From it were shipped to distant markets large quantities of sugar cane, syrup, cotton, live stock and more recently, sweet potatoes. Today railroad facilities have declined, but have been replaced by bus and truck transportation. The growing of sugar cane and manufacturing of sugar and syrup have practically disappeared but have been replaced with crops of cotton and sweet potatoes while dairying and cattle raising have developed into a new industry. The 1950 population of Carencro was 1587.

The town of Youngsville had its beginning about 1831 when J. J. Roy took up land there and brought with him in a wagon all his earthly possessions. Other lands there were taken up about the same time by P. Landry, A. L. Dyer, Dr. Young and others. In 1839 the town was laid out either by Mr. J. J. Roy or his son, Desiré Roy and named Royville. This name soon became so confused with that of a town named Rayville in North Louisiana that at the request of the Post Office Department, and in order to end the confusion, the name was changed to Youngsville, and by that name it has been known ever since. Youngsville was first incorporated in 1883 with Mr. A. L. Dyer as the first mayor. In 1880 the population was only 100; in 1920 about 500, and 1950 it was 769.

The first settler in what is now the town of Broussard was Mr. Valsin Broussard, who, soon after the Civil War acquired land on which the town is now located. Other early inhabitants on this site were Marcel Melancon, John Baptiste Malagarie, Martial Billeaud, and J. G. St. Julien. About 1870 Mr. Broussard employed Mr. F. J. Rosk, a surveyor, to lay out the town which was to be named after the owner of the land on which it was situated. In 1884 the town was duly incorporated as Broussard and was granted a charter which provided for a government consisting of council, mayor, clerk and marshal, all to be elected by popular vote. Two years later, in 1886 the people became dissatisfied with the government and elected no officials, thus allowing the charter to lapse. It was not until 1906 that the town was re-incorporated and a new government, similar to the old one put into operation. When the town was first laid out there was no post office there and the citizens received their mail from a stage coach which travelled between Lafayette and New Iberia. The post office was established in 1878 with Mr. J. B. Malagarie as the first postmaster. In 1950 the population of Broussard was 1,237.

One of the earliest inhabitants of the present village of Scott was Mr. V. Cayret, a native of France who, prior to 1880, took up land in what is now the town of Scott. In that year he refused to the Louisiana Western Railroad a right of way through his land unless the officials would agree to place a station on his land and thus encourage the building of a town there. The railroad officials agreed to this; and the day the first rails for the track arrived Mr. Alcide Judice opened near the right-of-way a small grocery store. The primitive state of this country at that time may be illustrated by a story long told in connection with the founding of the town and the building of the railroad. It was said that one old settler was much averse to having such a beast as a railway train run rampant across the prairie. To stop this invasion of his domain he devised the plan of hiding in the tall grass near the tracks with a white sheet thrown over his body. Then when the snorting monster came along he would jump suddenly out at it and thus give it such a scare that it would never return. He made all preparations for carrying out his scheme, but as the train continued to make its daily trips it is supposed that he and not the train did the running away.

From these humble beginnings Scott grew and developed into the flourishing town that it is today, with stores, cotton gins, sweet potato processing plants, modern schools and churches. The railroad station still stands but fewer passenger trains stop there than formerly. The name Scott was given to the town in honor of Mr. G. P. Scott, who was at one time division superintendent of the Southern Pacific Railroad. The village was never formally surveyed into blocks and streets but like Topsy just "grew up." In 1904 it was granted a charter which provides a government by mayor and alderman. For many years citizens of Scott have frequently said to the people of Lafayette, "Scott is where the West begins."

It is not known definitely when the village of Milton was first settled. Some of the ancestors of persons now living there took up lands there as early as 1823, the same year the parish was organized. They were Baptiste Denais, a shoemaker, and his brother Jean Denais, Desiré Broussard, Aledon Broussard and a Mr. Montet. The town was named after Milton Cushman, a younger son of John Cushman, who settled in Milton about 1870 and became one of its leading citizens. Young Milton Cushman studied medicine and as late as 1923 was a practicing physician in New York City. The town was not laid out formally until 1910, when Dr. A. K. Burkett, who owned much property in and around the village, employed a surveyor to mark out regular blocks and streets. It has only recently been incorporated.

CHAPTER XII

THE FOUNDING OF CHURCHES

CATHOLIC CHURCHES

To the citizen of modern Lafayette it seems strange to learn that the first settlers of the territory in which he lives were not legally entitled to freedom of conscience. Such was the case, however, as we read in the Black Code of Bienville, which reflected the then existing laws of France, that only the Catholic religion was to be practiced in Louisiana. This rule worked a hardship on very few, however, as most of the inhabitants were already of that faith and there is no record of anyone's being punished for a violation of that law. In truth one of the early Spanish governors publicly suspended the law in order to induce English settlers from the Carolinas and Mississippi to migrate here. As a matter of fact those early settlers were a liberty loving people and would not tolerate any too strict regulation in religious matters. Such an attitude was characteristic of most people who first founded homes in an American frontier community.

For some time it appears that the first citizens of this region were without religious advantages. The nearest church was at the Poste des Attakapas and had been established there some time before the Spanish occupancy. Though the present church there was built in 1765 it had no resident pastor before 1782 and had been cared for by missionary priests who travelled from place to place. It was not until Father Barriére became the pastor of St. Martinville in 1795 that the residents of the Lafayette area began to enjoy the ministrations of a priest. It was Father Barriére who first began to make pastoral visits to the families of this district and to gather about him in private homes his devout followers for Christian worship, or for administering the rites of christening, marriage and burial. Meantime there had been built on the present site of St. John's Cathedral, on land owned by Jean Mouton, a small chapel which was, until 1821, only a mission of St. Martin.

On March 21, 1821, Jean Mouton donated to the Catholic congregation the site on which this first church stood, together with 5.54 arpents of land. The act of donation was witnessed by Valery Martin, Ancelet Richard, and accepted for the church by Father Francois Carmouche. It was acknowledged by Judge Paul Briant, Judge of St. Martin Parish, and recorded the next day in the St. Martin Parish courthouse. According to Father Barriére, the church was dedicated on December 30, 1821 as "de l'eglise St. Jean du Vermilion." On May 15, 1822 Bishop DuBourg made Vermilion the center of a new parish comprising the present parishes of Lafayette, Vermilion and part of Acadia.

Just why the name St. Jean was selected for the new church is still not definitely known. The late Judge Paul Debaillon, who did much research in the histories of the church and the Mouton family, developed the theory that, since the name Jean and Baptiste appeared so frequently among the forebears of Jean Mouton, St. John the Baptist had been regarded as the family saint and protector. With this in mind, therefore, Jean Mouton had used his influence to have the church given the name St. Jean. It must be remembered that all these events occurred before Jean Mouton laid out the village which was subsequently called Vermilionville.

The first pastor of the newly established church and parish was no other than the beloved missionary priest. Father Barriére, who served until 1824 when he returned to France. The church thus founded did not grow rapidly, nor was it free from difficulties. During this early period when the population was sparse, the problem of financing the church was a difficult one. However, the congregation was able to raise some money, because on October 8, 1832 it purchased from Alexandre, Césaire, and Antoine Emile Mouton, for $2400.00, the land occupied now by the St. John cemetery. Because of internal dissensions no resident priest after the departure of Father Barriére had been able to satisfy either the parishioners or the Bishop. Between 1842 and 1853, however, during the pastorate of Father A. D. Mégret, the internal dissensions were composed and plans completed for building a new and larger church to replace the original one. During the pastorate of Father Forge, who began his work in 1881, the church, built thirty years before, was greatly enlarged and improved and the grounds beautified. Father Forge converted the plot of ground between the church and the rectory into a magnificent rose garden. It is said that over one hundred varieties of roses were cultivated by him and that he knew the name of each. People came from far and near to see the beautiful garden and visit the flower-loving priest. By 1913 the congregation had completely outgrown this structure, which had reached a state of decay; and plans were matured for the construction of the present imposing edifice, which adorns the site of the original chapel. The cornerstone of this last church was laid in 1913 and the structure completed in 1916. The plans and specifications, prepared by E. A. Cousins, were inspired by the Reverend Monseigneur W. J. Teurlings, V.G., who directed their execution.

In less than two years after the completion of the new church, Southwest Louisiana was detached from the Archdiocese of New Orleans and formed into an independent diocese with Lafayette as its Episcopal city. St. John's Church became St. John's Cathedral, with a native son, the Right Reverend Jules Jeanmard, as its first bishop.

After the Catholic Church became well established here Vermilionville became the center of all religious activity in the new parish. Since it was not possible for all parishioners to come to Vermilionville to worship it was necessary for the pastor to make visits to the surrounding settlements. These missionary visits led to the founding of other religious centers in the parish, which became the bases for future churches. The first of these to materialize was the one at Youngsville. This church was organized in 1859 by Father Foltier and a small chapel built. A few years later this chapel was enlarged to its present size; and in 1956 it was completely inclosed in brick and converted into the beautiful edifice one sees there today. The next church built in the parish was in Carencro. This church was built under the direction of Father Guillot in 1874, but was burned to the ground a year later. Another one was constructed and shortly met the fate of the first one. A third one, larger than the others was soon built, but it seemed doomed by the old adage of "threes" and was blown down by a tornado. The present church in Carencro is the fourth one and was constructed in 1900 under the able direction of Father Grimaud. Recently it has been remodeled and greatly improved. The church at Broussard was organized in 1883 and a small chapel built, of which Father Cuny was the first pastor. Two years later this chapel burned to the ground, and for near twenty years, no other church was erected in its place; and during that time the members had to attend religious services at Lafayette, Youngsville or St. Martinville. In 1903, however, a movement to erect another church was inaugurated by Father Roguet. This large church was completed the following year. In 1956 this church was replaced by the handsome one now occupying the same site. The church at Scott was founded in 1897 with Father Durhon as the first resident pastor.

During the administration of the late Bishop Jeanmard the facilities required to nurture the spiritual and educational needs of a rapidly growing Catholic population have been greatly expanded. At least six new churches have been built in the City of Lafayette alone.

A Courageous Priest

The history of the churches of Lafayette would not be complete without a glimpse at the Reverend Antoine Desire Mégret, pastor of the Church of St. John in Vermilionville from 1842 to 1853, and his efforts to develop the spiritual and educational resources of the community. A reading of his letters and a glimpse at his portrait, now hanging in Mount Carmel Academy, will convince one that he was a man of resolution and action. Since the departure of Father Barriére for France in 1824 no resident priest assigned to the Catholic Church in Vermilionville had been able to satisfy the parishioners, the "Marguillers" or the bishop and vicar general. Certain reforms proposed by the administrators of the mother church were supported by the pastor and certain parishioners, but strenuously opposed by others led by several members of the Board of Marguillers, who served as lay administrators of the local church. This spirit of independence had no doubt developed during frontier days when missionary priests had little time to enforce all the rules of the church.

Father Mégret, having been fully informed of the situation before his assignment, came determined to carry out the ordinances of the church as he understood them. The result was a long and bitter contest which at times broke into physical violence in which the good father was assaulted on the street. One of Mégret's good friends was Césaire Mouton who, fearing for the priest's life, presented him with two loaded pistols, counselling him to use them in his own defense should occasion arise. A few years after this testimonial of friendship Césaire died. Somewhat later Césaire's son, William Mouton, was at the parish court house to receive his inheritance of $30,000.00 in gold. Father Mégret, knowing of William's presence there, came also and handed William the two loaded pistols, in the same condition as when they had been given to him by the father, and said: "Here my boy is something that belongs to you. Your father had given me these to defend myself. Thank God I never needed them."

"What do you want me to do with them Father?" asked the astonished young man.

"What you wish," was the reply.

"Well, then, let us go and bury them at father's feet," said William; and so it was done in the presence of a few witnesses.

The contest between Father Mégret and the faction opposing him was long and bitter. In the end, however, says Father C. M. Souvay in his article "Rummaging Through Old Parish Records," by refusing to say mass in the church and risking his life in support of its ordinances, he finally convinced a majority of the parishioners that the laws of the church, as he understood them, came first. Finally, with the cooperation of his supporters, and strategy on his part, he at last succeeded in taking the affairs of the church out of the obstructing Board of Marguillers. His victory, however, brought him little happiness, even though plans were under way to build a new church to replace the original chapel. At the Confirmation ceremonies in Vermilionville on August 22, 1853, Father Mégret begged Archbishop Blanc to relieve him of his pastorate at the Church of St. John the Evangelist. One week later his request was granted; and he made plans immediately to establish himself at Perry's Bridge, three miles below Abbeville on Bayou Vermilion. In the midst of his preparations to leave, a fearful epidemic, believed to be yellow fever, broke out and carried off people daily, first by two's or three's, then by sixes and eights, and twelves, with no distinction of age, race or color. All who could fled their homes and sought safety elsewhere. Father Mégret himself found refuge at the plantation home of Mr. Paul de Saint-Julien on the banks of Bayou Vermilion. There he held mass under the umbrella trees. From there he went to stay at the home of Dr. V. Gauthier. It was here that his mulatto slave died and was buried in the plantation yard; and it was from here too, broken-hearted, he hastened back to the village of the people he had abandoned, but to whom he was ever ready to administer the last sacraments.

Alexander Borde, one of the editors of *Le Creole* in St. Martinville and the author of "Les Comités de Vigilantes," was dining with Father Mégret when he was notified that a man of the Protestant faith named Girard was dying. He hastened immediately to the stricken man's bedside to utter words of divine consolation. A very few days later Father Mégret, said to be the last victim of the plague, was called by his Maker. The date was December 5, 1853. The people of both Vermilionville and Perry's Bridge had lost a true friend.

PROTESTANT CHURCHES

Practically all of the early French or Spanish settlers of Lafayette Parish were of the Catholic faith. It was not until long after the purchase of Louisiana by the United States in 1803 that newcomers from other states of the Union began to arrive. It happened quite frequently that these brought with them the ideals and beliefs of some of the Protestant churches. It was still a long time before they had come in sufficient numbers to enable the adherents of any one faith to found a church of their own in Vermilionville. The first group that became strong enough to organize its own church was composed of those who adhered to the doctrines of the Methodist Episcopal Church. For several years before the founding of their church, perhaps as early as 1837, these pious people had been visited from time to time by a travelling elder who assembled them in a private home for an occasional religious service or for christenings, marriages, or funerals. In 1858, however, the congregation had become numerous enough to require the services of a regular minister. In that year a site for the first church was donated by Benjamin Porter Paxton, at the corner of Congress and Washington Streets, now occupied by the office of J. Y. Foreman. Trustees of the new organization were Gideon Stephens, James Higginbotham, and Doctor John W. Chevis. From that time on the growth of the congregation was steady, with the result that the membership and resources had increased to such an extent that it was able in 1925 to build the present imposing church at the corner of Lee Avenue and East Main Street. There are now two other Methodist Churches, one on Jefferson Boulevard and one on the Abbeville highway.

The next group to establish a church was made up of Presbyterians. This event was quite natural in view of the fact that it was this church that had shaped the religious and social ideals in a great portion of the South in ante-bellum days. The idea of organizing a Presbyterian Church in Vermilionville apparently originated in the mind of Mrs. A. C. Hayes; for it was she, who with some lady friends, addressed a circular letter to the Sunday Schools of the Assembly appealing for funds with which to build a church in Vermilionville. This letter resulted in a donation of $150.00, to which the Sustenation Committee of the Assembly added $300. This appeal and the response must have aroused the Presbytery of Louisiana because, at the spring meeting it appointed two ministers, the Reverends A. L. Young and Matthew B. Shaw to visit the field west of the Mississippi River to establish churches.

These two ministers came first to Opelousas where they organized a church. Then, with the elder of that church, Captain A. L. Black, they came to Vermilionville where they held a series of meetings. At a congregational meeting held on August 23, 1875, and attended by the two ministers named above, there was organized the Presbyterian Church of Vermilionville. Those who attended the meeting and thus became the first members of the church were: Mr. and Mrs. J. T. Hayes, Mr. and Mrs. John D. Torrance and their two sons, Benjamin B. and John E.; Miss H. G. Greig, Miss Eliza Jamerson, Mr. and Mrs. T. A. McFadden, Mrs. Mary E. Kennedy and Mr. J. H. Adams. At this meeting J. T. Hayes was elected elder and T. A. McFadden and J. H. Adams deacons.

In March of 1876 the Reverend Edward Carter became state supply minister for the Opelousas and Vermilionville churches. He conducted services in each place twice each month, and served until his death in Opelousas in the autumn of 1878. During these years church services were held in Hebert's hall, the basement of the Masonic hall and in the school room of F. A. Rogan. At this time it was customary for each member with his entire family to attend both the Sunday School and the sermon each Sunday.

In the spring of 1878 Elder F. S. Mudd donated to the congregation the lot in Buchanan Street where presently stands at No. 407 a service station. Here was built the first Presbyterian Church, a wooden structure to which were added Sunday School rooms in 1927 and 1929. In 1922 the congregation purchased at the corner of Johnston Street and College Avenue a large lot on which to build a manse and a future new church. The manse was completed in that year, but the present handsome church and student center was not completed until 1946 at an approximate cost of $80,000.

The Baptist Congregation was organized to form a church on November 3, 1902 in the former Presbyterian church on Buchanan Street. There were present for this purpose the Reverend gentlemen, E. K. Robinson, A. L. Johnston, and E. O. Ware. The five charter members were Mrs. I. A. Broussard, Mr. and Mrs. V. L. Roy, and the Messrs. F. K. Hopkins and O. B. Hopkins. The Reverend Robinson became the first pastor. For several years the meetings for worship were held in the Presbyterian Church and in the Masonic Hall. It was not until 1909 that the congregation was strong enough to build on the corner of Lee Avenue and Oak Street, where the American Bank now stands, a small but attractive brick church. This was constructed during the pastorate of Rev. J. L. Kendrick, who at the age of ninety is living in peaceful retirement with his daughter, Mrs. H. R. Bodemuller. Some years later it was necessary to build a wooden annex to accommodate a rapidly growing congregation. By 1948 the membership had completely outgrown these two buildings, and began, under the direction of Rev. R. H. Holmes the construction, on the corner of Lee Avenue and Barry Street, of the present handsome church and adjoining structure to house the Sunday School and other church activities. In recent years, to accommodate the expanding congregation two other Baptist churches have been built, one on Jefferson Boulevard and one on the Abbeville highway.

The Episcopalians in the community had, for some time prior to 1901, held religious services in the Presbyterian Church under the leadership of a visiting minister. In 1901, however, on a lot at the corner of Jefferson and Garfield Streets, donated by Judge Parkerson, they built a small but attractive brick church which served until 1950. In that year the congregation sold it and purchased the former home and grounds of the late N. P. Moss on Johnston Street, which with some alterations and additions, has served as a church until the present. However there has just been completed on these grounds a new church designed to accommodate a rapidly growing congregation.

For some years prior to 1883 the members of the Jewish congregation in Lafayette met in private homes to hold their religious services. In 1883, however, the members effected a formal organization and began plans for building a temple. Those participating in this organization were Messrs. B. Falk, Lazarus Levy, Joseph Plonsky, Leon Plonsky, Haas, Morris Rosenfield, Edmond Kiam and Joseph Wise. In that same year the present temple was constructed on a lot given them by Governor Alexandre Mouton. To meet the needs of a growing congregation this church was remodeled and redecorated some years later.

The next religious group to organize a church consisted of those who adhered to the teachings of Christian Science. In the winter of 1928 a group of Christian Science students began to meet every

Wednesday evening at the home of Mr. and Mrs. T. B. Hopkins at 1310 Johnston Street. These meetings were continued until January, 1929, when there was felt a need for a more central meeting place. Accordingly a hall on the second floor of the Delhomme building at 202 Lincoln Avenue was rented where Sunday morning services, Sunday School and Wednesday evening meetings were held for the next eighteen months. In the summer of 1930 a lot on Voorhies Street was purchased and a small bungalow type of church building was erected on it at a cost of $2000. This then became the permanent church home in August 1930. In this same year the congregation was officially recognized as a branch of the mother church in Boston, and officially incorporated as the Christian Science Society of Lafayette, Louisiana.

With the selection of Lafayette as a center for the oil industry there has been a large influx of new residents from many states. Among them members of other Protestant denominations have organized and built their churches in the city. Those recently established churches are: Assembly of God; Christian; Church of Christ; Latter Day Saints; Lutheran; Methodist Episcopal; Nazarene and Salvation Army.

CHAPTER XIII

TRANSPORTATION AND TRAVEL

EARLY METHODS

The evolution of travel and transportation in Lafayette Parish and environs presents a most interesting subject of study. As we have already seen the Acadians came to their future homes in pirogues and flat boats or barges. In the absence of good roads, such was the almost universal mode of moving persons and goods in this entire region, from the time of the first settlements until long after the invention of the steamboat in 1807. The earliest trapper went the round of his snares in a pirogue and in this silent craft carried his peltries to market and brought home his new supplies and necessities. The English trader built his miniature store on a barge which he rowed, poled or dragged on the numerous bayous from settlement to settlement, there exchanging his lead, gunpowder, traps, tea, cutlery and other such articles for furs, hides and other products as the settlers could persuade him were marketable. Boating in this early period became a regular business and owners of barges made regular trips between settlements on the banks of bayous and lakes.

A trip from Lafayette Parish to New Orleans was a long and expensive undertaking. Only the rich could afford it. The barge on which one made this long and tedious journey was drawn by ropes tied to slaves or horses walking along the shore of lake or stream. If the journey were down stream all hands got on board and floated with the current. If it were upstream the barge had to be drawn as described above. The barge was open and the boatmen undertook to furnish only the actual transportation of the persons taking passage with him. It travelled only in the daytime and was tied up to the bank of the bayou or lake where night happened to overtake it. There the travellers had to go on shore, where they, with their servants, put up their tents for shelter and cooked the food which each must carry with him. After supper each traveller slept or whiled away the night talking or gaming with his companions as the notion suited him. Pirogues could go wherever there was even shallow water, but these large barges could go only on navigable streams. Consequently the only points at which the inhabitants of Lafayette could secure barge service were at Pin Hook on the Vermilion, New Iberia or Breaux's Bridge on Bayou Têche and Washington on Bayou Courtableau.

Fortunately for the early citizens horses were both plentiful and cheap. In fact the first settlers found them roaming wild on the prairies of this region and to be had only for the taking. They had no doubt escaped from the early Spanish settlements in Mexico and had multiplied in this uninhabited country. Everyone rode horseback in those days even on long journeys. Carriages were few because of the absence of good roads, though, by the time of the Civil War stage coaches had regular routes from Lafayette to Opelousas and New Iberia. The building of some roads, however, was encouraged by the later French and by the Spanish governors. These officials required every one who received a grant of land fronting on a stream to build a levee in front of it, if needed, and maintain on the levee a road. Under the Spanish regime, in order to maintain communications between Florida and northern Mexico, there was gradually blazed and cleared the Old Spanish Trail leading from Pensacola, Florida to New Orleans and thence through the Attakapas District to San Antonio, now Highway 90. Thus the cattleman who desired to deliver his cattle to the New Orleans market must drive them on foot at least a part of the way over this trail.

It was not until 1836 that the police jury of Lafayette Parish, which then included the present Parish of Vermilion, felt the need of a parish wide system of roads that would lead to neighboring settlements. It was on September 10 of that year that the police jury, presided over by Basil C. Crow, appointed a committee, consisting of Jean Bernard, Joseph Bernard, John Giroir, and Baptiste Comeaux, to meet with a similar committee from St. Martin Parish to lay out a road from Vermilionville to New Iberia. On March 6, the following year the same police jury appointed several committees to lay out roads: one from the Vermilion bridge to Perry's bridge below the present town of Abbeville; one from the Vermilion bridge to the bridge at Madam Caddy St. Julien's bridge; one from the Vermilion bridge to New Town on the border of St. Martin Parish; one to lay out a road from Vermilionville to the Bayou

Carencro bridge; one to lay out a road from Vermilionville to Bayou Queue Tortue.* At the same meeting the police jury enacted an ordinance requiring all able bodied men from eighteen to forty-five years of age to work up to six days a year on these roads, and appointed in each ward an overseer to supervise their construction. Thus was inaugurated the step that led eventually to the building of the roads that connect the present city of Lafayette with Abbeville, New Iberia, St. Martinville, Opelousas and Crowley. All these roads had been completed by the time of the Civil War, though they were crooked, dusty, and, in rainy weather, frequently impassable.

It was long after the invention of the steamboat that the barges on the Louisiana streams were replaced by these newer vessels propelled by steam. It is not known when the first steamboat came up the Bayou Vermilion to Pin Hook, but it was well before the Civil War. Such craft, however, could travel up that stream only during rainy seasons when the bayou was high. Even then they had to risk the danger of being damaged or disabled by submerged logs, trees or stumps. So anxious were the people of Lafayette Parish to have regular steamboat service that between the years 1840 and 1850 the police jury appropriated the sum of $4,000.00 to have the obstructions in the bayou cleared from the Pin Hook bridge to Vermilion Bay.

Years ago one of the older citizens told the writer of a trip he made on one of these boats. On the deck of the boat were piled several coops of chickens. While leaving the landing at Pin Hook a lurch of the boat caused some of these coops to be overturned and broken open, with the result that many of the chickens escaped and flew into the branches of the trees overhanging the bayou banks. Then as the boat started downstream several of the passengers and crewmen grabbed guns and amused themselves by shooting the frightened chickens in the trees. During low water, however, the only steamboat landings that could be depended on were at Breaux Bridge, New Iberia on Bayou Têche and Washington on Bayou Courtableau. For years, therefore, before and after the Civil War those three landings were the only points from which the farmers of Lafayette Parish could ship their cotton, sugar and other products, and at which they and the merchants could receive their incoming freight and mail.

Transportation facilities were considerably improved when the

---

*A small stream just west of Duson, meaning turtle tail.

New Orleans, Opelousas and Great Western Railroad was completed from New Orleans to Morgan City in 1850. From this terminus Morgan's steamboats carried freight and passengers up the numerous navigable streams in this section of the country. Even this service was interrupted in 1862 when the Union military forces, having captured New Orleans, took possession of both the railroad and Morgan's boat lines, which they operated for military purposes until 1866.

THE FIRST RAILROAD

In 1869, however, was inaugurated the step which was to bring the first railroad to Lafayette Parish. In that year Charles Morgan bought at marshal's sale the property of the New Orleans Opelousas and Great Western Railroad. The road had been badly damaged by the Union armies and much of its equipment worn out or destroyed. This road, originally projected to Lafayette, was not only repaired but steps were taken to carry out the original plan and rush it to completion. After overcoming many difficulties encountered in building it through miles of swamps it was finally opened up to Lafayette in 1880. The coming of the first train was a great event, not only for the railroad officials, but for the citizens of Lafayette Parish and vicinity who had been active in the organization and promotion of this enterprise. Among those from this section may be named Governor Alexandre Mouton, Conrad Debaillon, Alexander deClouet, Joaquin Revillon, E. H. Martin, Robert Cade, and John H. Overton who was judge of the district which included Lafayette Parish. Overton resigned his judgeship in 1852 to become the second president of this pioneer railroad at a salary of $330.00 per month, a position he held for twenty-five years. Elected as permanent secretary of the corporation was Benjamin F. Flanders of Connecticut, whose descendants are now living in Lafayette Parish. Soon after the first trains entered Lafayette, the company invited Governor Mouton, his associates and friends to be its guests on a trip to New Orleans in a special car set aside for that purpose. In New Orleans they were wined and dined, all in appreciation of their services in making the completion of this vast undertaking a reality.

In the same year that the trains reached Lafayette there was organized the Louisiana and Western Railroad, which purchased an old grade belonging to the New Orleans, Mobile and Texas Rail-

Plantation home of Antoine Emile Mouton, married to Gadrat Rousseau, granddaughter of Governor Jacques Dupre.

"This plantation was next to the home of Gerazin Bernard who died of yellow fever in 1867. On the walls of the large center hall were murals of Indians and buffaloes and scenes of wild western life. Adjoining Mr. Gerazin Bernard's plantation was that of Horace Voorhies, the brother of Cornelius Voorhies, chief justice of Louisiana's Supreme Court. Adjoining Horace Voorhies' plantation was that of the father of my father, the senior Jean Sosthene Mouton. The plantations were strictly cotton plantations. Uncle Emile was the only one who cultivated cane and made sugar." — From the unpublished "Memoirs of Alexandre Mouton"

(Photograph courtesy of Mr. and Mrs. John Givens Torian)

Below) The Richard Chargois Home at 514 Buchanan Street was built by Richard in 851. It is now occupied by a granddaughter, Miss Josette Salles.

Seller's House built 1835. "We'll split the house in half; each will take his half and have the walls repaired", and so today two separate houses stand, about seven miles from Lafayette on Route 1. In this manner, the two sons of Andrew Mathew Sellers, from Canada, established their ownership at the time of his death.

road Company, lying between Lafayette and the Sabine River near Orange, Texas. Work on the Louisiana Western began in 1873 and was completed in 1881, along with the six mile link between the Sabine River and Orange, known as the Louisiana Western Extension. The Louisiana Extension in turn made connection at Orange with the newly completed Texas and New Orleans Railroad between Orange, Houston and other Texas cities. It was now possible for one to travel by train from New Orleans, through Lafayette to Houston. The first train from New Orleans through Lafayette to San Antonio reached its destination on February 7, 1883, at which point it was met a day later by a similar train from San Francisco. Since that time trains from New Orleans to San Francisco have run regularly through Lafayette. The engine, "Sabine", which pulled this first train was restored and for many years stood in a park adjoining the railroad station in Lafayette; but during World War II the railroad officials, in a burst of patriotism, surrendering it to be broken into scrap.

The original Morgan line was designated to be built from New Orleans through Lafayette to Cheneyville in Rapides Parish, and there connect with the Texas and Pacific. But when the plans were changed to continue from Lafayette to Texas, that part of the road has been known as the Alexandria Branch. It was begun in 1880 and completed in 1882. In 1906 began the construction of a railroad between Lafayette and Baton Rouge. This was soon completed and for many years there were regular passenger and freight trains between the two cities. The flood of 1927, however, destroyed the bridge which carried this road across the Atchafalaya River and it was never rebuilt, thus bringing to an end through service on this branch.

A great advance in the development of the parish transportation system came with the building of the first gravel surfaced roads in 1915, to replace the dirt roads which frequently became impassable during a season of rain. The initiative in this progressive step had been taken the year before by the city of Lafayette which voted bonds in the amount of $75,000.00 for such roads in the city and a few miles of main roads into the country. Three years later a parish-wide bond issue gave $300,000.00 for a system of gravel roads to connect the city of Lafayette with other roads leading to the seats of all adjoining parishes. To this sum the state and federal governments added $200,000.00. In 1920 the first ward voted $36,000.00, and the second ward $125,000.00 for lateral roads.

A year later the fourth ward voted $125,000.00 and the seventh ward $50,000.00 for the same purpose. With these large sums of money converted into gravel roads there was by 1923 scarcely a town or hamlet in the parish that was not safely accessible by motor within a very short time, whether the weather be fair or rainy. With the extension of these roads to the neighboring cities of Abbeville, New Iberia, St. Martinville, Opelousas and Crowley they too were brought much nearer to Lafayette which by this time was developing into a trade center of large proportions.

With the rapid increase in the number who owned automobiles and depended on them for transportation, the gravel roads came to be regarded as an inadequate and unsatisfactory highway for automobile traffic. When, therefore, Governor Huey P. Long in 1928 proposed a $100,000,000.00 state-wide bond issue to build a state-wide system of bridges and paved roads and, as he said, "lift Louisiana out of the mud," the plan received hearty support in Lafayette Parish. In pursuance to this program U. S. Highway 90, known as the Old Spanish Trail, had been paved entirely through the parish and on to Lake Charles by 1931, and the roads to Breaux Bridge and Carencro by 1932. By 1938 the pavement had been completed to Abbeville and Opelousas. Since then the surfacing of the lateral roads in the parish with either cement or black top has freed the motorist of the mud and dust that plagued him in the past. The result is that today Lafayette, the parish seat, is a vertible hub from which radiates five concrete highways running east, west, south, north and northeast. Those five outbound highways are part of a state-wide system and connect with other great regional or national routes.

WATERWAYS

The officials of Lafayette Parish have long been interested in securing improved water transportation for this area. Beginning as early as 1840 the police jury made occasional appropriations for the clearing of stumps and driftwood from Vermilion Bayou. At one time it subscribed to stock in a company that proposed to dredge a canal to connect Bayous Vermilion and Têche. In recent years citizens and officials of parish and city have worked hard to promote the intercoastal canal and other waterways. Their efforts were finally crowned with success in 1944 when the federal engineers began the dredging of Vermilion Bayou from its mouth at Vermilion Bay to a point several miles north of Pin Hook. The project was soon completed so that the bayou now has a depth of nine feet and a bottom width of 100 feet. Traffic is now regularly conducted in barges and light boats. A city bond issue in 1949 set aside $50,000.00 for the construction of public wharves. This sum is yet to be expended pending the acquisition of a site.

NEW MEANS OF TRANSPORTATION

Lafayette Parish owes its enviable position as an aviation center to the unselfish efforts of a few World I fliers who endured severe personal inconveniences to maintain the integrity of the Lafayette Municipal Airport during the years of public apathy. The airport is located a mile southeast of the city limits, and had its beginnings in 1929 when the city of Lafayette voted a bond issue of $25,000.00 to purchase the first 152 acres of the present airfield. In recognition of the parish-wide significance of an airfield the parish in 1941 voted a bond issue to buy enough additional land to give the field a total of 925 acres. Soon thereafter a private flying school was established on the field and thus enabled the city and parish to contribute to the trained manpower needs of the Army Air Corps at the time of its expansion when every available flier was needed.

At the outbreak of World War II the airport was in 1941 expanded and improved with funds from the federal government. The runways were lengthened and paved, hangars and a control tower were constructed and other necessary facilities installed.

A private firm then contracted for the use of the field and during the war conducted a school in which, under federal contract, hundreds of young men were trained for the U. S. Air Force. After the war the field was used for some time as an army air base. It was then returned to the management of the Lafayette Airport Commission which enters into contracts for its use. Several types of privately owned air services are based there. The largest user, however, is Eastern Air Lines which operates passenger and freight plans both east and west with several flights daily in both directions. During the war the 120 acre Girard Field on the Carencro road was established as an auxiliary port and was maintained for several years as a private flying school and field.

When the writer came to Lafayette in 1912 there was no such thing as an automobile for hire. A rickety, horse-drawn bus stood in front of the Gordon Hotel to carry guests to and from the hotel to the railroad station. To go anywhere in town one went in his own horse-drawn buggy or hired one from one of the livery stables. With the building of good roads, however, and the improvement of motor driven vehicles, a great change took place. Passenger carrying buses and freight hauling trucks soon appeared on the highways and in the city. By 1952 there were serving the city and parish of Lafayette three passenger bus lines, including the local transit company, five freight transportation lines, and six taxi operators with a total of thirty-two cabs.

CHAPTER XIV

THE SCHOOLS OF CITY AND PARISH

Early Schools

During the early days there were no schools in the city or parish of Lafayette except those organized and taught by private teachers. One of the first of these teachers was Alexandre Bard who later was an editor of *Le Creole* in St. Martinville and the author of "Les Comites de Vigilantes." Some of the older residents can recall the private schools taught by F. A. Rogan and W. A. Lerosen. Early in 1890, before the first high school was built Mr. Robert Greig taught a public school in a building located on the lot now occupied by the home of Mr. Laurent Pellerin at 319 East Main Street. Later Mr. Greig opened a private school on St. John Street opposite the Lafayette Sanitarium. Some of the well-to-do families sent their daughters to a girls finishing school conducted by Madame de St. Laurent in St. Martinville. Those who desired to learn more than the mere rudiments were compelled to go to colleges in New Orleans or some distant state.

In 1821 the Academy of the Sacred Heart at Grand Coteau was opened for the education of young girls; and in 1835 St. Charles College at the same place became available to young men. Many young men and women of Lafayette Parish were educated at these two schools.

As a result of a national trend to have an academy in every community a group of public spirited men secured on February 8, 1840 a legislative act granting "a sum of money to the trustees of Vermilionville Academy" in the town of Vermilionville. On February 28, 1842 legislative act number 66 provided for the incorporation of the above named academy. By its terms Joseph Breaux, Basil C. Crow, Charles Mouton, John Greig, Robert Cade, Daniel McCaskill, Lucien Guilheaud, Francis Breaux, Domartin Pellerin and their successors were incorporated as a body politic under the name and style of the Vermilionville Academy. Meantime, Robert

Cade, John Greig, B. C. Crow, Charles Mouton and Joseph Breaux, having been named commissioners of the Academy under the act of February 8, purchased from "Madame Maria Crow, widow of the Hon. T. B. Brashear" four lots, together with her residence, storeroom, carriage house, and other buildings for the use of the Academy. This location, on the corner of Jefferson and Vermilion Streets and now occupied by the Moss building, became thrice significant: it was the home of the first parish judge, the place where the policy jury held its first meeting, and finally the location of what was probably the first public school in Vermilionville. The Academy continued to exist until 1872 when the trustees were empowered to dispose of it by private or public sale and to devote the proceeds to the use of free schools in the town of Vermilionville.

PAROCHIAL SCHOOLS

One of the ambitions of Father Mégret, who served as pastor of the Church of St. John from 1842 to 1853, was to provide here in Vermilionville educational advantages for the children of his parishioners so that they would not have to incur the expense of leaving home. Accordingly he began in 1843 to acquire the property on which Mt. Carmel Convent now stands. First he bought from Césaire Mouton, son of Jean, lots 136, 137, 138 and 139, together with all fences, a large house of wood with a porch and an edifice of brick. As part payment Father Megret bound himself to deposit each year for four years at St. Charles College in Grand Coteau a certain sum to pay for the education of Césaire's son, Guillaume Mouton. The act of sale was notarized by Joachim Revillon. A year later Father Mégret bought from Vincent Bertrand lot number 135 for $140. He then in 1843 purchased from Thomas McBride lots 132 and 133 and the home on it, but not the boutique (store), which McBride reserved to be moved. It was in this house that the Academy of Mt. Carmel on September 8, 1846 opened its doors to eight young ladies who became its first pupils. The first principal was Rev. Mother St. Paul Aucoin, assisted by Sisters Du Carmel and Rose. The school grew rapidly, so that a few years later Father Mégret bought the old Masonic hall, which must have occupied lot 134, as this was the only remaining lot in the block that Mégret had not previously bought. Later Father Mégret transferred all these grounds and buildings to the Mt. Carmel Foundation. It was not until 1873 that a large frame two-story building was completed in which to conduct the school. This with some additions was completely outgrown by 1924, when the present brick building was completed at a cost of about ninety thousand dollars. In 1952 other buildings including a handsome gymnasium were added. In 1946 from April 28 to May 5 Mount Carmel celebrated its Centenary Jubilee, which was featured by the crowning of Jubilee Kings and Queens and the presentation by the citizens of Lafayette of a purse of $10,000.00, received for the school by Mother Superior M. Dolores.

In 1859 Father Etienne Jules Foltier founded a school to which was given the name St. Joseph's Academy. It was located on the present site of the Lafayette Sanitarium, but closed after a brief duration. Mr. Joseph A. Chargois, who was ninety-one years of age in 1937, attended St. Joseph's Academy as a boy and when it closed he then attended the Vermilionville Academy. In 1881 Father Forge took charge of the parish and gave immediate attention to the founding of a boys' school for young men too old to attend the convent. To that end he built St. John's College at the northeast corner of the church grounds. After many attempts at making this school succeed it had to be closed because of lack of patronage. The building was then moved west of the presbytery to be used as a dining room on state occasions. It was not until 1918 that the ambition of Father Forge for a boys school was realized in the founding of the present Cathedral High School. The modern building occupied by this school was completed in 1924, and the Isenberg Gymnasium and auditorium in 1951. In 1955 the high school building was remodelled and enlarged and a home for the teaching brothers built. Other parochial schools in the city include, for white children, St. Genevieve School, Lady of Fatima School, and Father Teurlings High School; for colored children, the Holy Rosary Institute, St. Paul's School and the Immaculate Heart of Mary School.

The first of the parochial schools to be established in the parish outside the city was in Carencro, when, in 1897 there was organized in that town a convent to be conducted by the Sisters of Mt. Carmel. The St. Cecilia Parochial School in Broussard was organized in 1909 with the assistance of Bishop Drossarts, and the present two-story brick building constructed at a cost of $25,000. After the city of Lafayette became the center of a new diocese there arose a need for certain training schools. As a consequence there has been established recently on the Breaux Bridge road, just byond the city limits, the DeLaSalle Normal School for the training of teaching brothers, and the Immaculata Seminary for the training of priests. In 1953 there were five Catholic high schools in the parish and fourteen Catholic elementary schools. One of the high schools and seven of the elementary schools are for Negro children. Ten of the Catholic schools in the parish are located in the city of Lafayette.

Public Schools

The development of a public school system in Lafayette Parish has been attended by many difficulties. Due to lack of public interest few free public schools were built prior to the Civil War, and these were poorly taught and attended. Prior to 1845 the state offered only $600.00 for public education in this parish; and there is no record that this amount was utilized. The first police jury appointed a committee of five of its members to supervise education but it was long before it began to function. The constitution of 1845 authorized the parish to levy a tax for the support of schools and to appoint a superintendent of education at the munificent salary of $400.00 a year. Under this law a one room school was opened in 1847 at about where the City Pharmacy now stands in the city of Lafayette. In 1852 the office of parish superintendent was abolished and his duties, together with the salary, transferred to the parish treasurer. The carpetbag constitution of 1868 provided for a school in the parish, but, since it was to be open to both white and colored children, it was attended only by Negroes. By the law of 1879 the office of parish superintendent was recreated with a salary of $200.00 a year, a parish school board was appointed by the governor, and all poll taxes collected were to go to the support of public schools. It was under this law that the first so-called high school was erected in the town of Lafayette in 1894 at a cost of $3000. This building stood where the Lafayette Lumber Company is now located and consisted of a two-story wood structure containing two rooms and an auditorium. By this time there were about thirty one or two-room schools in the parish.

In Carencro one of the first schools was a private one taught by a Mrs. Melchior in her own home. In 1874, however, a small one-room public school was built on the present site of the school farm. This school was later moved to the lot where the fire bell later stood; but, because of lack of drainage, was soon moved to the location of the present public school. The first teacher in this school was a German named Herchershine. In 1889 a new school with three rooms was built. Only two of these rooms, however, were used. In 1899 this school was enlarged by the addition of a second story. By 1917 the capacity of this building had been exceeded and a new brick building, containing fifteen rooms and costing $30,000.00 was completed.

The first public school in Broussard was opened in 1884 in a building of two rooms which was donated by the Farmer's Alliance. For the first few years there were only two teachers but as the attendance grew other rooms and teachers were added to the school. By 1916 the capacity of this building had become inadequate to meet the ever-increasing number of students who applied for admittance. After a spirited contest a bond issue of $30,000.00 was voted for a new building. This structure of brick, containing eight classrooms, was completed the following year.

The first public school in the town of Scott was built in 1895 under the encouragement of Mr. Alcide Judice on land belonging to Mr. Breaux. This was a one-room school in which the pupils were taught by Mr. Philip Martin. A few years later a two-story building was erected on the same site. This school offered only courses in the elementary grades. With the completion of a new high school building this school became an accredited high school in 1921.

It was not until 1898 that the state organic law made possible the building of a real system of public schools in the city and parish. In addition to the poll tax it provided for a state-wide levy of one and one fourth mills for public school purposes. It also authorized parishes, municipalities, wards and school districts to tax themselves more liberally for public education as long as the total of such taxes did not exceed ten mills. The same law permitted the parish to pay as much as $1200.00 a year for a parish superintendent. Under this law the parish soon began to take rapid strides in educational progress. In 1900 the people taxed themselves $80,000.00 to secure the location of Southwestern in the city of Lafayette. Three years later the city voted bonds in the amount of $24,000.00 for the construction of the Southside High School, recently demolished to make way for Lafayette's new post office. In 1906 the parish secured in Mr. L. J. Alleman its first professionally trained parish superintendent; and in 1910 was built the

Northside Primary School at a cost of $20,000. The Central School was built in 1919 at a cost of $75,000.

Meantime the wards and school districts out in the parish had voted bonds for the building of high schools in Broussard, Carencro, Scott and Youngsville. This remarkable educational development was given further impetus in 1927 when the citizens of the parish voted a bond issue to be used in retiring outstanding city and ward school bonds and the building of new schools. This issue was for $1,000,000.00 and from it were constructed the N. P. Moss School at a cost of $75,000.00 and the present Junior High School at a cost of $140,000. In the other towns the existing schools were enlarged and new high schools built at Judice and Youngsville. In 1940 another bond issue of $45,000.00 made possible the building of Myrtle Place Elementary School.

By 1950 practically all schools in the parish, due to the rapid growth of population, had become overcrowded, outmoded, and greatly in need of repairs. To meet these conditions the voters authorized, in 1950, a bond issue of $2,558,000.00 to build new schools and enlarge and modernize existing ones. From this fund have been built in the city a high school and two elementary schools for white children and a high school and elementary school for Negro children. Out in the parish a new elementary school was built in Scott and additional rooms, cafeterias and gymnasia added to others. As this is being written plans are under way to build many other schools with the proceeds of a $7,000,000.00 bond issue which the voters have recently authorized. With the completion of this new building program, Lafayette Parish will have a physical plant that is a far cry from the one-room school that stood on the corner of Jefferson and Vermilion Streets in 1847.

SOUTHWESTERN LOUISIANA INSTITUTE

Education in Lafayette Parish and the surrounding areas was given great impetus when the General Assembly of Louisiana, by act 162 of 1898, authorized the establishment of Southwestern Louisiana Industrial Institute. This act was introduced by the late Robert Martin of St. Martin Parish and provided that the Institute should be located in that Parish of the Thirteenth Senatorial District which offered to the Board of Trustees the best inducement therefor. The first two meetings of the board were held January 3 and 5, 1900 in Lafayette and New Iberia respectively. The competition between the two cities resulted in favor of Lafayette which offered the following inducements: twenty-five acres of land donated by Mr. Crow Girard and his mother Mrs. Maxim A. Girard; three thousand dollars in cash from the citizens of town and parish; and a tax of two mills for ten years to yield approximately eighty thousand dollars. With the proceeds of these donations, supplemented by legislative appropriations, Martin Hall, Foster Hall and a shop building were erected and the first session opened September 18, 1901.

The legislative act which created the school gave it its name and provided that it should be administered by a board of trustees appointed by the governor of which the governor was to be ex-officio chairman. The first board was appointed by Governor Foster in 1899. This board thereupon named as the first president Edwin Lewis Stephens, who began his duties January 1, 1900, and opened the first session September 18, 1901. President Stephens directed the destinies of the Institute for the next thirty-eight years. It was he who during this period, designed the basic pattern for future physical and scholastic development. This pattern was so brilliantly conceived, and proved to be so sound that succeeding administrations have found little cause to change it.

The Louisiana Constitution of 1921 designated the Institute as one of the institutions of higher learning in Louisiana and changed its name to Southwestern Louisiana Institute, with the subtitle of "Liberal and Technical Learning." The same constitution abolished the old board of trustees and placed the Institute, along with certain other state colleges, under the administration of the reorganized State Board of Education. This board consisted of eleven members, eight elected from the eight congressional districts and three to be appointed by the governor, and to serve concurrently with him. A later amendment now provides that the three appointive members shall be elected, one from each of the three public service districts of the state. With the rank of a senior college, authority to confer baccalaureate degrees, and a non-political board to administer its affairs, the Institute soon advanced to a position from which it could command greater academic respect and thus larger appropriations from the legislature. The first degrees were granted in 1921.

President Stephens served as president until his retirement as President Emeritus in 1938. Since then the Institute has had two presidents: Lether Edward Frazar from 1938 to 1941 and the present executive, Joel Lafayette Fletcher, who assumed his duties January 1, 1941.

Since the erection of the original buildings subsequent appropriations by the legislature have made possible a vast expansion of the physical plant. During the administration of President Stephens there were built DeClouet Hall in 1904; a frame residence for the president in 1908; Brown Ayres Hall in 1909; the purchase of a dairy farm of one hundred and twenty-five acres in 1918; the construction of Girard Hall to house the College of Liberal Arts and furnish larger quarters for the library in 1922; the erection of Lee Hall in 1925; the completion of Buchanan and Judice Halls as dormitories for women and men in 1927; the purchase of thirty acres of land for horticultural purposes near the campus in 1931; and several unnamed subsidiary structures on farms and campus for the rapidly expanding activities of the Institute.

In 1935 the Institute initiated a cooperative plan to meet the needs of young men who desired a college education, but were unable because of the depression to pay the usual charges for board and room. Under this plan each participating member of a cooperative club paid his prorated share of the cost of board or performed a prescribed amount of work on the dairy and horticulture farms, if he were unable to meet this cost. The first students to participate in this plan were housed temporarily in the agricultural exhibits building which is now the laundry. With assistance from the Works Progress Administration the Institute was soon able to build a more permanent cooperative dormitory which accommodated one hundred and twenty students; and subsequently with more federal aid it was able to add two more such dormitories and a cooperative dining hall.

Beginning in 1936 and extending through 1938 the State pursued a policy of enlarging and improving the physical plants of all the state colleges. To implement this policy at the Institute the legislature appropriated substantial sums of money. With some of this money additional land was purchased for campus and for agricultural uses: the Whittington farm of one hundred and eighty acres situated on the Abbeville road one mile south of the campus, and thirty-five acres to connect the campus with the thirty-acre horticulture farm purchased in 1931. By 1940 these funds had also made possible the completion of the following buildings on the campus: the men's gymnasium, Harris Hall, Evangeline Hall, the Hugh D. McLaurin Gymnasium, a student center, Mouton Hall,

Stephens Memorial Library, Broussard Hall, Saucier Infirmary, Parker Hall, Burke Hall, F. M. Hamilton Elementary Training School, McNaspy Stadium and a new residence for the president. In addition to those new buildings, Foster Hall and Buchanan Hall were in part rebuilt and renovated and the campus in other respects extensively improved. Since 1940 a paved boulevard had been built through the campus and a system of concrete walks laid along the outer boundaries of the main campus and connecting all the buildings.

After World War II Southwestern enjoyed a phenomenal growth and had to build to meet the increased educational demands made upon it by the hundreds of veterans seeking educational advantages after their discharge from the armed forces. Additional living quarters for single and married veterans were provided with aid from the Federal Public Housing authority. These buildings are now the property of the Institute and are now used for faculty and student housing. Another federal program placed on the campus numerous temporary classroom, laboratory and shop buildings for science, business administration, engineering, industrial arts, and agriculture.

The sums appropriated by the legislature to meet this postwar growth have been used to provide many new facilities: the acquisition of an additional 345 acres of land adjoining the Whittington farm; the purchase and equipment of 70 acres on the Bertrand road for instruction in poultry husbandry; Beverly Randolph Hall, Emile Huger Hall and Lucy Baker Hall, dormitories for women; Blackham Coliseum, with a seating capacity of over 5000, to be used by the Mid-Winter Fair Association and by the Institute for athletic and other school events; and one of the finest and best equipped dairy industry plants to be found in the state. A new modern laundry has been installed at the south end of the campus; the old farm dining hall has been completely transformed to provide classrooms and offices for the United States Air Force Reserve Officers Training Corps and for the United States Department of Interior.

One million dollars appropriated for the biennium of 1948-50 has been used for major repairs and improvements to the Allen Dining Hall, the paving of St. Mary Boulevard and the construction and equiping of a much needed chemistry building which is among the most modern and complete to be found in the South.

As this is being written there has just been completed a handsome and modernistic Memorial Student Union Building and two large men's dormitories. Under construction are an Engineering building with full equipment for Civil, Electrical, Mechanical, Chemical and Petroleum Engineering; and a Biology building with complete laboratories for all the biological sciences. With the completion of these buildings Southwestern will be prepared to train in the fields of science and engineering the men for which an industralized South is so urgently calling.

The primary purpose of the State in founding the Institute was to give the stimulus of state assistance to the development of education in the South and southwestern section of Louisiana, which hitherto had had only meager educational opportunities for its large population. Emphasis was placed upon technical training along with basic academic studies, because of its value in earning a livelihood. The requirements for admission were accordingly low. But by gradually raising the entrance requirements from year to year the status of the Institute has been successively advanced from elementary to high school grade, then to junior college rank, and finally to that of standard senior college conferring baccalaureate degrees. This last rank was attained in 1921.

As soon as the courses had been graded to a point sufficiently high to meet college standards a teacher training department was organized. This was inaugurated in 1912 in response to the demand of the public schools of the state for a much larger number of trained teachers than existing training facilities could supply. This department developed rapidly into a standard two year normal school which was recognized in 1915 by the State Department of Education by granting to its graduates professional teachers certificates. On the attainment of full senior college standing by the Institute this department was elevated to the position of a four-year teachers college now designated as the College of Education, granting to its graduates professional degrees in practically all fields of subject matter now taught in schools of elementary and high school grade.

Meanwhile the academic and technical courses, which included agriculture, commerce and manual training, had been reorganized and strengthened to meet college standards and were so consolidated as to form that central organization of the Institute now designated as the College of Liberal Arts. This college offered curricula in the arts and sciences, agriculture, commerce and engineering, all leading to appropriate college degrees. Under this organization, President Stephens chose as the first dean of the College of Liberal Arts Dr. Harry Lewis Griffin and the first dean of the College of Education Irving P. Foote.

By 1938 the student enrollment in the Institute had grown to such proportions that serious consideration was given to the elevation of some of the larger technical departments to the status of colleges. Accordingly in 1938 the Departments of Agriculture and Home Economics were detached from the two existing colleges and organized into a College of Agriculture with its own faculty and administration. In 1940 the Department of Engineering was similarily separated from the College of Liberal Arts and set up as the College of Engineering with its own faculty and administration. In September, 1952, the College of Commerce was similarly organized by the separation from the College of Liberal Arts of the Department of Economics and Business Administration. In this manner, therefore, have five of the early departments of the Institute grown into independent colleges. While the College of Liberal Arts maintains its own curricula and grants its own degrees it continues to be the central service college for the other four colleges and for the sixth college which was organized in 1951. This last one is the College of Nursing.

Evidence that the standards followed in the building of the curricula have been kept on a high plane is found in the fact that the Institute has won the approval of various accrediting and professional agencies by being admitted to membership in the following: The Southern Association of Colleges and Secondary Schools, in 1925; American Association of Colleges, in 1926; American Council on Education, in 1927; American Association of Colleges for Teacher Education, in 1932; The National Association of Schools of Music, in 1950; National Council for Accrediting Teacher Education, in 1954; and Engineering Council for Professional Development, with accrediting in Chemical, Civil, Electrical and Mechanical Engineering, in 1956. The Institute is also on the approved list of the New York State Department of Education.

Under the leadership of President Stephens Southwestern soon began to exert a powerful influence in developing the latent educational and cultural resources of Southwest Louisiana and particularly of the City and Parish of Lafayette. Among the older families of Acadian and French decent there was still preserved much of the culture of old France, which lay dormant and often unexpressed. Among their children who came to the Institute there was much intellectual and artistic talent. Through its programs of instruction in literature, art, music, history and dramatics, the Institute provided a means of discovering and developing abilities which had lain neglected and uncultivated. Based on these native abilities there soon sprang up on the campus any number of literary societies, dramatic clubs, choral societies and lecture programs. In many cases talented citizens of the community were invited to participate in these offerings with the result that popular interest in intellectual and artistic subjects was greatly stimulated. One of the early instances of this common effort occurred when, in 1907, a number of local persons joined with faculty and students in staging the popular Mikado, photographs of which are still treasured by some of the participants. The intellectual interests of Lafayette were heightened in 1910, when President Stephens joined with local townsmen in the organization of a Public Forum, which met monthly in a room above what is now the City Pharmacy on Jefferson Street. At the meeting of the Forum, which continued for several years, were presented musical programs, stimulating lectures, and discussions of current subjects. The work thus began has continued through the years. In this manner has Southwestern built on the native love for learning and culture, all of which has created an atmosphere that enabled it to become the great institution it is today.

The residence of Jules Revillon, built about 1880, was on South Washington Street around the corner from the store. On the porch from left to right are: (1) Joachim, who never married, (2) Julie, married Jules Krauss, (3) Joe Ducote, who married Caroline Martin, (4) Lucille, who married George McClure, (5) Alix Judice (Mrs. J. Alfred Mouton) who had come to give Louise a music lesson, (6) Louise, who married Edward Ferran, (7) Marie, who married John Marsh, (8) Mrs. Jules J. Revillion, their mother.

(At Right) Couret Home — the old Gerassin Bernard home off the Carencro highway, built around 1852.

An ancient plantation home against a background of trees. The house was built by Mrs. William Couret's greatgrandmother Eugenie Mouton, who was the granddaughter of Jean Mouton and Gerassin Bernard. Eugenie was born in the nearby home of her father, Francois Mouton, in 1804. She died in 1897,

The timbers for the house were cut by slaves from the bank of the Mermentau River, forty-five miles away. The bricks were made by the slaves. The house was designed by Paxton & Noillon architects of Vermilionville. Mrs. William Couret and her daughter, Lucille, now live in the family home.

— Courtesy of Lucille Couret

The Eastin Home, later the office and residence of Dr. J. D. Trahan at 820 S. Washington Street. The lumber from which it was built was brought from the St. Martinville swamps in wagons drawn by oxen. Razin Wallis was the builder and architect. Mrs. (Dr.) Henri L. Ducrocq, Dr. Trahan's daughter, lives in the house next to this one.

(Below) Residence of Charles Mouton, built about 1850, later the home of Judge James G. Parkerson. It is on Garfield Street at the intersection of Polk Street. On old city map this area is referred to as the Mansion Block.

CHAPTER XV

FINANCE AND INDUSTRY

CATTLE, SUGAR, COTTON AND OIL

The earliest commercial activities in what is now Lafayette Parish consisted of transactions between those who came here to exchange beads and other trinkets with the Indians for their furs. Then came the trapper who tried his own hand at catching the fur-bearing animals, at first with little success, because he did not know how to preserve his peltries in warm and rainy weather. Many a novice spent the winter in wood and swamp accumulating valuable skins only to lose the whole season's catch when the warm spring came before he could get his precious store to market.

With the coming of the Acadians to the territory centering in Vermilionville, the new industry of raising cattle and horses soon took first rank. All the pioneer had to do was to acquire from the government a small grant of land and on this plant the nucleus of a small herd of cattle. In every direction stretched the boundless prairies still unclaimed and covered with green verdure. Turned loose on such pastures his small herd soon multiplied and grew fat. His only care was to round them up occasionally and brand as his own the new-born calves. In the old brand book for the Opelousas and Attakapas Districts, which may be seen in the library at Southwestern Louisiana Institute, appear the names and brands of these early pioneers in the cattle industry. By 1827 over forty brands had been registered for Lafayette Parish alone. It has been said that a few individuals had as many as three thousand calves and a thousand colts to brand each year. At five dollars for a steer and eight for a horse such a one could count on no mean income.

By 1830, however, the pastures were beginning to be plowed up and planted to cotton and sugar cane. At the outbreak of the Civil War these two industries had become well established. Both crops were cultivated largely with slave labor and on a comparatively small scale. Rice was then grown only in small quantities for domestic use, and its culture in this parish did not become important until after it had been exploited in Acadia Parish by Mr. Joseph Fabacher shortly after 1880. Soon thereafter the wide prairies were plowed up and the cattle industry pushed westward into Texas.

The development of the sugar industry in the parish is worthy of special mention. In the early days of the industry, nearly every farmer had his "cane patch" and a small mill propelled by horse power. In this mill he crushed from his cane the juice which he boiled in open kettles either for sugar or syrup. By 1840 a few planters had steam propelled mills which were capable of turning out large quantities of raw sugar. Governor Mouton had such a mill on his plantation at Vermilionville. Since only large planters could finance a steam mill it soon came about that many small farmers brought their cane to such a mill to be converted into sugar and syrup on a toll basis. The industry prospered until the Civil War practically destroyed it. After the war it recovered slowly. In 1870 Lafayette Parish produced only 12,800 pounds of sugar and 715 gallons of syrup. Ten years later this amount had increased to 631,000 pounds of sugar and 20,000 gallons of syrup. In 1940 the production was 27,000,000 pounds of sugar and 9,865 gallons of syrup. The census of 1950 showed the production of sugar alone to be over 21,000,000 pounds. There are now in Lafayette Parish only two large sugar factories and several mills that produce syrup for local consumption.

The first of these great factories was begun in 1889 by Mr. Martial Billeaud of Broussard. The capital was fifty thousand dollars and the daily capacity was four hundred tons of cane. The capacity has been gradually increased so that today it can process two thousand tons of cane daily. The factory now represents an investment of a million dollars. A second one was incorporated in 1895 by the late Colonel Gustave Breaux, A. B. Denbo and others with a capital of seventy-five thousand dollars. This factory stood by the railroad on the ground now occupied by the Braun Welding establishment at 1815 Oak Avenue. After several years of operation under the management of Mr. Denbo, the factory was purchased by a group of New Orleans capitalists. Representing the new owners in Lafayette was Mr. G. von Tresco, a native of Germany who is remembered by older citizens as a most interesting person. The New Orleans owners continued to operate the plant under the old name of Lafayette Sugar Factory until 1922 when it was destroyed by fire. Although the capital remained at seven-five thousand dollars the factory was valued at over three quarters of a million dollars at the time of its destruction. The third factory is located at Youngsville. It was organized in 1907 by Roy O. Young and his associates for the purpose of making syrup. In 1909 it began making sugar also; and in 1910 was reorganized as the Youngsville Sugar Factory with a capital of $150,000. With this enlarged capital the capacity of the plant was increased to 1000 tons of sugar cane daily. This concern has also grown with the result that the plant, with earned improvements, represents an investment of well over half a million dollars.

The planting of cotton in the parish has steadily increased since 1830. In 1870 the product amounted to 6,234 bales. Today a single concern will gin almost that amount in a single season. Before 1876 cotton gins were run by horsepower. In that year probably the first steam powered gin was constructed at Carencro by Mr. Avignac Arceneaux with a capacity of five bales daily. Subsequently two other gins were constructed there, each with a capacity of thirty-five to forty bales daily. The first cotton gin in Youngsville was built in 1890 by Mr. P. B. Roy. Other gins are located in Scott, Duson, Broussard, Milton, Ridge and Lafayette. In 1952 the nineteen gins in the parish processed cotton to the value of six million dollars. In 1896 was founded by T. M. Boissat, C. M. Parkerson and C. D. Caffery the Peoples Cotton Oil Company. From cottonseed this plant manufactures cotton-seed cake, meal, linters, and oil.

DEVELOPMENT OF BANKING

The industrial development of the city and parish has been influenced very largely by the establishment of banks. Before 1841 there was none in the parish. If one had money he must either hide it or send it to a state bank either in St. Martinville or New Orleans. If he wished to borrow money he must resort to one of the aforesaid institutions or, worse yet, to a private money lender. In 1830 the police jury had to borrow from the state bank in St. Martinville and pay ten per cent interest. If one were so unlucky as to have to borrow from one of the money lenders he might have to pay from two to five per cent a month for his loan. In 1832, however, as a result of the efforts of certain community leaders, Governor Roman on April 2, signed a legislative bill labelled "An Act to incorporate the Subscribers to the Union Bank of Louisiana." Section 33 of this act authorized the subscribers to establish eight offices of discount and deposit in the state, one of which was to be located "in Vermilionville in the Parish of Lafayette," where with a capital of $200,000.00 it was to serve the parishes of Lafayette and St. Landry.

Evidence seems to indicate, however, that the office of Discount and Deposit of the Union Bank of Vermilionville was not opened until some time in 1841, as evidenced by the first promissory note which reads as follows:

No. 1

$1500. Twelve months after date I promise to pay to the order of T. and A. Lastrapes, at the office of Discount and Deposit of the Union Bank of Vermilionville the sum of fifteen hundred dollars, value received.
Vermilionville, 17th May, 1841
Signed, R. Garland
Endorsed, T. and A. Lastrapes
C. L. Swayze
Credit of the Drawer
C.L.G.

On the back of the note is written:
2373 Rice Garland $1500
1842 May 17/20

Just how the Vermilionville branch of the Union Bank of Louisiana was managed and how long it existed is not clear from the records found in the Lafayette Parish Courthouse. It seems that the discounts were recorded by Joachim Revillon and loans were made as late as December 15, 1848. On that date two notes were executed: Number one was for $160.00, signed by E. I. Gregnon and endorsed by Cahe Neveu and Ursin Hebert; number two was for $50.00, signed by A. Richard and endorsed by E. Reeves. Most of the notes were for small amounts. The largest one was for $1850.00, signed by Marin Brashear and endorsed by Martin Demaret, B. C. Crow and Robert Cade.

After the financial crash of 1837 many banks in Louisiana were forced to close their doors. During this period and long after the Civil War people in the parish were forced to patronize private banks and money lenders. Among those who engaged in this business in Lafayette Parish during the post war period may be named Eloi Girard, P. B. Roy, Walter Torian, John O. Mouton, Leo Doucet, and William Clegg. Mr. Clegg conducted a kind of private bank for the lending of money in an office on St. John Street in the block now occupied by the Christian Brothers School. The rate of interest charged by the private bankers usually began at ten per cent.

It was not until 1891 that there was established in Lafayette a bank such as we know it today. This was the People's State Bank of Lafayette with a capital of twenty-five thousand dollars. The first officers were: Judge Conrad Debaillon, president, C. C. Brown, vice-president, George L. McClure, cashier and S. R. Parkerson, assistant cashier. On the board of directors were: Judge Conrad Debaillon, A. J. Moss, J. G. Parkerson, C. C. Brown, G. B. Petty, G. L. McClure, N. P. Moss, William Campbell and Pierre Gerac. After twenty-seven months of operation the deposits of one hundred and fifty-three depositors amounted to $63,308.01.

The People's State Bank was reorganized as the First National Bank in 1895 and the capital increased to fifty thousand dollars. As a national bank its first officers were: Crow Girard, president; S. R. Parkerson, cashier; and Pierre B. Roy, auditor. The following persons made up the board of directors: Pierre B. Roy, A. J. Moss, Alcide Judice, Crow Girard, J. G. Parkerson, N. P. Moss, Felix Demanade, John S. Whittington and C. C. Brown.

In 1904 the capital was increased to one hundred thousand dollars; to two hundred thousand in 1919; and in 1953 the capital stood at five hundred thousand dollars with an equal amount as surplus. By 1908 the deposits of the reorganized bank had reached four hundred thousand dollars; over two million in 1920; and to twenty and a half millions in 1953. In spite of the difficult years following World War I and the depression of 1930, this bank had in 1935 resources of three and one half millions. In 1953 its resources were over twenty-one and three quarters millions.

The next bank to be organized was the Bank of Lafayette which opened for business in 1898. This bank was promoted by J. J. Davidson, C. O. Mouton and their associates. The initial capital of $25,000.00 was increased to $50,000.00 in 1915 and to $250,000.00 in 1921. In 1920 the name had been changed to the Bank of Lafayette and Trust Company, and the banks of Scott, Carencro, Youngsville and Broussard were absorbed by the enlarged financial institution. About the same time this bank also established branches in Duson and Maurice. The rapid expansion of this bank is seen by a glance at its deposits. At the end of the first year the deposits amounted to slightly over thirty-two and one half thousands of dollars. In 1910 they had increased to over two hundred thirty thousand; and in 1920 to over three and a quarter millions.

During the post war period and the depression, however, this bank suffered such severe reverses that it was forced into liquidation.

The friends of the defunct Bank of Lafayette and Trust Company were not content to see the home of this bank unoccupied. Accordingly in 1937 there was organized the Guaranty Bank and Trust Company with a capital of $100,000.00 and surplus of $200,000.00. With the growth of Lafayette it has prospered and in 1953 had assets of over twelve and one half millions.

The latest bank to be organized in Lafayette was the American Bank and Trust Company. It opened for business on February 8, 1956, with a capital of $500,000.00 and a surplus of $250,000. Officers and directors were: J. Maxime Roy, Chairman of the Board; Paul Blanchet, President; J. B. Hutchinson, Executive Vice-President; Alfred F. Boustany, Vice-President; Bennett J. Voorhies, Attorney. Other directors were: Robert Angelle, Dr. J. J. Burdin, W. D. Huff, Joe Huval, A. R. Johnson, W. B. Landry, and W. K. Rainbolt. The first statement issued June 31, 1956, showed resources of over six million. The last statement issued June 10, 1959, lists the resources at considerably over ten millions.

The material development of city and parish has been greatly facilitated by the organization of building and loan associations. Such an organization was founded as early as 1888 by local and outside interests with an authorized capital of $300,000. This concern, however, did not prove to be permanent and was followed by the Popular Loan and Building Company of Cincinnati, which remained in business until 1907.

In the meantime there had been organized on February 12, 1900 the Lafayette Building Association with an authorized capital of one million dollars. This enterprise was conceived by B. N. Corona, and the first officers were: Julian Mouton, president; A. B. Denbo, vice-president; S. R. Parkerson, treasurer; and D. S. Schwartz, secretary. In 1935 the resources of the association were over one and a half millions and by 1952 had climbed to over nine millions.

In 1908 was organized the Home Building Association with J. P. Colomb as president; J. F. Jeanmard as secretary; J. C. Barry, treasurer, and E. G. Voorhies, attorney. This rapidly grown institution in 1935 had total resources of over nine hundred fifty thousand dollars. By 1953 this had grown to over six and one half millions.

RISE OF BUSINESS AND INDUSTRY

In 1899 a group of progressive minded men of Lafayette organized themselves into the Lafayette Improvement Association. This group was composed of Dr. N. P. Moss, S. R. Parkerson, C. M. Parkerson, C. D. Caffery, P. B. Roy, Frank Moss, Felix Demanade, Alcide Judice, O. C. Mouton and others. The assembling of these men may be said to mark the beginning of the present chamber of commerce. Their purpose was the improvement of the town. These gentlemen worked unceasingly to have Southwestern Louisiana Institute located in Lafayette. It was this group that supported the first big bond issue for extending the electric light and water systems and for building the first modern high school. These were the men who decided that Lafayette should have a modern hotel and theatre. Accordingly they organized the stock company which, in 1904, built the Gordon Hotel and the Jefferson Theatre at a cost of $100,000. The spirit manifested by them was not permitted to die. In 1915 was organized a Chamber of Commerce, backed by all the leading businessmen of the parish and supplied with enough money to advertise the advantages of the community and to employ a paid secretary. Since that time the parish has not been without this valuable organization which has expanded to keep pace with the growing population. With a paid membership of eight hundred in 1958, and a capable office force the Chamber exercises a powerful and aggressive influence in all phases of community development.

Space does not permit the writer to tell here in detail the entire story of the exploitation of the resources of this rich community. We know that there have been small saw-mills in Carencro and along the banks of Bayou Vermilion in Lafayette Parish long before the Civil War. It was only in 1920 that the Baldwin Lumber Company, owned by Messrs. Allen, Earl, and Robert Barnett, built a large mill here. From logs taken from the swamps around Lake Martin this mill sawed lumber at the rate of 100,000 board feet daily for several years, and gave employment to six hundred men. The site of that mill is now occupied by the B. F. Trappey and Sons canning factory.

It was not until after 1900 that the value of Lafayette as a distributing center was fully realized. In 1903 was organized by Felix Demanade, N. P. Moss, S. R. Parkerson, T. M. Boissat and Raoul Jeanmard the first wholesale grocery under the name of the Merchants Grocery Company. The original capital was $50,000.00, but in 1920 this was increased to $150,000.00. Four years later a second one, the Lafayette Wholesale Grocery Company, was organized by E. L. Berde, Julius Goldsmith, and A. W. Prudhomme with a capital of $50,000.00, which in 1918 was increased to $150,000. The success of these two enterprises and other similar ones gave indication that Lafayette had a promising future as a distributing point for merchandise. With the development of improved highways and rapid growth of population the number of wholesale distributors of merchandise increased rapidly. By 1948 there were in Lafayette Parish one hundred and sixteen wholesale establishments, distributing everything from drugs, cigars and cigarettes, building materials, radios and televisions, to confections, farm machinery and petroleum products.

Eyes Turned on Lafayette

On October 15, 16, 17, 1936 there was held on the campus of Southwestern in Lafayette a conference that was to have far-reaching results in the industrial development of Lafayette, South Louisiana, and the entire Gulf Coast. On those three days was held the Southern Chemurgic Conference under the sponsorship of the Farm Chemurgic Council of Dearborn, Michigan. The conference was organized jointly by the Lafayette and Beaumont, Texas, Chambers of Commerce. On the committee on arrangements for the Lafayette chamber were Dean H. L. Griffin, Chairman, T. M. Callahan, V. O. Griffin, J. R. Jeanmard, J. L. Fletcher, L. L. Judice, Elmo Hodges, and J. Maxine Roy. Heading the Beaumont committee was P. B. Doty, President of the First National Bank of Beaumont, who also presided as general chairman. Attending the conference either as speakers or observers were hundreds of persons from many parts of the country representing agriculture, finance, industry and science.

On the first day of the conference guests were taken on a motor tour of the Evangeline Country and shown its rich resources. They visited the sugar factories, rice mills, salt mines and oil fields. All were enthusiastic over what they saw. On the two succeeding days at the various sessions there were presented by outstanding authorities in their fields twenty-five prepared papers on the resources of South Louisiana and their possible uses in industry. As each paper was read there were present special representatives of

Science Press and the Associated Press to flash the contents to appropriate publications all over the United States. Among those who presented papers were Dr. Henry G. Knight, Chief of the Bureau of Chemistry and Soils, U. S. Department of Agriculture; A. B. Connor, Director, Texas Agricultural Experiment Station; J. Arthur Brock, Saginaw, Michigan, Editor of Sugar Beet Journal; Walter Godchaux, Vice-president, Godchaux Sugars, Inc.; Wheeler McMillen, Editor, the Country Home, New York, New York; James A. Lee, Editor, Chemical and Metallurgical Engineering, New York, New York; Dr. Charles H. Herty, Director, Pulp and Paper Laboratory, Savannah, Georgia; and William W. Buffum, Treasurer and General Manager of the Chemical Foundation.

During this conference the citizens of Lafayette displayed their most generous hospitality in entertaining those in attendance and on the program so that not only were the resources of this rich region flashed to the world but also the hospitality and friendliness of its citizens which have been demonstrated on so many other occasions. This conference and a subsequent one held in Beaumont, Texas, had much to do with directing the attention of the captains of industry to the rich resources of South Louisiana and the Gulf Coast.

In concluding this chapter it should be pointed out that the development of the city and parish of Lafayette may be attributed to a few key events: the completion of the Southern Pacific Railroad through Lafayette in 1883; the opening of Southwestern Louisiana Institute in 1901; the establishment of banks and building associations between 1891 and 1908; and the paving of all highways leading into Lafayette in 1936. The event that started the Lafayette community on its greatest expansion program in finance, industry and population came in 1940 when oil companies began to establish offices in Lafayette, drawn here by the central location of the city with respect to their various activities, and by the friendly hospitality of Lafayette's citizens. As the oil companies moved into Lafayette with their lease men, production men, field supervisors, geologists, engineers, marketing supervisors and other personnel and, followed by a host of concerns that service oil operations such as supply stores and trucking firms, many proposals for furnishing them with suitable office space were made, but none of them seemed satisfactory because of the lack of parking space. Finally on June 18, 1952 an oil man suggested to Mr. Maurice Heymann the idea of an oil city or center. Mr. Heymann at once became interested in the suggeston and, after consultation with several company representatives, found that they preferred offices removed from down town, and in a location where they could have lots of ground floor space and plenty of nearby room for parking. The suggestion by Mr. Heymann that he could provide such facilities on the grounds of his nursery, which lay between Pin Hook Road, Girard Park and St. Mary Boulevard, met with their approval. The result was that, after architect Hays Town had drawn up preliminary plans for a four building unit, Mr. Heymann, on Friday, June 20, 1952, told the Lafayette *Advertiser* that he was building a million dollar oil center. After the plans were changed to include two more buildings in the oil center complex, construction began in late September 1952; and by October all of the space had been leased. Thus began the move that has made Lafayette the oil center of all South Louisiana and has changed the face and character of the city. This development has continued to grow until the number of buildings totals approximately thirty, and now involves an investment of over three and one half million dollars. The influx of oil men with their familes has been largely responsible for the recent rapid increase in the population of the City of Lafayette.

CHAPTER XVI

COMMUNICATIONS

The Post Office

There was a post office at Vermilion several years before Jean Mouton mapped the plans for his village. An inquiry directed to the office of the Deputy Postmaster General concerning the early post office here brought forth the following information:

"The Lafayette post office was originally established at Vermilion Bridge on February 6, 1817, with Abel Terrill appointed the first postmaster. The following is a list of the postmasters and the dates of appointment to office:

Postmaster	Date of appointment
Abel Terrill	February 6, 1817
Robert Cade	September 19, 1823

Post office changed to Vermilionville January 27, 1825

I. I. Nevin	April 17, 1825
Emile Charx	October 21, 1828
Allan Smith	January 20, 1838
Daniel O'Bryan	March 23, 1839
James M. Moore	August 5, 1840
Joachim Revillon	January 14, 1846
William P. Thomas	March 23, 1855
Enoch P. Kemper	September 2, 1856
John Rykoski	December 20, 1858
Louis A. Roussel	February 2, 1866
John H. Chargois	June 8, 1866
August H. Monier	July 17, 1866
Alphonse Neveu	July 8, 1867
Jean J. Neveu	August 8, 1867
Alphonse Neveu	May 12, 1871
Auguste Monnier	October 17, 1881
Marshall T. Martin	February 24, 1882

Post office name changed to LaFayette, June 2, 1884

Marshall T. Martin	June 2, 1884
Samuel F. Simpsen	June 29, 1885
Paul Demande	March 12, 1890
Charles O. Menton (Mouton)	April 14, 1894
Paul Demande	August 8, 1898
Joseph R. Domengeaux	March 27, 1903
Ambrose L. Marshall	May 7, 1916
Joseph R. Domengeaux	December 20, 1921

Spelling of name changed to Lafayette, January 1, 1925

Robert L. Monton (Mouton)	May 18, 1929
Walter Guidry	November 17, 1930
Edwin A. O'Brien	April 26, 1931
Sidney L. Voorhies	May 4, 1936
Leon J. Guidry	May 23, 1949
Edwin A. O'Brien (acting)	September 30, 1954
Edwin A. O'Brien (regular)	September 30, 1955 to date."

Prior to 1836, the year the Lafayette Parish Police Jury planned the first roads to connect Vermilionville with the surrounding towns, mail was probably delivered to the post office by courier on horseback, the postage often being paid by the one who received it. Beginning in 1837, however, the mail was carried to Vermilionville in a four horse post coach from either New Iberia or Washington to which it came by boat. This manner of delivery continued until the railroad was completed from New Orleans to Vermilionville in 1880. Thereafter mail was transported by train. With the establishment of regular flights by Eastern Air Lines on August 3, 1948 citizens of Lafayette have been privileged to send and receive their mail by air. It is now possible to send packages by air mail express.

NEWSPAPERS

The writer has not been able to find copies of any newspaper published in Vermilionville prior to 1850. For many years before that time, notices of sales, proclamations and other legal transactions were posted on the doors of the church and court house, or published in some paper in a neighboring town. There is ample evidence, however, that newspapers were published in Vermilionville before the above date.

It was on March 3, 1843, that Father Mégret, pastor of the Church of St. John, wrote Bishop Blanc and complained of the "Diabolical spirit of the paper in Vermilionville." In this same letter he says:

"Two young Frenchmen, one twenty-five and the other twenty-eight years of age, both men of remarkable talent, were called about two months ago to the office of this paper."

On August 4, 1843, Mégret again wrote to Bishop Blanc and said: "Guegnon received some more money to put in the paper the article against me."

The Guegnon mentioned in this letter is the same E. J. Guegnon named in connection with the Union Bank of Louisiana in Vermilionville in 1848. It was he who was said to have published *Le*

RESIDENCE OF PIERRE GERAC

Jean and Pierre Gerac were from France, the sons of Pierre and Mary Bellau. Pierre, born in 1837, came to New Orleans with Jean in 1851 — then on to Lafayette Parish in 1855.

Pierre served in the 22nd La. Infantry during the Civil War. In 1868 he married, in Mexico, Francesco Y'Chaves, a native of that country.

The Geracs became large landowners, and operated many business enterprises. The old Gerac store stood at the SE corner of Vermilion and St. John Street.

Their home was sold to Bishop Jeanmard for the present building of the Bishopric. The house was moved across the street, facing the property. It is now owned by Walter H. David. On the porch, from left to right, are the Gerac family:

1. Henri, married (1) Frances Adar, (2) Evelyn Darby
2. Estelle, married (1) Gus Lacoste (2) Leonard Dugas
3. Raoul, married Mary Miller
4. and 5. Mr. and Mrs. Pierre Gerac
6. On the railing Robert, who died young
7. Pierre, married Mathilde Richard
8. Louise, married Leon Delhomme
9. Felix, married Louise Hitter
10. Helene, married Rene Delhomme

RESIDENCE OF EDMOND MOUTON, JR., 1866, AT MOUTON SWITCH

The residence of his father, Edmond Mouton, Sr., was on the border of "Beau Bassin," a place called by the early Acadian settlers "Pretty Basin," a beautiful spot where a stream forms nearly a circle surrounded by hills covered with luxuriant vegetation and the whole studded with magnificent live oaks. This area is about a mile east of Carencro. One of the very earliest homes, it was dragged from Mermentau by oxen on seven hundred split rails, which were used to build rafts to float the house across the river, the oxen dragging the rafts. This took seven to eight months. The house was dismantled about ten years ago. The home of Edmond Mouton, Jr. is divided by a wide hall, separating one side of the house from the other. One side is one half of the home of General Alfred Mouton and the other side is built of lumber that Edmond Mouton, Jr. bought from "Coquelin" Latiolais who had

Meridional first in St. Martinville and later in Vermilionville, where he served as judge; and last in Abbeville where in 1856 he purchased the *Independent* and changed its name to *Le Meridional*. Judge Eugene Isadore Guegnon was known as a man who expressed himself freely in the columns of his paper; and for his frankness he was challenged to several pistol duels in two of which he was wounded. He died in Abbeville in 1862 at the approximate age of forty-seven years.

Court records of notarial acts indicate also that a paper by the designation of *Impartial* was the next one published in Vermilionville. These records testify that such legal notices as sales were ordered by the court to be published in the *Impartial* on September 26, 1846; October 5, 1846; November 16, 1846; March 30, 1847; February 1, 1848; and January 10, 1850.

The next paper known to be published was *L'Echo de Vermilionville*, a weekly printed in both English and French. Notarial acts prove conclusively that it was being published as early as 1856. The French editor was Eraste Mouton and the English editor Abijah Bailey. During the war between the states both men served in the Confederate army, but the paper continued to be published as late as 1863 by Columbus Bailey, a younger brother of Abijah Bailey. The shop in which the paper was printed stood on Buchanan Street directly across from the residence of the late Judge Paul Debaillon at 821 South Buchanan.

In 1865 Mr. William Bailey, who had in 1856 apparently bought the interest of Eraste Mouton in *L'Echo de Vermilionville*, founded a newspaper that was destined to have a long and distinguished career. This was the *Lafayette Advertiser*, which he published for the next twenty-seven years. It was after a brilliant career in the Confederate army that he returned to begin the publication of this paper. He had already before the war had experience in connection with both the *Echo in Vermilionville* and the *Teche Courier* in St. Martinville. The *Advertiser* was begun as a four page paper, being issued every Saturday. For many years it was published in both English and French. One has only to read its faded columns to be impressed with the high purposes of its editor. Mr. Bailey strove constantly to bring about self government in Louisiana during the troublesome days of Reconstruction; and, through editorials, to promote the social and material development of South Louisiana.

In 1892 Mr. Bailey severed his connection with the *Advertiser* and soon thereafter accepted from Governor Foster an appointment to the position of clerk of court for the parish of Lafayette. He did not survive long after this and died in 1896. Mr. Bailey, whose wife was Penelope Queen, was the father of the late Mrs. Arthur Roy, the mother of Maxime Roy, Mrs. Emile Soulier, Mrs. W. W. Hawkins of this city and Mrs. Ben Thibodeaux of Washington, D. C.

After the *Advertiser* was given up by Mr. Bailey it was acquired by Mr. H. A. Van der Cruyssen who continued its publication for some years. Later it was purchased and published by Mr. James A. Alpha and Mr. W. A. LeRosen, first as a weekly, then a semi-weekly; and after 1912 as a daily. It continued under this management until acquired by the present publishers in 1921.

Meantime there had been founded on March 11, 1893 by Mr. Charles A. Thomas and Mr. Homer Mouton another newspaper. This was the *Lafayette Gazette*, a small seven column paper of four pages. While this paper had no national press service, one cannot help being impressed with the faithful manner in which its editors collected and featured local and state news. In its columns can be found much of what happened in Lafayette and Louisiana in the years between 1895 and 1908.

Homer Mouton soon bought the share of his partner, Mr. Thomas and thus became the sole owner and publisher. At his death his brothers, Jerome and Philip Mouton, who had been associated with him, continued its publication. They later sold it to Mr. Andrew A. McBride. He published it for several years and then sold it to Mr. O. A. Fournet who employed Mr. J. Davidson as editor. Under this management the *Gazette* continued as a weekly until June 1, 1921. On that date the *Gazette* was acquired by the new owners of the *Daily Advertiser* and consolidated with that newly reorganized newspaper.

These are advertisements from the Lafayette Gazette, March 25, 1899.

> As an inducement to buyers, Levy Brothers are giving one ticket to everyone who purchases a $3.00 pair of shoes. This ticket entitles the bearer to ten "shines."
>
> * * * * * *
>
> Engineer Melchert informs the Gazette that he hopes to use the ARC lights by the first of April.

The present newspaper, the *Daily Advertiser*, has thus fallen heir to the traditions of two old and well known newspapers in

Lafayette. Fortunately the new owners of the consolidated paper were well able financially not only to perpetuate these traditions but to enlarge them in a worthy manner. With adequate capital at their command the new owners formed a publishing firm under the name, "Lafayette Advertiser-Gazette Incorporated." Under the able direction of Mr. Morgan Murphy of Wisconsin, president of the corporation, and the late Thomas M. Callahan, editor and publisher, the *Daily Advertiser* soon became one of the leading dailies of all South Louisiana.

In 1938 Mr. James A. Alpha, who had been publishing in Jeanerette a newspaper, the *Progress*, moved to Lafayette with his paper and began publishing it as a weekly under the caption, the *Lafayette Progress*. At Mr. Alpha's death in 1948 the paper descended to his daughter, Hazel Alpha. She then sold the paper to Mr. Burton Grimstaff who continued to published it as a weekly. Mr. Grimstaff also published a Sunday paper entitled the *Pictorial*. In 1948 Mr. Grimstaff sold the paper to a newly organized corporation designated the Lafayette Publishing Company which continued the publication of both the *Progress* and the *Pictorial* as weeklies until January 1, 1949, when publication of the *Pictorial* was discontinued. The *Progress* now appears on Saturday, and, since the discontinuance of the Saturday edition of the *Advertiser*, performs, with its summary of the week's news, a very valuable service. Its columns carry not only the official notices of parish and city but a record of real estate transactions and historical articles of great local interest.

NEWS BY WIRE AND AIR

The citizens of Lafayette sent and received messages by telegraph first over the wires of Morgan's Louisiana and Texas railroad. From 1880 until 1891 the only telegraphic access to the outside world was over the wires along the railroad tracks. It was not until 1891 that the first telegraph office was established in Lafayette with Miss Mary Littel as the first manager and operator. Miss Littel's sister also served as telegrapher at the rail station in Carencro at the same time. There must have been a shortage of telegraphers in those days, because soon after its opening Southwestern employed a teacher to give instruction in telegraphy and continued to do so until World War I. By 1923 the number of messages coming into and through Lafayette had become so great that Western Union found it necessary to transform its Lafayette office into a relay station. With this change the station remained in continuous operation with commercial service open until midnight. The Postal Telegraph established an office in Lafayette in 1933, but, after a brief existence, that office with its parent corporation were absorbed by Western Union.

The citizens of Lafayette have enjoyed telephone service for the last sixty-five years. The first telephones were installed in 1893 by the Hoggasett Telephone Company, a local concern with headquarters in New Iberia. Its first subscriber was the First National Bank which was given the call number one, a number it retained for many years. The Hoggasett Company continued to operate in Lafayette until 1904 when it abandoned the field to a competitor. This competitor was the Cumberland Telephone Company which, on February 3, 1896, secured a franchise to operate in the Lafayette territory. Shortly thereafter it built an exchange and began business with fifty subscribers. On July 1, 1926 the Cumberland Company was merged with the Southern Bell Telephone and Telegraph system which presently conducts all telephone operations in the city and parish of Lafayette.

The expansion and improvement of telephone service by this company has kept pace with the rapid growth of the city. In 1924 the company converted its Lafayette exchange into a group headquarters for Lafayette, Opelousas, Eunice, Crowley, Abbeville and intervening territory. A year later the flash system was substituted for the old magneto (crank) phones. In 1927, to house the new exchange, the company constructed the first unit of the present large headquarters building, which, with equipment, cost approximately two hundred thousand dollars. To service economically the growing population it converted the manually operated telephones to dial ones. This last step, coupled in 1955 with the changing of all telephone numbers in the area to two letters and five digits, was preparatory to the next proposed improvement. This proposal, when consummated, will enable the subscriber, from his home or office, to dial station to station numbers without the assistance of a long distance operator. The fifty subscribers of 1896 have grown to seven hundred and eighty-two in 1920, to nine thousand, four hundred and forty-three in 1950 and to over twenty-five thousand on November 1, 1958.

Lafayette's contacts with the outside world were greatly improved in 1936 when George Thomas and his associates organized the Evangeline Broadcasting Company which gave Lafayette its first radio station, KVOL. This station, since the above date, has kept its listeners informed on current events and entertained with the best in music, theatre, and sports. The great desire of local citizens for a local television station was finally satisfied in June 1955, when the Camellia Broadcasting Company went on the air with a permit for Channel Ten. In addition to its own local programs this station carries the programs of the Columbia Broadcasting Company.

CHAPTER XVII

DOCTORS, DENTISTS AND DISEASE

Early Doctors

Probably the first doctor to reside in the Parish of Lafayette was no other than Dr. Antoine Bordat, ex-surgeon of the French army, the father of Marie Marthe Bordat who became the wife of Jean Mouton. Dr. Bordat in early life lived and practiced his profession in New Orleans. After the death of his wife and when he was quite old, he came to live in the home of his son-in-law, Jean Mouton, on Bayou Carencro. The date of his removal there is not known, it was probably around the year 1800. Nor is it known whether he practiced his profession there. The date of his death and place of burial are also not known.

In the first decade of the nineteenth century, Doctor Matthew Creighton, from Kent County Maryland, settled in Kentucky for a short period then came on the Grand Prairie, the name given to the country around Vermilionville. The land on which he built his home and office, presently known as Myrtle Plantation, is about a mile from town on the airport road. This originally included a portion of the present Lafayette Airport. The old home and office still stand across the railroad tracks from the airport. This property, which came into the possession of the late Hugh Wallis, a grandson of Dr. Creighton's daughter, is still occupied by the Wallis family.

The Wallis home, built by Dr. Creighton in 1811, has frequently been the center of interest because of the beautiful murals painted on the canvas covered walls of the dining room. The panelled paintings, depicting rural scenes, were executed by a French artist named Charles de Busuire, who had been brought to New Orleans to paint the scenes in the French Opera House. Having been employed by the Creighton family soon after the Civil War, he is said to have spent two years in painting the scenes which are now faded and dim.

The late Alexander Mouton, grandson and namesake of Governor Mouton, related to me how, as a boy of ten years, he went to the old doctor for treatment of a stone bruise on his heel which had become badly infected. Encouraged and calmed by the kindly words of the good doctor, he finally stretched full length on the porch floor with his face down, and, while he, with gritting teeth, grasped the end boards of the floor with all his strength, the doctor lanced the offending spot on his foot.

The second doctor to administer to the sick of the infant settlement was probably Doctor V. Gauthier on whose plantation Father Mégret sought refuge during the yellow fever epidemic of 1853. It was here that Abbe Mégret's slave died and was buried.

Vermilionville's third doctor was Dr. F. S. Mudd who was born in Kentucky March 12, 1829. In 1850 he had started to practice in what is now Vermilion Parish. After seven years there he moved to Vermilionville where he continued to practice until his death about 1910. In 1872 Dr. Francis Stirling Mudd was married to Martha Greig, the daughter of John Greig.

During the yellow fever epidemic of 1858, to the home of Antoine Emile Mouton fled many relatives from Vermilionville. Running from the scourge proved to be no sure escape for seven of the refugees went down with the dread disease. Living in Carencro at that time was Dr. Francez, a charming old gentleman from France. When called upon for help he conscientiously said he would nurse them the best he knew how, but assured them he did not know the cure, and certainly did not want to kill anyone. The treatment at that time was a light purgative and hot foot bath, after which the patient was wrapped in hot wool blankets, and then left to sweat it out until the fever left him. After the fever had subsided the patient, if he survived, was cautioned to eat very lightly. Those who recovered from the dread disease could not recall any severe pain but remember quite vividly how ravenously hungry they were. In view of the fact that a victim's house had frequently been deserted, the inability of the convalescent to get prepared food aided him in obeying the doctor's orders.

Prominent among the contemporaries of Dr. Mudd were Dr. T. B. Hopkins, Dr. J. D. Trahan, Dr. G. W. Scranton, Dr. Percy M. Girard, Dr. William Ware Lesley, and Dr. Romain Francez of Carencro.

Dr. Thomas Benjamin Hopkins (1832-1922) — the family originally from Ireland—came to Vermilionville from Claiborne Parish with Dr. John Bailey Kennedy shortly after the Civil War. They were accompanied by their families. Educated at the Medical Department of the University of Pennsylvania, Dr. Hopkins was on the medicall staff of the 20th Arkansas Regiment of the Confederate Army as assistant surgeon. He first married Mary Willis Kennedy. After her death he married Susan Kennedy, both daughters of Dr. John Kennedy whose wife was Lydia Elizabeth Cobb. Dr. Kennedy practiced medicine but one year in Vermilionville, dying in the yellow fever epidemic of 1858.

Dr. Hopkins practiced medicine for fifty years. Each evening he posted his visits of the day at these rates:

Office visits	$1.00
House calls	2.00
Night calls after midnight	3.00
Delivering a baby including three calls after birth	10.00

All calls included the cost of medicines; all bills payable at the convenience of the patient, which usually meant after the crops had been harvested.

Dr. J. D. Trahan was born on the Whittington plantation on Bayou Vermilion near the Mauriceville Road. He married Rose Celeste Alice Laribeau in the St. Louis Cathedral. He completed his studies at Tulane University, numbering among his friends the famous Dr. Matas and Dr. Ernest S. Lewis. Dr. Trahan was on the staff of General Alfred Mouton. Lafayette was his home. A son, Dr. Raoul Anatole Trahan, followed in his father's footsteps. Two daughters of Dr. J. D. Trahan married physicians. Haydée Trahan married Doctor Henri Louis Ducrocq of France (1871-1917), who finished at the College de Louis le Grande in Paris. Later he came to New Orleans, completing his medical studies at Tulane. Another daughter of Dr. Trahan, Stella, married Dr. Raney of Crowley. Dr. J. D. Trahan died in 1921.

Dr. George Washington Scranton (1849-1909) came to Louisiana from Madison, Connecticut, shortly after the Civil War in search of a warmer climate. He was a law graduate of Yale, but, after coming to Louisiana, he studied medicine at Tulane University. He married Anatalie Breaux of Scott, Louisiana, sister of Colonel Gus Breaux, and practiced medicine in Lafayette Parish. His practice was continued by his son Dr. George Washington Pierre Soule Scranton who is still remembered by the older residents of the parish. The son was named after his father and his father's friend Pierre Soule of New Orleans. He married Nina Duplex of Youngsville. The Duplexes were wine importers from Bordeaux, France.

Dr. Romain J. Francez (1817-1892) was born in Algerix, France and migrated to Carencro about the time of the Civil War where he practiced his profession, giving relief to victims of yellow fever in 1858. He also played a leading role in the development of Carencro. He was married to Anatasie Bernard, daughter of Gerasin Bernard, and was the grandfather of Mrs. William Couret who now occupies the old Bernard home on Pierce Street.

Dr. William Ware Lesley (1848-1928) was born and reared in southern Illinois. He first began the study of medicine at the Medical College of Louisville, Kentucky. After coming to Louisiana he completed his studies at the medical department of the University of Louisiana in New Orleans before it became Tulane. He came to Carencro in 1875. He was married to Miss Caroline Hays of Mississippi in 1879.

Dr. Percy M. Girard (1859-1944) was a native of Lafayette Parish. He was married to Miss Lela Singleton. After completing his medical studies at Tulane University he practiced his profession in Lafayette until ill health forced his retirement. He spent his last years managing his plantation on the Pin Hook Road on which is now located the Heyman Oil Center.

Among those who continued the good work of the doctors mentioned above were: Dr. L. Oran Clark, Dr. George R. DeLaureal, Dr. Henri L. Ducrocq, Dr. Felix E. Girard, Dr. J. Franklin Mouton, Sr., Dr. Louis A. Prejean, Dr. Merrick E. Saucier, Dr. George Washington Pierre Soule Scranton, Dr. Frederick R. Tolson and Dr. Robert D. Voorhies.

The lives of these men were lives of courage and sacrifice, dirt roads and sometimes no roads—narrow broken bridges, dilapidated plantation gates, everlasting blinding rains in which their ways were lost and their horses had to take them home.

THE FIRST DENTISTS

A revealing view of the early practice of dentistry in Vermilionville was given us by the late Doctor Paul Salles in a radio address which he gave as a part of the program celebrating the one hundredth anniversary of the founding of the City of Lafayette. He related that itinerant dentists first performed that much needed service for the early inhabitants long before the time of a resident dentist.

Before the coming of dentists the self care of the teeth began with the use of althea sticks shaped much like modern orange wood sticks and used with or without soda or charcoal to clean and polish the teeth. But in Vermilionville as early as 1846 there were tooth brushes being sold by a Mr. Couguet in his drug store in a brick building at the northwest corner of Lafayette and Convent Streets.

Following the itinerants were the band-wagon dentists who extracted teeth while a band played during the operation. This procedure was followed so that those standing by could not hear the groans and screams of the ones being operated on, and thus be scared into refusing their patronage.

Among the first of the itinerant dentists was Dehamel, a Frenchman from St. Martinville who on his visits stopped at the boarding house of Martonne, "a mulatresse libre," on Lafayette Street. This house stood opposite the large home of the late Doctor Franklin Mouton, Sr. Instead of patients coming to him, Dehamel travelled from plantation to plantation where he seemed to have done extractions only. Following Dehamel was Doremus of St. Landry, who did extractions and with a foot propelled drill prepared cavities for amalgam fillings. He also made dentures.

Next came Derbonne from Washington, Louisiana, followed by Parker from Opelousas; and later Demouly from Cuba. Demouly operated a drug store on the south side of Court House Square, near the present law offices of Waldo Dugas. He extracted teeth and also sold prepared chalk for polishing them.

In 1883 the number of college trained dentists in the United States was only three hundred and ninety-four. One of this number was Dr. H. O. Salles who had recently graduated from the University of Baltimore and came to Lafayette, where he opened up his office on West Vermilion Street next to the residence of the late Mr. Edward Martin. He later moved his office to Buchanan Street where it still stands by his home across the street from K.V.O.L. broadcasting station. For many years he was the only resident dentist in Lafayette Parish. After his death many years ago his practice was taken over and carried on by his son the late Doctor Paul Salles, author of the broadcast referred to above. Dr. Salles was married to Sarah Philomena Buchanan, the daughter of Captain John Charles Buchanan and Josephine Eugénie Mouton.

Captain Buchanan came to Lafayette from Virginia as a civil engineer for the Texas and New Orleans railroad.

SICKNESS AND DISEASE

In the early period described above there were no hospitals in Lafayette. The nearest surgeons were in New Orleans and patients often died before they could be taken there. Little was known about such diseases as appendicitis, diphtheria, typhoid, tuberculosis and yellow fever. Many died of what was called stomach ache when in reality the killer was appendicitis. Vaccine for typhoid and diphtheria had not yet been discovered. Plagues which turned out to be yellow fever, with its dreaded black vomit, carried away hundreds of persons. Reference has already been made to the epidemic which in 1853 carried away Father Mégret, his slave and dozens of citizens. Yellow fever was thought to be carried in the air, so people burned sulphur in their homes to drive away the dread disease.

The last epidemic of yellow fever occurred in Lafayette in 1905. So frightened were the people that the disease would spread that the authorities of Lafayette placed armed guards at the railroad station and at all roads leading into town to keep travellers from entering.

THE FIRST HOSPITALS

It was not until comparatively recent times that Lafayette could boast of a hospital. It was in the year 1906 that three doctors of the parish decided that Lafayette should have one. They were Dr. L. A. Prejean of Scott and Dr. J. Franklin Mouton and Dr. L. O. Clark of Lafayette. In 1906 these three organized the Lafayette Sanitarium. It was not until 1911, however, that the hospital became a reality, opening on the present site with five or six beds. The facilities at first were limited, but under the direction of these three doctors the hospital gained rapidly in fame and physical conveniences. Many lives have been saved there by Lafayette's surgeon, Dr. Clark. The hospital has been enlarged four times so that today, with ninety-six beds and the most modern equipment it continues to serve an ever increasing number of patients.

The present officers are: Dr. C. E. Hamilton, President, and Dr. F. H. Davis, vice-president .Members of the board of directors are: Dr. Ralph Bourgeois, Dr. Edgar P. Breaux, Dr. J. J. Burdin,

Dr. O. P. Daly III, Dr. J. O. Duhon, Miss A. R. Glaudi, Dr. J. Franklin Mouton and Dr. Lee J. Sonnier.

About the time of the opening of the Lafayette Sanitarium, Dr. F. E. Girard opened the first eye, ear, nose and throat clinic in Lafayette. It was located in a frame building on Lafayette Street across from the building occupied by Beadle's feed and seed store facing the court house square. He continued to operate it for several years. The building is now operated as a rooming house.

In 1914 a group of doctors, headed by the late Dr. R. D. Voorhies, invited Dr. O. P. Daly, who had conducted a hospital in Opelousas and who had gained a wide reputation as a surgeon, to come to Lafayette to organize a second hospital in the city. As a result there was organized the Attakapas Sanitarium which was first located in the former home of Dr. Tolson at 1108 Johnston Street. Unfortunately this hospital burned and the Attakapas Sanitarium was moved to the building formerly occupied by Dr. Girard's eye, ear and throat clinic, referred to above. There it continued to operate until about 1926, when it was discontinued. In that year, however, Dr. O. P. Daly bought the ground where the main building of the Charity Hospital stands and there built a two story brick hospital to which he gave the name St. John's Hospital. This hospital, which succeeded the Attakapas Sanitarium, continued to serve the community until 1937 when Dr. Daly sold it to the state to form the nucleus of the present Charity Hospital, which had its beginning at that time.

Since the building of these hospitals, the rapid growth of population has forced such an expansion of medical facilities that Lafayette has become an important health and medical center. There are now five hospitals in Lafayette with a total of over five hundred and fifty beds, including one hundred and fifteen for tuberculosis patients. In the parish there were in 1953 sixty-nine practicing physicians, all but four of whom are in the city of Lafayette. Of these thirty-three were general practitioners and thirty-six specialists. As evidence of the progress made since the days of one doctor and the travelling dentist, it can be pointed out that there were also in the parish in 1953 fifteen dentists, eighty-seven registered graduate nurses, fifty-four registered practical nurses, eight registered laboratory technicians and six x-ray technicians.

In the early days little or no effort was made toward the prevention of disease. For several years now Lafayette Parish has maintained a Health Unit. Located in the modern Health Center building, constructed as a memorial to those who lost their lives in the two world wars, the personnel of this unit gives, free of charge, immunization against whooping cough, diptheria, tetanus, polio, smallpox, and typhoid fever, to all who apply. Health Unit activities in general sanitation such as the protection of water, food, milk, and drug supplies decrease considerably the chances of spreading communicable diseases from such sources.

CHAPTER XVIII

LAW AND THE COURTS

LAW OF THE FRONTIER

Among those who settled the Attakapas country were people from many lands; Acadia, France, Spain, San Domingo, and the Canary Islands. Subsequent to the purchase of Louisiana by the United States in 1803 they were joined by adventurers from the states of the union and other countries. Among this mixture were many who were unable to understand American laws and customs, or were criminally inclined. Moreover the country was still sparsely populated and the seats of justice far removed from the people and their activities. Consequently the law was frequently violated with impunity. However, a large majority of the population consisted of peaceful and law abiding citizens who were content and anxious to cultivate their lands and lead lives of simplicity and industry. Yet as time progressed the activities of the criminally-inclined and law-breaking class assumed such large proportions just before the Civil War that the inability of courts to bring them to justice caused the law abiding citizens to become greatly alarmed.

At first the depredations of these outlaws were infrequent and well concealed, but when the desperados learned that the hands of justice were slow and uncertain they became bolder and more open. Their earliest crimes consisted of petty thievery but their later offenses were often overt acts of brigandage, in which stores were robbed, houses were burned, and often whole herds of cattle corralled and driven away. In numerous instances the helpless victims were murdered. The most significant thing about these depredations was that all of them seemed to be directed by some master mind or central organization, so thorough and far flung that it was practically impossible to secure a conviction of the offenders. In fact later investigations proved that the individual criminals were banded together into organizations, each having its officers and regular head who directed the activities of the subordinate bands, and planned regular campaigns of crime.

The punishment of the criminals was rendered still more difficult by the misused ability of one or two well known criminal lawyers in the Attakapas country. These lawyers were natives and were so well versed in the customs and traditions of the people of that section, and enjoyed such wide acquaintance and favor among even the lowest classes, that in nearly every case, they were able to select a jury which they knew beforehand would return a verdict favorable to the defendant, no matter how revolting the crime he had committed.

Many examples of the manner in which the law was flouted can be given. Two instances of this miscarriage of justice are graphically recorded in the unpublished papers of the late Judge Felix Voorhies, author of "Acadian Reminiscences." Judge Voorhies, the father of the late Dr. R. D. Voorhies, was closely associated with the Vigilance Committees as a young lawyer. His account follows:

> On one occasion a planter came upon a "neighbor" who had just killed a steer and was in the act of carrying away the meat. "This is my steer," said the planter. "I shall have you prosecuted for larceny."
> "Pshaw!" said the neighbor, "you are too intelligent to do that."
> "Too intelligent! Why do you mean to say that this is not my steer?"
> "It may have been yours once," was the reply, "but it is mine now."
> "What!," said the planter, "This is your steer?"
> "Certainly it is; you have sold it to me and I have paid you the price in the presence of witnesses."
> "Monstrous! They will swear to a lie; you know this steer belongs to me. I will prosecute you just the same."
> "As you please," said the neighbor, shrugging his shoulders as he went away with the meat.
> He was prosecuted, but true to his word, he produced in court seven witnesses who testified that he had purchased the steer from the planter and had paid him in their presence. Needless to say he was acquitted.
> On another occasion a planter missed his favorite cow. Riding on the prairie in search of her he came to a store kept by a Frenchman and was much surprised to see the skin of his cow hanging on the fence.
> "Where did you get that skin?," he asked the merchant.
> "I have just bought it."
> "From whom? It is the skin of my cow that was stolen last night."

"Had you come a little sooner, you would have seen the person who sold it to me. He has just left, but I cannot give his name."

"Be careful," said the planter. "The skin in your possession is strong presumption that you yourself have stolen the cow; the more so that you refuse to give his name."

"I can't give you his name," said the merchant.

"Very well, the grand jury will investigate the matter."

The merchant was indicted for larceny by the next grand jury, and, though warned by his attorney to disclose the name of the thief, he steadfastly refused to do so. At the trial the evidence against the merchant was direct and conclusive, yet he was acquitted. Throughout the trial he had shown no concern over his precarious position and his acquittal did not seem to surprise him. However, when asked by his counsel how it was possible for a jury to acquit him in the face of such conclusive evidence of guilt, he merely smiled and said: "I can talk now, although I will give no names. The man who sold me that skin was on the jury, and there were, besides him, five others who belong to his gang. I was sure of an acquittal. Had I given his name, my store would now be in ashes and I would probably be dead. I thought it more prudent to take my chances."

The foregoing instances are sufficient to explain the conditions that prompted the peace loving citizens of a large and growing section of the state to take the law into their own hands, in direct disobedience to the commands of the highest district and state officials. At that time many good and sensible citizens held that the state officers and courts were capable of handling the situation. Still there was a large majority of the population in the afflicted district who were strongly in favor of taking the law into their own hands, defending their stand on the principle that all authority finally emanates from the people.

It was in January, 1859 that the plan of organizing Committees of Vigilance was first suggested. Not until March of that year was the first committee organized at Cote-Gelée in Lafayette Parish. This organization was soon followed by others in the territory comprising the present parishes of Acadia, Iberia, Lafayette, St. Landry, St. Martin and Vermilion. In all seven committees were organized. In defense of this action one of the executives issued a proclamation which in part follows:

Fellow Citizens:

Having organized ourselves as Vigilance Committees, that is, having constituted ourselves a tribunal entirely independent of the other judicial tribunals created by law, we owe it to

AN ACADIAN HOUSE

Typical of the early homes of the Acadian settlers. An outside stairway leads to the attic where the boys of the family slept. The chimney was made of mud.

BAYOU TECHE — ST. MARTINVILLE, LOUISIANA

Mrs. Homer Bailey's School — 1870 — was "kept" by Mrs. Fleming and her daughter, Mrs. Homer Bailey, both highly educated ladies from Martinique. Mrs. Fleming, from the rocking chair in her bedroom, taught the little boys and girls as they sat on their stools around her from the first to the sixth grade. Writing was taught on the dining room table. Catechism was emphasized. Most of the children were from the prominent families. Mr. Homer Bailey was the brother of Mr. William Bailey, the father of Mrs. J. Arthur Roy. Today the location is marked by a parking lot at the northeast corner of South Washington and West Main.

(Below) Joachem Revillion's General Merchandise Store, built about 1850, dismantled in 1900, was on the Southwest corner of West Main and South Washington Streets. Born in Pierreclos, lept. Saone and Loire, France in 1804; he died in Lafayette in 1897. After seven years in the French Navy he came to New Orleans, then to Lafayette. He taught school for several years then became the partner of a Mr. Chaix in the ownership of this store. Later he became the owner of the business. He married Ismene Dejean of Opelousas. They had three sons, Jules, who later owned the store, Pierre, and Philobert. Among those in the front of the store are: Mim Neveu (little boy), Hebert Billeaud, Henry Roy, Joe Ducote, Pierre Revillion, Jacko, a colored porter.

ourselves, as well as to you, to give the reasons that have driven us into the revolutionary movement that we have inaugurated..... We would blush to give any explanation either to the bandits who infest the district or to their friends or accomplices..... Fellow Citizens: We have been subjected to a system of rapine and plunder without parallel in this country; our property is destroyed daily and hourly; our houses are burglarized and rifled of their contents; crime has its army in our midst with its generals, officers and soldiers. We will tell you bluntly how it is that crime holds high carnival in our midst: the jury has failed most miserably in its mission. It has been guilty, in the face of God and society, of the abominable crime of perjury, for when jurors acquit those whose guilt is established beyond peradventure, they commit the crime of perjury, and place themselves on a level with those whom they have acquitted....

Now, fellow citizens if you still hope to save from rapine and plunder that which you have earned by your labors; if you wish to restore our corrupt society to a healthy standard, by branding with the infamy of exile or of the lash the men whose presence in our midst is an insult to public morality and a danger to our families, follow our example; join us, fellow citizens in our holy crusade against vice and immorality; against rapine, murder and incendiarism, and let us, with the lash, print on the backs of those wretches a catalogue of their crimes.

While the organization, purposes and methods of these committees were much alike, yet they were under the direction of no central head. Each as a rule elected a president, a secretary and an assistant secretary. In most instances there was an executive committee and a marshal to carry out its orders. Regular meetings were held at which new members were received and administered an oath to keep secret all the proceedings of the committee. In some instances the committees recruited a miniature force of armed men which met in the towns regularly to drill. Major Aurelian Saint-Julien was made commander of all forces of all committees, and General Alfred Mouton, a graduate of West Point, who was subsequently killed at the battle of Mansfield, was appointed drillmaster of all the forces. These forces were recruited in order to meet any mass armed resistance, which it was feared the bandits might possibly offer. They numbered in all about four thousand armed and disciplined men. The force at Vermilionville had, as part of its equipment, a four pound brass cannon nicknamed "Betsy," used regularly in their drills.

As has been stated the punishments generally agreed on consisted of banishment, the lash, and the rope. Punishments might or might not correspond with those designated in the state criminal code. The usual procedure was for certain members of a committee in whose jurisdiction the crime had been committed to meet informally to determine the guilt or innocence of the accused, without giving him the privilege of a defense. This treatment was accorded especially to those who, in the belief of the committee, had been acquitted by a packed jury, or one that had based its decision on the evidence of perjured witnesses. No consideration was shown to such persons accused.

The punishments administered were extremely severe. One suspected by the committee was notified by an emissary to leave the district within a given time. If he disregarded the order, he was waylaid and severely lashed. Then if he did not obey he was given a still worse beating; and that punishment was repeated until he was glad to leave. As many as a hundred lashes with a trace or bridal rein were often inflicted on a single victim. On one occasion a suspect, charged with several crimes, was waylaid by twenty-two members of one of these committees, who surrounded him before he was aware of their presence. After having dragged the miserable wretch into their midst they began to rain blows upon him with their whips. "There," said one as he struck him a terrific blow, "that is for my cotton mill you burned."

"Take that," said another, "for stealing my horse."

"That," said a third, "for driving away my cattle and selling them."

"And that and that," said all the others as they took their turns at applying their lashes.

In this manner was the punishment continued until the wretched victim was completely overcome and ready to pledge himself to leave the country. The death penalty was also inflicted by these committees and more than one poor rascal was left swinging to a tree or lying in a crumpled heap as the result of the deadly aim of a firing squad.

The whipping scene described above was dramatically reenacted in 1936 in one of the episodes of the pageant presented in celebration of the one hundreth anniversary of the founding of Lafayette. Directing the group of acting vigilantes was no other than the famed G. A. "Bedon" (High Hat) Martin. Having counted the lashes applied to the cringing victims, he brought the scene to a close with a resounding "and one for lagniappe."*

The radical and unorthodox methods of these committees soon attracted the notice of the press, the state authorities, and men of public affairs. Probably without exception, all the papers in the parishes where the committees operated gave them their strongest support. The *Courier* of Opelousas, the *Democrat* of St. Martinville and the *Echo* of Vermilionville defended the committees and their propaganda in the strongest terms. The New Orleans papers were divided in their attitude, the *New Orleans Times* supporting the state authorities against them. Governor Robert C. Wickliffe and the state prosecutor of the district affected, Mr. A. Olivier, denounced them in most uncompromising terms as rebels against the law and order of the state. In fact many prominent and influential citizens of the district took the side of the state authorities, to the extent that the sons of some of them, seeking adventure, joined the bandits in a few of their forays. On the other hand the committees received the strong support of such men as ex-Governor Alexandre Mouton, General Alfred Mouton, Major Aurelean St. Julien, Mr. Alcée Judice and many others, all of whom took an active part in the work of the committees. Finally on May 28, 1859 Governor Wickliffe gave official notice of his opposition in a proclamation in which he charged the committees with violating the law and committing outrages on citizens and their property. He then ordered the committees to disband and disperse; and called upon "all good citizens of the state to lend their assistance for the arrest and prosecution of these violators of the law."

The committees heeded not this proclamation of the governor. On the other hand it infused new life into the brigands, who became bolder and more insolent than ever. Believing that the governor meant to come to their aid with the state militia, they called themselves anti-vigilants, and began to make plans for an open military campaign against those identified with the Vigilance Committees. To this end they brought together stores of arms and ammunition on a certain farm at Bayou Queue Tortue near Vermilionville. It was suspected that they intended to attack, pillage and burn the town of Vermilionville; and such proved to be the case. The Vigilance Committees, not to be taken by surprise, inaugurated at once a movement to disperse them, and, if possible,

---

*Lagniappe, Spanish for a little gift when a purchase was made — a bit of candy, an additional pepper or sprig of parsley.

in one supreme effort, to break their power completely and drive them from the district. Accordingly the committees began to assemble levies of armed men. These forces, led by Major Saint Julien, advanced from Vermilionville to make the attack. His forces, numbering seven hundred men, were fully armed, well drilled, and had with them the brass cannon called "Betsy". The anti-vigilants numbered, according to some estimates, eighteen hundred. Having refused a demand to surrender, they seemed determined to fight; but when the brass cannon was unmasked in the final encounter, which took place on September 3, 1859, most of them took to their heels. In the chase that followed about two hundred of them were finally captured. There were taken also by the forces of the committee near a thousand small arms of various kinds. Of the two hundred prisoners taken all but eighty were released on their solemn pledge never again to molest the peace of the district. These eighty were then bound and, according to the report of eye witnesses, laid with their faces to the ground and lashed until they promised to leave the state never to return.

The power of the bandits was thus completely crushed. Hundreds of them had been driven from the state and the others had been beaten and scared into submission. There was no further trouble on their account, and conditions resumed again their normal and peaceful aspect. The task of the committees having been accomplished, they disbanded, thus bringing to a close a movement which, for a period of nearly six months, had threatened to plunge the state into civil war.

Lawyers and Judges

The people of Lafayette, from the beginning, have had their lives regulated by several systems of law. The first settlers were governed by early French law which had been developed from the Roman system of law and the code of Justinian. During the Spanish regime the legal system of Spain was introduced and enforced throughout Louisiana much to the dismay of the French population. Though the Spanish system had also descended from Roman law it was different in many ways from the French due to the fact that it had been influenced largely by ecclesiastical law. When Louisiana was acquired by the United States in 1803, a new element, trial by jury, was introduced and as time went on many features of the English Common law were added, though the French law, improved by the Code Napoleon in 1804, and modified by statute, still constitutes the basic law of the state.

When the parish of Lafayette was organized, one of the first projects of the police jury was the selection of a site for a temple of justice in which the legal business of the parish might be carried on and the records kept. The story of the first site selected and its moving to the present one has already been told. On the lots donated by Jean Mouton for a parish courthouse was a modest frame building thirty-six feet wide and forty-one feet deep, which was used as a courthouse until 1835. It probably stood on the southeast corner of the present courthouse property as Main Street at that time ran straight through the present courthouse grounds. In 1835 the police jury let the contract for the construction of a new courthouse to cost $6000. In order to carry out the plan of Jean Mouton, donor of grounds for both church and courthouse, that the courthouse should face the church, Main Street was divided into north and south Main with the courthouse square between the two.

This second courthouse served its purpose well until 1859 when a contract was signed with Paxton and Templeton for the building of a new and larger one. Antoine Lacoste signed as surety to the contractors and Francois Daigle and W. Brandt represented the police jury in the transaction. The two story frame building was in colonial style and, with its massive white columns and bell tower, faced the same old church. The four live oaks which had been planted at each corner of the square soon grew to great size and, for many years, provided shade for the citizens resting or loitering to pass the time or exchanging greetings with friends. Some years later there was built at the corner of South Main and Buchanan Streets a two story brick jail; and at the corner of South Maine and Lafayette a one story brick office, with storage vaults, for the clerk of court.

By 1927 the third courthouse had become entirely inadequate for the rapidly expanding business of the parish. In that year, therefore, the citizens voted a bond issue of $300,000.00 for the construction of the present imposing edifice. Since this building was to occupy a greater portion of the square it became necessary to demolish not only the old courthouse, jail, and clerk's office but to destroy the four beautiful live oak trees that stood on each of the four corners, though four magnolia trees were later planted in their place. All the previous courthouses had been equipped with a bell which, at each court session summoned the lawyers from their numerous offices which had sprung up around the courthouse square. For some reason this bell had not been installed in the new courthouse but had been discarded with the ancient furnishings of the old one. However, it was not long before the lawyers began to long for its familiar sound. Soon their complaints grew so insistent that the old bell was salvaged from its dusty hiding place and hung out from a window outside the present court room so that its peal might again summon the waiting lawyers to the bar of justice.

The boundaries of the judicial district in which Lafayette is located have been changed many times. At one time they extended far westward to include Cameron Parish. The judges who presided over these early districts had to endure many hardships and inconveniences, having to travel often on horseback or by boat to reach places where they were to hold court. Lafayette Parish, however, has been honored in having had capable, honest, and efficient judges. The first judge to serve the parish was Thomas B. Brashear. Among others who have served the parish with distinction are H. N. Bullard, Henry Boyze, Ephriam K. Wilson, George R. King, Eugene E. Mouton, C. M. Olivier, L. Dupre, Seth Lewis, B. A. Martel, John Clegg, Eraste Mouton, Conrad Debaillon, Martin F. Rigues, John H. Overton, Adolph Bailey, Orther A. Mouton, N. N. Edwards, W. W. Bailey, William Campbell, Philip Pugh, J. M. Porter, Paul Debaillon and Edward Meaux.

With the creation of Lafayette Parish in 1823 and the establishment of the first courthouse the Lafayette Bar Association came into being, for without lawyers courts and governments cannot function. Soon thereafter lawyers row began to rise around the seat of justice. Many of their names have been forgotten but they all played their part in building the community. Among the early lawyers who practiced before the bar, we find the following names: the law firm of Bowen, Simon and Crow; Brownson and Davis; C. J. Craig, Basil Crow, Cornelius Voorhies; W. Eugene Mouton; Edward Eugene Mouton; Fred H. Davis; John Brownson; Alexander Mouton; Charles Homer Mouton; Eraste Mouton; L. Philibert Revillon; Edward Simon; Gustave A. Breaux; Alcibiades DeBlanc; L. Dupré; William Mouton; Martin Voorhies; Felix Voorhies; Michel Eloi Girard; Martin F. Rigues; J. C. Briant; Conrad Debaillon; Crow Girard; Edward G. Voorhies; William Campbell; Orther C. Mouton; Jerome Mouton; Julian Mouton; Charles D. Caffery; Joseph A. Chargois; Ralph Elliott, and J. E. Poche. In more recent years the name of John L. Kennedy is remembered as that of a brilliant criminal lawyer; and the late Dan Debaillon, a man of lovable disposition and of sound professional integrity, is still hailed as the greatest factor in recent years in fostering cordial relations among the members of the Lafayette Bar.

FAMOUS CRIMINAL TRIALS

In the last century the Lafayette courthouse has been the scene of a number of famous criminal trials, three of which are worthy of mention. Just prior to the Civil War three Negroes killed and robbed a Jewish peddler, taking his money and the merchandise in his pack, dividing it among themselves. They were apprehended, tried and sentenced to hang. The sheriff at that time was Edmond Mouton, a kind hearted man, whose duty it was to do the hanging. On the day of the execution a large crowd was assembled and followed the three condemned men from the jail to the gallows. In the crowd was an old Negro woman selling cakes, popcorn and pralines. One of the prisoners asked the sheriff if he could have some cakes. Sheriff Mouton said, "Certainly," and then halted the procession. The Negro then took one cake, but was urged by the sheriff to take all he wanted. With his hands full he then asked if he could call Jean Louis, and was told he could. Having been called, Jean Louis stepped from the crowd. The poor convict then took from around his neck a red bandana handkerchief, and, laying it on the ground, he placed the cakes in it. These he handed to Jean Louis saying, "Give these to my little ones."

In 1856 the village was shocked by the disappearance from her home at 415 West Main Street of the widow Veuve Missonier. After a brief search her body was found at the bottom of a deep well in her yard. It was quickly revealed that she had been murdered by her own slave who had placed it there. He was quickly apprehended and, as he was being tried in the courthouse, the nearby church bell tolled for the funeral of his unfortunate victim. It is needless to say that he was convicted and sentenced to be hanged in the parish courtyard.

Perhaps the most sensational murder in the whole history of the parish occurred in 1896. On the night of April 23 of that year two young French brothers, Ernest and Alexis Blanc, laborers on the plantation of Col. A. D. Boudreaux, after lengthy planning, entered the store of Martin Begnaud on the pretense of buying a package of tobacco. Begnaud was a highly respected and prosperous merchant of Scott and was known to have money. Having been admitted to the store they overpowered and bound Begnaud, forcing him at pistol point to tell them where the keys to his safe were. Having secured something over $3000.00, and wishing to leave no witness to their crime, they then stabbed Begnaud to death with a makeshift dagger. It was reported that fifty-two stab wounds were found on Begnaud's body. They then returned to their home where they hid the money and the improvised dagger.

When the murder was discovered suspicion was not turned on the Blanc brothers but on two others who were arrested and thrown in jail, being held there while the frantic search for the real murderers went on, stimulated by the offer of a $1000.00 reward posted by the family of Begnaud. While this search was going on the Blanc brothers disappeared, and it was not until then that the eye of suspicion was turned toward them; then no one knew where to look for them. According to their later confessions they traveled over much of the United States, Mexico, and even returned to their native France.

The two suspects, Gustave Balin and Hemp Benton had been in jail many months when, on the night of January 1, 1897, the two Blanc brothers stepped off the train in Scott and went to the plantation of their old employer, Col. Boudreaux, having been, for some inexplicable reason, drawn back to the scene of their heinous crime. Two days later, through the efforts of Sheriff Isaac Broussard and his chief deputy, A. M. Thomas Mouton, they were in jail. After intense questioning by these two officers and others both the accused, one after the other, confessed; and their trial was set for February 17, 1897.

On the day of the trial hundreds of people were in Lafayette to follow the proceedings. They were disappointed, however, because the two lawyers appointed by the court to defend them withdrew from the case. The court thereupon appointed C. H. Mouton, and Col. Gustave A. Breaux to defend them, and postponed the trial until February 25 in order to give the newly appointed lawyers time to prepare their defense. The trial was held on the above date; they were both convicted of the murder of Martin Begnaud and, by Judge Conrad Debaillon, sentenced to be hanged. The date set for their execution was April 2, 1897.

As the day of execution approached excitement spread throughout the parish and even to other parts of the state. Because of their youth considerable sympathy had been stirred up on behalf of the condemned brothers. The French consul in New Orleans and a number of French societies appealed to Governor Foster to commute their sentences, but he declined to intervene.

On the execution day Lafayette was crowded with several thousand spectators hoping to get a glimpse of the condemned young men. People began to assemble around the courthouse square very early in the morning, many of them having brought their lunches with them as if it were a holiday. In order to get a glimpse of the unhappy pair, many sought vantage points in the trees and houses surrounding the court square. Negro women went through the crowd selling cakes, pralines, boudin and oreilles de cochon. Such was the setting in which the murderers of Martin Begnaud expiated their crime.

A Eulogy by the Supreme Court of New Orleans

On October 8, 1912 the Supreme Court in New Orleans heard eulogies, memorial services for members of the Bench and Bar who died during the year.

Chief Justice Breaux responded — Among those on whom eulogies were presented by the chairmen of the committees were as follows:

Lucius Garland Dupré, eulogy by E. B. Dubuisson; General Francis T. Nicholls, eulogy by W. S. Parkerson; C. Wickliffe, eulogy by H. Garland Dupre; Edward C. Voorhies, eulogy by O. C. Mouton.

Among the concluding words of Chief Justice Breaux,

"The year is momentous in the annals of the state. Distinguished lawyers are among the departed.

"Without the sweet memories of the past, life would have little for which to live.

"There is no present; its moments are immediately added to the past and the past urges us on to better and nobler ends."

CHAPTER XIX

LAFAYETTE PARISH IN WAR

The history of the City and Parish of Lafayette would not be complete without some reference to the part their loyal citizens have played in the wars which have been fought in defense of their country. Mention has been made already of the valiant action taken by Leon Latiolais in the War of 1812. Many others from this parish hastened from their homes to defend them against the British invader. Two companies from the Lafayette area were organized with Robert Perry and Shadrach Porter as captains. Following are the names of a few of the brave men who made up those two companies: John F. Bourque, Pierre Desormeaux, Charles Harrington, William Harrington, John B. Theall, P. P. Thibedeaux, Abram Abshire, Pierre Lapointe, Vidal Lapoint, and Zephirin Trahan.

A record of those who served in the Mexican War is not available. It is known, however, that General Frank Gardner, who subsequently married a daughter of Governor Mouton and made his home in Lafayette, played a conspicuous part in it. Having graduated from West Point Military Academy in 1843 in a class that included Generals U. S. Grant, Hardee, Ingalls, and others, he was considered a particularly skillful and efficient infantry officer. As one of the officers of the old Seventh United States Infantry he fought throughout the Mexican War, from the firing of the first gun at Fort Brown, until the surrender of Mexico City. For his acknowledged gallantry he was awarded brevets and subsequent promotions in the United States Army.

At the outbreak of the Civil War, having in the meantime married a southern lady, Mathilde Mouton, daughter of Louisiana's first democratic governor, Alexandre Mouton, General Gardner resigned his commission in the United States Army and linked his fortunes with the Confederacy. He rose rapidly to the rank and command of major-general and as such held many responsible positions. He gained fame for his stout defense of Port Hudson until compelled to surrender to a greatly superior force of the Union army. After the war he lived quietly in Lafayette until his death April 21, 1878. General Gardner Avenue is named in his honor.

The part played by the men of Lafayette Parish in the secession movement and the subsequent Civil War is an important one. The secession convention was presided over by Ex-Governor Mouton. When hostilities began many brave men hastened to fight for their homes and for the southern cause. The first body of troops from this parish to enter the Confederate army was composed of twenty-five men who went to St. Martinville to join the company enlisted there by Captain Alcibiades de Blanc. The first full company to be recruited from the parish was known as the Acadian Guards. Of this company Alfred Mouton was captain, William Mouton, first lieutenant, Polk Bailey, second lieutenant, and Telesmar Comeaux, third lieutenant. On the formation of the Eighteenth Louisiana Regiment the Acadian Guards became company one and its captain, Alfred Mouton, who was a West Point graduate, was promoted to colonel. This regiment did its first fighting at the battle of Shiloh, where Colonel Mouton was wounded. He was promoted shortly thereafter to the rank of brigadier general and with his brigade transferred to the trans-Mississippi department where his brigade became part of General Dick Taylor's division.

The next company recruited from the parish was commanded by Eraste Mouton, captain, with William Eastin first lieutenant, William Campbell, second lieutenant, and Ernest Martin, third lieutenant. The third company was recruited by Captain W. C. Crow. The other officers of this company were A. Moss, first lieutenant, Pancross Rein, second lieutenant, and Joseph Louvier, third lieutenant. The last two companies were attached to the twenty-sixth regiment and Captain Crow became the lieutenant colonel. After the going of this company only recruits to fill up the depleted ranks of the three companies were called upon to enlist.

Nor did Lafayette escape the bitter experience of invasion by the enemy. In the spring of 1863 General Banks advanced from New Orleans to drive out or destroy the Confederate forces holding the Teche Valley under General Taylor. Banks had twenty thousand men against Taylor's three thousand. Consequently all that Taylor could do was to retreat northward, doing all he could to retard the advance of Banks. The retreat led through the town of Vermilionville. It was at the bayou bridge at Pinhook that Taylor fought one of his desperate rear guard actions. Having destroyed the bridge, the retreating Confederates threw up breastworks, in what is now Girard Park, the remains of which could be plainly traced until recently. These they defended bravely but were forced to continue their retreat through Vermilionville, Opelousas and on to Mansfield where Taylor finally made a stand. There the army of Banks was decisively defeated by General Taylor. It was there that Vermilionville's hero, General Alfred Mouton, met his heroic death.

During this campaign federal troops camped near Vermilionville for several days. After crossing the bayou at Pin Hook, one of their first acts was to seize the Walnut Grove plantation home of Sosthene Mouton, who was away with the Confederate army, and throw out Mrs. Mouton with her family of six small children. They not only occupied the house but confiscated horses, wagons, carriages, harness and everything useful to them. The oldest of the children were Alexander and Bordat, ten and nine years old. Many years later Alexander in his memoirs describes the flight from this house:

> After the federals crossed the bayou, I can still see them swarming up the steep bank toward our home and soon they were all around our house. Mother's only thought was to seek refuge in the home of her father, Governor Mouton, at Isle Copal, a mile away down the Pin Hook road. The first problem was to find means of transportation for my frail mother and the small children, since all horses and vehicles had been taken. We finally found that the federals had left one decrepit old horse we called "Volan." In the barnyard was the chassis of an old surrey with wheels and shafts still intact. Having brought old Volan in we got him between the shafts and hitched him to the wreck of a carriage with a makeshift harness which we improvised by tearing burlap bags into strings, using them for traces and a collar. On the frame of the carriage we placed three boxes on which mother and the other four children sat. Then, with Bordat holding Volan by one side of a makeshift bit and I the other side, we started down the mile long road to Ile Copal. It was a slow procession and how we made the trip God only knows. The narrow, hedge-lined road was covered with dust about three inches deep, and as we urged Volan along in a slow walk, we were enveloped in clouds of dust stirred up as the federal cavalry and artillery rushed by on each side of us. That we were not run over and crushed must be due to a kind providence. In this manner we finally reached what we thought would be a safe refuge in our grandfather's mansion.
>
> The day after our arrival, however, the federals appeared

"The memories and deeds of our ancestors is security for the present."
— *General Richard Taylor, "Destruction and Reconstruction"*

A group of Confederate veterans photographed in the park of Major Jean Sosthene Mouton at Beau Séjour, his plantation home, in 1888. Seated, left to right: Judge Allen, Chris Steiner, William Clegg, Mr. Ware, Pierre Bernard, Martial Martin, Jean Sosthene Mouton, Sidney Greig, William B. Torian. Standing, left to right: Samuel Montgomery, Arthur Greig, Alexander Comeaux, Tibus Dugas, Lucien St. Julien, Louis Breaux, Leonidas Creighton, Joseph A. Chargois, Auguste Lisbony, J. C. Buchanan, Douglas Cochrane. Two little boys: In rear, Dave Church; in front, Frank Meyers. (See Appendix for genealogical data)

Public School taught in 1896 by Mr. Robert Greig in a building on the lot now occupied by the home

before my grandfather's house and camped all around it. Occupying the tents were General Banks, General Grover, General Whitisee, and General Franklin. They took over the kitchen, utensils, food supplies, and even the old cook, Edith. As for the rest of us we had to do our cooking in the fireplaces. Nevertheless, I shall always remember General Banks as having a kind and very pleasant face, due to an experience I had with him.

Food for us was very scarce and the older ones managed to get along with the fish and game we boys were able to catch. On more than one occasion we were forced to scrape from the feed troughs of the horses the grains of corn left, wash and parch them for food. The chief sufferers were the babies for whom there was no milk. This situation became so critical that it was decided that I should go to General Banks and ask for one of our cows. Accordingly I went to his tent and straightway a guard stopped me at the entrance and asked me who I was. My answer was, "I am a rebel, we are all rebels." At this point General Banks, who had overheard my answer, called to the guard to send me in. General Banks, who was surprised to see a small boy with such big talk, asked me what I wanted. I then explained to him about the babies and their need for milk, and asked him if we could have one of our cows. His immediate answer was, "Of course; and for your d--- impudence I'll let you have two cows"; and with that he called an orderly and told him to go in the field and bring two cows. It was not long until an orderly came down the dusty road leading two of our Jersey cows. The babies did not want for milk after that. Before the troops left they set fire to our home at Walnut Grove and it burned to the ground. I never believed it was done at the order of General Banks.

During his stay in Vermilionville General Banks had his officers billeted in a number of other private homes. Among them was the comfortable home of Hazard Eastin, which stood on the site now occupied by the home of Mrs. Ashby Trahan at 224 St. Landry Street. Mr. Eastin was the son of Herbert Eastin who had served as a member of General Andrew Jackson's staff at the Battle of New Orleans. He was a cousin of the famous Sam Houston. Mrs. Eastin who was inclined to sympathize with the Union cause always said she felt perfectly safe as long as the federal officers occupied her home.

In the battle of Pinhook bridge General Alfred Mouton, as commander of General Taylor's Louisiana Brigade was always in the thick of the fight. The successful retreat of Taylor's forces was due largely to his skillful leadership. So anxious was General Banks to capture him that he sent officers to search the private rooms of Governor Mouton's family, thinking he might be hiding there. So great was Taylor's confidence in General Mouton that he conferred on him the distinction of making the initial charge at the battle of Mansfield. Of the twenty-two hundred men under his command in this battle six hundred and seventy-two died with him.

It is said that at the end of the battle he stopped to protect a group of Federal soldiers who had thrown down their arms in surrender. While he sat on his black charger, "Têche," waving to his men not to fire some of Federals picked up their guns and fired at him. He was shot through the breast. He was buried temporarily at Mansfield but in 1866 two of his nephews, Sidney and Sosthene Mouton, brought his body to Lafayette where it now rests in the family plot in the Catholic cemetery. Many were the commendations he received from his Confederate superiors, especially from General Taylor who said of him: "He was modest, unselfish, and patriotic. He showed his best when in action, always leading his men."

When the news was flashed across the country that the United States had entered World War I to fight with the allies "to make the world safe for democracy" the response from the citizens of Lafayette Parish was prompt and enthusiastic. Many, including students at Southwestern, volunteered without waiting for the draft. A Students Army Training Corps was established on the campus where several hundred young men were given instruction preliminary to entering officer training camps. Many young men who could speak French were sent to France immediately as interpreters and billeting officers for the American forces. The total number of volunteers from the parish was fifty-one, of whom forty-one were white and ten colored. The number who entered under the Universal Service Act was four hundred and two. Of these two hundred were white and two hundred and two colored. Of the total of four hundred and fifty-three who enlisted in the service from Lafayette Parish twenty-four received commissions as officers. Twenty-seven either were killed or died in the service, and many others were wounded or disabled. The first to die in action was Louis Stanley Martin, son of the late Dr. G. A. Martin. It was in his honor that the Lafayette Post of the American Legion took the name, Stanley Martin Post, when it was first organized in 1919 through the efforts of the late Robert L. Mouton, a captain in the Marine Corps.

CHAPTER XX

THE NEGRO IN LAFAYETTE PARISH

Until the year 1712 France steadfastly refused to permit the introduction of Negro slaves into Louisiana. In that year, however, Louis XIV leased the colony to Anthony Crozat, together with exclusive trade rights in the territory. Among these rights was the privilege of sending one ship annually to Africa for Negroes. In the following year twenty Negro slaves had been brought into the colony. In 1717 the population, including soldiers sent by the King, and persons of all ages, sex, and color numbered only about seven hundred.

By 1717 Crozat had given up the colony and it had been turned over to John Law, who promoted the colossal scheme known as the "Mississippi Bubble." By terms of his grant Law was to bring into the colony in twenty-five years six thousand white settlers and three thousand slaves. During the first year one thousand slaves were shipped into the colony. As a result the Negro had become a permanent and essential element in the population and economy of Louisiana.

By 1724 the problems created by the presence of numerous Negroes, slaves and free, caused Bienville to issue a code subjecting them to certain regulations. This was the famous "Code Noir." This code was followed by several other more rigid ones in later Louisiana history. The Bienville Code dealt mainly with slaves though it also restricted the privileges of free Negroes. It required Catholic instruction and baptism for all slaves; forbade marriage or concubinage of white or free-born or manumitted Negroes with slaves; fixed the conditions by which slaves could marry; deprived slaves of the right to sue or be sued; forbade the shackling of slaves; declared Negroes movable property; stated the conditions under which they might be manumitted; and regulated in great detail the manner in which slaves might be punished. One of the earliest references to Negroes in the Attakapas District was made by Robin who spent the years 1804-5 at the Poste des Attakapas.

He wrote that about fifty years previously a man named Masse had settled near the Poste and brought with him some twenty Negroes. The earliest records in the Catholic Church there, beginning with 1756 before a church had been built, record the baptism of several of his slaves, no doubt in obedience to the "Code Noir." These baptisms prior to 1765 were celebrated by missionary priests.

In 1771 Governor O'Reilly, in setting forth conditions for the granting of land in the Attakapas District decreed that grants of a square league would be made only to those who owned one hundred head of horned cattle, *two slaves* and a few horses and sheep.

In 1773 Commandant Gabriel Fuselier prepared an inventory of the large indigo plantation of Captain de Vaugine at False Point on Bayou Teche. On this plantation, which was forty arpents front by forty deep on the east bank and forty by twenty on the west bank, there were thirty-three slaves consisting of thirteen men, ten women, and ten children. Special mention was made of a big thirty-three year old Louis who was frequently trusted by his master to collect debts due him in New Orleans. Thus did the Negro find his way into the Attakapas District and the Parish of Lafayette.

The growth of the Negro population is shown by the census records. A census of the Attakapas District taken by Daniel Clark and sent to Secretary of State James Madison in 1803 showed 2270 whites, 1266 slaves, and 210 free persons of color. The census of 1810 numbered 3959 whites and 3410 Negroes in the entire Attakapas District. Of the Negroes 191 were designated free persons of color. The 1830 census of Lafayette Parish, which then included the present Vermilion Parish, and the first census after its separation from St. Martin, showed a total of 5653 persons. Of these 2367 were slaves and 109 free persons of color. The census of 1860, the last before the Civil War, gave a total of 8934 persons. Of these 4319 were white, 4387 were slaves and 228 free persons of color. This is the only time that the colored population in Lafayette Parish exceeded the white. By the census of 1880 Lafayette Parish contained 7670 white persons, 4574 black persons and 988 mulatto persons. This disparity between the number of white persons and Negroes has continued to increase steadily with the result that, by the census of 1950, there were 42,011 white persons against only 15,727 Negroes. This disparity is due to several factors. After emancipation many of the freedmen wandered away from the parish. In more recent years many have left to seek higher wages in cities and industrial centers such as Orange, Port Arthur, and

Beaumont, Texas. In the last twenty years there has been a heavy influx of white persons into Lafayette drawn hither by a booming oil industry.

During the period of slavery Negroes contributed much to the economic development of the parish. There was an impression among the whites that only persons of color could withstand the intense heat while working in the fields. Consequently it was the Negro who cleared the fields, planted and harvested the crops, and performed the numerous manual tasks of the plantation. Many of them became skilled mechanics, working as coopers, blacksmiths, cobblers, and some actually served as overseers. They performed such essential services as nurses, cooks, dairymen and hostlers.

Many Negroes of Lafayette Parish display two characteristics not found outside of Louisiana. Having grown up among the Acadians great numbers of them speak French as their native tongue. In fact many of the older ones in rural sections today can understand and speak no other language. From the Acadians many of them acquired a gentleness of manner and a culture most unusual among members of their race. Under the French influence most of them were reared in the Catholic religion and still observe the rites of that Church. In the early days Negroes attended church with the whites and sat in pews set aside for them. Now they have their own churches. In the Parish of Lafayette the Negroes now have eight Catholic churches and chapels, three Baptist churches, two Methodist, and one Church of God.

In his thesis for the Master's degree, entitled Public Education in Lafayette Parish, the late Superintendent J. W. Faulk refers briefly to Negro education. Prior to 1868 there were no schools for Negroes in the parish. The Constitution of 1868 provided for public schools in the parish open to both colored and white pupils but of course only Negroes took advantage of them. By 1877 two schools for Negroes were taught by E. C. Dennister and W. H. Williams, and in 1880 there were six Negro schools in the parish. By 1885 W. H. Williams and Batiste Pierro were instructing one hundred and fifteen pupils in the Excelsior School. In 1887 the Negroes of Royville (now Youngsville) petitioned the school board to employ Paul Breaux to teach there, but there is no record of his employment. In 1900 there were 206 Negroes enrolled in the public schools and in 1922 there were ten colored teachers in the parish schools.

The statistics given above do not tell the whole story. Mrs.

Josephine Segura, a teacher in a Negro public school in the parish and a graduate student at Southwestern Louisiana Institute, (which has been accepting qualified Negro students since the fall of 1954) has written a most valuable term paper for a course in sociology in which she traces fully the development of Negro education in Lafayette Parish.

Prior to the Civil War about the only educational training Negro children had was in connection with their learning the Catechism and the rites of the Catholic Church. Soon after the Emancipation Proclamation Mr. Archille Figaro employed Miss Alice Mayne of New Orleans to teach his children. Soon thereafter she opened a private school in a room Mr. Figaro rented for that purpose. The private school in Lafayette continued to be taught for many years by members of the Figaro family. Meantime the Negroes organized private schools for their children in various parts of the parish. Such schools were conducted in Lafayette, Duson, Ridge, Youngsville and in a few other communities. Some of the leaders in the founding of these schools were Achille Figaro, W. H. Williams, Louis Anderson, Alice Mayne, and Paul Breaux.

In time the need for Negro education was recognized by the school board which began gradually to take over some of the private schools. Around 1885 the private school which W. H. Williams taught in the Good Hope Baptist church was taken over and financed by the parish. In early nineteen hundred the privately owned school at the corner of Washington and Simcoe streets was converted into a public school with Paul Breaux as teacher. In time therefore practically all of these private schools have been converted into publicly supported ones.

In recent years public support for Negro schools has increased enormously. The picture today is entirely different. At present there are in the parish seven public elementary schools and one consolidated high school, containing from two or three rooms to thirty. Most schools have gymnasiums, lunch rooms for free lunches, and free transportation to and from school. The new Paul Breaux High School, costing nearly $900,000.00, has a cafeteria, gymnasium, football field and industrial arts department in addition to the regular courses of study. Of the 6545 Negro educables between ages six to eighteen, 3469, in 1958, were enrolled in the elementary schools and 510 in the high school. Teaching these students are 104 teachers all but one of which have four or more years of college training. Nine of them hold master's degrees.

Many Negro students look to the Parochial schools for their education. The first of these schools for Negroes was established in Lafayette in 1903 by Sisters of the Holy Family. Their school was located in a hall which stood on the corner of Lee Avenue and East Convent Street now occupied by Blue's Laundry. This was the beginning of Catholic education for Negroes in Lafayette Parish. Since that time other such schools have been established in Lafayette, Broussard, Carencro and other centers of the parish. At present there are seven Catholic elementary schools and one high school. These schools occupy a prominent place in the educational system of the parish and are making a valuable contribution. The high school, which is known as the Holy Rosary Institute and Trade School, gives unusually effective training to young boys and girls. In addition to academic subjects and religion the girls receive specialized training in domestic science, music, typing, and art. The boys study farming, carpentry, tailoring or dietetics. Enrolled in this high school in 1958-59 were 315 students, and in the seven elementary schools were 1312.

Since World War II the economic condition has greatly improved for Negroes in the parish. In rural areas many now own their own farms. Large numbers, however, are share croppers and have their good and bad years. When crops are good and prices right they prosper; at other times their income drops and they must go the landlord for advances until another crop is made. A series of crop failures leaves them heavily in debt. In many instances they find jobs at fair wages which have risen greatly in recent years. Whereas they used to work for seventy-five or eighty cents a day, they now earn almost that much by the hour. Workers who harvest the sugar cane crop this fall will earn eighty cents an hour. Tractor drivers will get more. The average share cropper cultivates twenty to thirty acres in corn, cotton, and sweet potatoes. One third goes to the landlord for the use of house and land. Most own their own mules and farm implements and a few own tractors. Many of them own an automobile of some kind and send their children to school.

In the city of Lafayette many Negroes earn good wages as carpenters, brick layers, plumbers, electricians and service station attendants. In the skilled trades they are paid the same as white workers. As common laborers they earn from seventy-five cents to a dollar and a quarter an hour. A considerable number operate small stores, drinking places and night clubs. They have their own insurance societies which pay sick and death benefits to their subscribers. A number of women operate beauty parlors for members of their own race. There are two Negro doctors who have a numerous clientele; and Negro school teachers with equal qualifications receive the same pay as white ones. Negroes in both town and country are eligible for old age and survivors insurance, old age pensions, and unemployment insurance. Large numbers own their own homes.

Modern health and sanitation improvements have meant much to the Negroes of Lafayette, City and Parish. In the city all sections inhabited by them have sewerage, water, electricity and gas. Gas is available in all rural towns and electricity is distributed throughout the parish. The Lafayette Charity Hospital, maintained by the state, furnishes free hospital and medical service to those who are unable to pay. This service includes pre-natal care to expectant mothers and follow-up care to the new-born babies. The Tuberculosis hospital with one hundred fifteen beds is available to those afflicted with that dread disease. The modern Memorial Health Center gives free of charge immunization against whooping cough, diphtheria, tetanus, smallpox, typhoid fever, and polio to all who apply. Immunization clinics are conducted weekly in Duson, Broussard and Carencro, and venereal disease clinic in the Health Unit. A tuberculosis clinic is held also on Monday each week in conjunction with the Tuberculosis Annex Hospital of the State Department of Institutions.

In the city of Lafayette many recreational facilities are open to Negroes. There are four movie theatres for them. Adjoining the Paul Breaux High School is a large park with a modern swimming pool and other amusement and playground equipment. Scattered throughout the city are a dozen other parks and playgrounds. Several are lighted so that they can be used at night for various games.

CHAPTER XXI

THE FLOOD OF 1927

Early in the Spring of 1927 news came that the heavy winter snows in the head waters of the Mississippi, Missouri, Arkansas, Ohio, and other rivers that feed the father of waters had begun to melt earlier than usual. To swell the volume of melted snow that poured into these streams came heavy and prolonged rains that caused many of them to overflow their banks. Soon these streams, swollen to capacity, dumped their vast loads into the Mississippi, Atchafalaya and others that must channel them to the sea. It soon became doubtful if these streams could carry such a volume of water within their existing dykes and levees. As the crest of the rising flood rushed southward past Cairo, Ohio, and Memphis, Tennessee, fears of a disastrous flood spread throughout central and south Louisiana. These fears soon became a reality in the flood of 1927, an event in the history of Lafayette long to be remembered.

While the City of Lafayette and its immediate environs were on high ground and thus free from any danger, yet portions of the parish to the east and along Bayou Vermilion were so low they might be in danger should the protective levees along the Arkansas, Red and Atchafalaya Rivers fail to hold. It was not, however, the danger to Lafayette that makes this event worthy of historical record. It was the determined effort and unstinted sacrifices which the citizens of Lafayette City and Parish put forth to give aid and comfort to their unfortunate neighbors who were victims of this unprecedented calamity.

Attached to the weather bureau in New Orleans was a remarkable meteorologist in the person of Dr. I. M. Cline. Using a system of his own he skilfully kept track of the flood waters as they raced southward, measuring accurately their volume, rate of progress, and forecasting the areas that would be inundated should levees give way at designated places. On the basis of his calculations he issued daily warnings as to which sections might expect to be flooded. While many old-timers who had experienced previous floods refused to heed his predictions yet they proved to be remarkably accurate and resulted in the saving of many lives and much property. For his contributions he was highly commended by Secretary of Commerce Herbert Hoover, who represented President Coolidge in the care of flood victims.

The area north and east of Lafayette, for flood protection, including much of St. Landry, all of St. Martin, and much of St. Mary Parishes, depended upon the levee system along the west bank of the Atchafalaya River which stretched northward from the vicinity of Henderson through Krotz Springs, Melville, and on beyond Simmsport. As the crest of the flood rolled southward all efforts were centered on holding this line and the Mississippi levees beyond.

Meantime, after a conference with federal officials the National Red Cross headquarters issued a call to the nation for help. It was on the basis of this call that Lafayette's Mayor, Robert L. Mouton, seconded by Trustee of Finance, Louis Chopin, and Wilson Peck, Trustee of Public Property, issued the following Proclamation on April 26, 1927:

"Whereas: A National Proclamation by President Coolidge directing attention to the people of the nation to the sad plight of thousands of fellow citizens in the flooded areas of the Mississippi River and its tributaries, and urging generous contributions of the whole nation for the alleviation of the suffering of the people in the flooded areas which directly affects eight states and indirectly the whole nation. This flood is the most extensive in the history of our country and threatens to be one of the greatest catastrophies this country has ever known, despite the almost superhuman efforts being made to avert it, and,

"Whereas the burden of providing relief in case of disaster rests upon the American National Red Cross, the agency designated by our National Charter for this work. In a joint conference of a committee composed of members of President Coolidge's cabinet and of the American National Red Cross, it was estimated that a minimum of Five Million Dollars would be required for the relief of the Mississippi flood victims, the quota of this parish is One Thousand and Five Hundred Dollars, and it must be put over big.

"Now therefore, I, Robert L. Mouton, Mayor of the City of Lafayette, do hereby call upon every citizen of this City and Parish to contribute to his utmost and assist in this most humanitarian cause. If you cannot help financially, give clothing or provisions.

Bring your offerings to the Red Cross above the Lafayette Building and Loan offices. Any donation however small will be appreciated.

        Robert L. Mouton, Mayor."

The response of the citizens of the City and Parish was immediate. The fifteen hundred dollar quota was soon raised and, when the Red Cross doubled the quota on May 2, all out efforts were made to raise it. The theatres and civic groups organized special programs to help raise the money. The new quota was soon raised and later exceeded by nearly fifteen hundred dollars.

On April 27, Mrs. F. E. Davis, Chairman of the Lafayette Parish Chapter of the Red Cross, called a meeting of citizens to discuss the approaching danger. Besides Mrs. Davis and the executive secretary of the local Red Cross, Miss Gertrude McDowell, there were present among others O. B. Hopkins, Rev. W. J. Teurlings, the Rev. Chancellor John Vigliero, T. L. Evans, Mrs. Luke LeBlanc, Felix H. Mouton, and E. E. Soulier. It appeared that the most immediate need was workers for flood duty on the endangered levees at Henderson, Port Barre, Melville and other threatened points. The group thereupon appointed Mr. E. E. Soulier to recruit additional workers; and Lafayette responded readily to his call. That same day the Lafayette Company B of the National Guard, sixty-six strong, under the command of Captain Wilfred Moss, Captain Leo Davis, and Lieutenant Harry J. Stahl, left for New Roads to help hold the levees against the waters loosed by a break in the Arkansas River dykes. The next day the Stanley H. Martin Post of the American Legion announced its readiness to help in the crisis. By May 2, nine hundred men were working furiously to strengthen the levees from Bayou Cypremort and Henderson to Port Barre. On May 4 a volunteer company of eighty-six Southwestern students under command of Coach T. Ray Mobley announced its readiness to labor on the levees. On May 8, eighty men from Mauriceville contributed their labor; and on May 10 one hundred nineteen from Lafayette under foreman Dan. J. Mouton left to join other workers in the frantic efforts to hold back the flood. They were joined a day later by near a hundred from Youngsville. These workers were carried to the threatened points in cars and trucks furnished free by individuals and business houses, and by special trains donated by the Southern Pacific Railroad. One such train carried six hundred workers. When volunteer workers failed to meet the demand many citizens and firms contributed hundreds of dollars to a fund from which Mr. Soulier could hire laborers at two dollars a day. Such was only a portion of the effort extended by the citizens of Lafayette Parish to protect their friends and neighbors from the threatened dangers of this gigantic flood. But more was to come.

Despite the desperate efforts of thousands of workers to hold the levees the pressure of the mighty flood soon broke them down one by one. On May 2 the Mississippi levee at Vidalia, between Natchez and Vicksburg, gave way and on May 12 the one at Bayou des Glaises broke, loosing the impounded waters to rush down the Atchafalaya basin. On May 17 the Atchafalaya levee at Melville broke also. The waters loosed by these breaks soon caused the levees on the west side of the Atchafalaya to crumble away and all efforts to hold them were abandoned. As the waters began to spread Louisiana flood director, former Governor Parker, predicted that the waters would overflow the lower half of Avoyelles Parish, 1/3 of St. Landry, 2/3 of St. Martin, 2/5 of Iberville and much of Iberia and St. Mary. This prediction was confirmed by Dr. I. M. Cline, meteorologist of the New Orleans Weather Bureau. In the face of these conditions all efforts were now concentrated on rescuing and caring for the thousands whose lives and property were endangered.

On May 14 Mayor Robert L. Mouton and Mike Donlon of the Chamber of Commerce wired flood director, former Governor John M. Parker, offering the cooperation of the City of Lafayette in any manner the situation might demand; and stating that Lafayette was ready to provide a site for a refugee camp if desired. A similar telegram was sent by the local chapter of the Red Cross.

Meantime there had been formed under the auspices of the local Red Cross a Flood Relief Committee under the chairmanship of Mr. O. B. Hopkins, with the following sub-committees: Executive Committee: O. B. Hopkins, J. Allen Barnett, I. B. Bendel, J. R. Jeanmard. Transportation Committee: H. V. Mielly for the Southern Pacific Railroad; and for Trucks: E. E. Soulier, R. H. Broussard, L. P. DeBlanc, and A. E. Gauthier. Food Supplies and Cooks: M. Heyman, C. B. Billeaud, A. E. Prudhomme, Rene T. Boudreaux, J. R. Jeanmard. Stenographic and Secretarial Help: Adele Elias and Lucy Webre. Housing: E. E. Soulier, Dan J. Mouton, F. V. Mouton, Mayor Robert L. Mouton, and City Trustee of Property Wilson J. Peck. Sanitation and Medical: Dr. Marc M. Mouton and Dr. G. R. DeLaureal. Nurses: Mrs. A. A. Morgan, Jr. The rescue and care of livestock: J. C. Nickerson and Wickliffe Vennard. These committees held themselves ready at a moment's notice to respond to a call for help.

On Sunday, May 15, Miss Gertrude McDowell, executive secretary of the Lafayette Red Cross Chapter, was called to the phone and told that two representatives of the National Red Cross were on their way to Lafayette and requested that she have the local Disaster Committee meet with them within half an hour. Miss McDowell started phoning the members, now scattered about town, but with the aid of several policemen she had in the Red Cross office within twenty minutes thirty-five committee members and business men ready for emergency work. The two Red Cross representatives were L. D. MacIntyre and H. B. Atkinson of the Mississippi Disaster Relief Staff. They were accompanied by Marcel J. Voorhies of the St. Martin Parish Relief Committee. They said that within forty-eight hours refugees would begin to arrive in Lafayette. While the committee was in session word came that the levee at Henderson had broken and attempts to hold it had to be abandoned. Following the departure of the three visitors an appeal for help came from Opelousas.

Spurred by the tremendous task that confronted it the committee worked all night long collecting trucks and boats and sending them out to bring in the refugees ahead of the rushing waters. All the while the local Disaster Committee was establishing lines of industry ready to begin work by daylight. By nine o'clock the next morning headquarters had been established in the old Heyman store building across Jefferson Street from the present one, and a local warehouse cleared. Each sub-committee chairman of the General Disaster Committee set up previously knew exactly what his duties were. About 8:30 Sunday morning a young man from Henderson came in the Red Cross Office to ask what he should do, as his family home was behind the levee and water was coming into his yard. He was told to rush back and bring his family here, that it would be cared for. Thus began the flow of refugees that was to treble the population of Lafayette in a few days.

As the magnitude of the task of rescue spread offers of help came from many sources. P. J. Voorhies of the Lafayette Lumber Company offered several boats and others offered hurriedly to build them. Hundreds of local men piloted the boats through the dangerous waters to rescue those marooned on high spots and roof tops. Every village as far as Beaumont, Texas, volunteered boats and trucks. Beaumont posed an example of splendid volunteer service and organized effort. At midnight the local Red Cross office phoned the executive secretary of the Beaumont Red Cross that our Disaster Committee needed trucks and drivers. The secretary there immediately got in touch with the Mayor of Beaumont. Through his efforts a special train was secured from the Southern Pacific Railroad. Fifty volunteer trucks were loaded on this train with a driver for each truck and several relief drivers. In a few hours this train was on its way to Lafayette. Beaumont also sent a delegation of business men, headed by the Mayor, a volunteer doctor and several other helpers. Leaving the train at Lake Charles and transferring to automobiles this group was in the Lafayette Red Cross office when the train with the trucks arrived in Lafayette at ten o'clock the next morning. The Red Cross Chapter at Orange, Texas, sent aid in the form of an ambulance and driver. From Texas also came cowboys to assist in rounding up cattle and transporting them to places of safety.

Confronted with the task of rescuing, housing and feeding thousands of refugees, the Disaster Committee went to work immediately. A survey of buildings in which to house them temporarily and of possible sites for camps was made. Orders were sent to Memphis for a thousand tents and blankets. A plea was made for outboard motors to drive the rescue boats. A Red Cross Production Unit for the collection and distribution of clothing, under the direction of Mrs. Harold Demanade, was set up in a building where Woolworth's store now stands at 524 Jefferson Street. The committee on housing selected three locations for camps: One on the old fair grounds, now the municipal golf course and recreation center; one at Greenville on the abandoned property of the Baldwin Lumber Company, now occupied by Trappey's canning factory; and one for Negroes on the grounds of the Negro School. A crew under the direction of Trustee of Public Property, Wilson J. Peck, began running water and electric lines to furnish the proposed camps with water and light. The sanitation committee constructed latrines for the camps, and work was begun on the construction of barracks-like buildings to supplement the tents and provide kitchens and dining areas.

Before all the above plans could be carried out, however, beginning May 15, refugees began to pour into the city. From then on all through the night headquarters was the scene of many activities. Members of the American Legion and others volunteered to keep headquarters open as long as necessary. Typewriters from the

Southwestern Commerce Department were installed at headquarters and several faculty members and students assigned to assist with the registration. Members of the Home Economics Department and the N.S.K. Sorority volunteered and were assigned to special duty. Pathetic scenes were presented as cars, trucks, mule-drawn wagons, one after another, arrived in front of the headquarters building loaded with refugees, their household goods and other movable property including chickens, pigs, dogs, and in many cases, their all. Many children were among the victims, as many as eleven in one family being registered at headquarters.

Sympathetic relief workers attended to their comforts, distributing sandwiches and coffee for adults, and milk for the children. After registration they were sent to the Greenville Camp. Live stock and poultry brought by many of them were tagged and taken to the fair grounds and placed in pens and barns pending further arrangements for their care or sale. By 10:00 A.M. Tuesday, May 17, the registration had reached three hundred fifty. The camp at Greenville soon filled, and as the refugees swarmed in before the tents arrived, it was necessary to place them temporarily in public buildings such as the Central High, Elks Home, Masonic Temple, Knights of Columbus Home, Woodmen Hall, and others. By 11:00 A.M. the next day the number had mounted to 4062.

The enormity of the task now began to dawn upon the officials. Fortunately the tents came and the citizens of Lafayette awoke on the morning of May 18 to see on the fair grounds a tent city of over 275 tents, erected in orderly rows during the night under the direction of Boy Scout Executive H. F. Coty. But many more were needed. To house the ever increasing numbers the Red Cross officials headed by L. D. MacIntyre arranged for the hurried construction of temporary buildings with 500 rooms twelve by fourteen feet to house those who had been placed in public buildings. A tent camp for Negroes was erected on the grounds of the Holy Rosary Institute. Dr. Marc M. Mouton and nurses worked day and night with health problems, establishing a general hospital at the N. P. Moss School, a hospital for Negroes at the colored public school, an isolation hospital at Greenville, and a maternity hospital in the Convent of the Most Holy Sacrament on St. Mary Boulevard, to be operated in connection with St. John's Hospital which stood on the grounds now occupied by the Lafayette Charity Hospital. Arrangements were made to vaccinate the refugees against smallpox and typhoid, 1255 being vaccinated in one day. The National

Red Cross sent Miss Ann C. Munn to assist in nursing and hospital work.

On May 19 word came that the waters were spreading rapidly in the Cecilia and Henderson section and that over 1000 families would have to be evacuated between Arnaudville and Breaux Bridge; and that the roads were jammed with cattle being driven to high ground. On Friday, May 20, Herbert Hoover arrived in Lafayette in a special train. After a conference with relief officials here and an inspection trip through St. Martin Parish he said: "The Red Cross and the many citizens in charge of the relief program are doing a wonderful work."

However, he went on to say: "There will be 15,000 refugees in Lafayette within the next seven days"; and referring to the bulletins issued by Dr. I. M. Cline, added:

"The Teche Ridge is going under and residents of all that section are being warned. Many do not seem to take the situation seriously enough, however. They could be taken out on boats but unless the flood warning is heeded much live stock will be drowned. The Southern Pacific is giving active cooperation in the emergency and is placing cars in readiness for the evacuation work."

Secretary Hoover also said that he would recommend that more National Guard troops be sent here for duty and also that more physicians and medical supplies be rushed to this section. As a result of this recommendation forty members of Breaux Bridge National Guard Company F, under command of Lt. R. E. Chaplin were sent here; and Adjutant-General L. A. Toombs established an office in Lafayette and ordered out more National Guard troops for touring the threatened sections and warning residents to flee.

As a result of this new danger all efforts were speeded up. Headquarters issued a call for more workers, to type, to register; and for helpers both white and colored to help at the camps. City and Parish officials cast aside all but the most pressing duties to join the Red Cross and other officials in the care of refugees. Mayor Mouton closed his office and headed for Arnaudville in charge of a fleet of rescue boats to warn residents of the approaching flood. Trustee of Property Wilson J. Peck redoubled his efforts to get water and light to the camps, while Trustee of Finance Chopin spent much time at the camps helping all he could. The police under Chief A. E. Chargois and parish officers under Sheriff J. D. Trahan remained on duty many hours each day. "Relief first and other things second," was their slogan. Then on May 21, Presi-

A Picnic at Chargois Springs about 1898. The back row: (1) George Bailey, (2) Anita Hohorst (Mrs. J. Franklin Mouton), (3) J. Alfred Mouton, (4) Stella Raney, (5) Neveu, (6) Alix Judice (Mrs. J. Alfred Mouton), (7) Ned Mouton (brother of Vavaseur), (8) Louise Judice (sister of Alix Judice), (9) Dr. Gabriel Salles (Josette Salles brother), (10) Frank Moss. Sitting: (1) Florian Cornay, (2) ?, (3) Albert Judice (brother of Louise and Alix Judice), (4) Martha Mouton (back), (5) Marie Revillion (front, Mrs. Marsh), (6) Felix Salles (front), (7) Sidney Mouton (back), (8) Emily Moss (Mrs. George deBlanc), (9) Johnny LeBesque (end). "Souvenir offert a Stella Trahan (the daughter of Dr. Trahan) par un ami sincere et devoue, Sidney Mouton," is written on the back of this photograph.

Above — *Jefferson Caffery*

Reverend Charles Burt Mouton, son of Xavi Mouton.

Below — The late Most Rev. Jules B. Jeanmard, D.D., first bishop of the Diocese of Lafayette.

dent Edwin L. Stephens announced the closing of Southwestern and the assignment of buildings and staff to be utilized for relief.

The writer of this story was a member of President Stephen's staff at Southwestern and was appointed to receive the refugees and assign them to rooms in the college buildings. The refugees began to arrive on Sunday, May 22, the day of torrential rains. With a staff at the entrance to Martin Hall to register the incoming refugees, I stood in front of the entrance to direct them to the registrars and then to assign them to rooms in the buildings on the campus. All day long I stood there in the heavy rain to receive them. It was a heart-breaking sight to see them drive up in their wagons and trucks with their scanty possessions soaked with the rain. On many of the wagons were placed, first, their beds and beddings, with other household articles. Tied to the back end might be a coop of chickens. Placed among the articles of furniture were the children, while the father and mother sat on the front seat. Tucked in odd corners might be a pig or pet dog. After a family had been registered, each one was given a blanket and assigned to a room. In some cases it was necessary to place as many as twenty in the larger class rooms. Where possible, however, women and children were assigned to rooms in the dormitories where there were beds. Those in the class rooms had to sleep on the floor with only a blanket. During that day and night twelve hundred refugees were checked into the college buildings, most of them drenched with the rain. That night, although the weather was warm, furnaces in many of the buildings were lighted in order that their clothing might dry. The next day, when the sun came out, lines were stretched from buildings and trees on which the refugees hung clothes and bedding. The campus looked as if a huge laundry operation had been performed.

During this trying ordeal there were many incidents both pathetic and humorous. One man called me aside and asked if he and his family could be placed away from the others as he had a little crazy girl who might disturb the others. I placed them in a large cloak room at the far end of a building. The little "crazy girl" proved to be a full grown young woman. One confused woman being registered was asked if she were married. She said she was but could not find her husband who was lost in the crowd. She thereupon began to wail and call upon those present to find her husband. Investigation proved she had never been married. That night, making a late inspection, I turned on the lights in one room to see if the windows were up in that heated building. Those sleeping on the floor sat up immediately and turned their eyes on a young man and woman sitting in the middle of the floor. When I asked if anything was wrong, all replied, "They were just married this morning." One morning, on a tour of inspection I walked into the wood working shop in Brown Ayres Hall where a number had been placed among the work tables, lathes and other machines. Sitting side by side on a work bench were two teen age girls with their legs dangling and dressed in their best. I said, "Good morning, who are you and where are you from?" With a mischievous look in their eyes, they replied in unison: "We are high water flappers." These refugees remained on the campus for several weeks until they could be moved to the tented city that arose on the fair grounds.

As the waters rose in the east refugees continued to pour into Lafayette. It was not until May 24 that the number coming in began to decline. On that date at 10:00 A.M. the number registered stood at 16,733 including 3280 families. Those brought in after that time consisted mostly of those who tarried behind and were rescued from high spots and roof tops, and those brought in from a camp abandoned at New Iberia. The disaster committees settled down then to minister to the needs of those under their care. Many difficulties, however, arose to complicate the task. On May 22 and May 28, torrential rains hampered all relief efforts. For many days thereafter Lafayette was cut off from the rest of the world with only transport by rail remaining. On Sunday, May 28 Lafayette was flooded with a rainfall of 6.07 inches on top of 3.80 inches which had fallen the two previous days, making 9.57 inches in three days. The fair grounds, having poor drainage, became a veritable lake with several inches of water in many of the tents. It became necessary to move the women and children to schools and other public buildings in town, a difficult task which involved the separation of families. Thereafter the tents were provided with raised wooden floors. That day has been designated "Black Sunday."

While few lives were lost, there were many tales of narrow escapes. When the waters from the Bayou des Glaises area swept down the Vermilion Bayou there were many cars on the road between Lafayette and Breaux Bridge which were stalled as the rushing waters engulfed the road. The occupants found safety by clinging to the tops of their cars until rescued by boats. In one car was the late L. L. Judice of Scott. In another car were Professor G. G. Hughes and W. B. (Daddy) Stokes of Southwestern. Seeing the waters rising swifty, Professor Hughes turned around and headed back toward Breaux Bridge, hoping to reach Lafayette by way of St. Martinville and Broussard. Professor Stokes, however, fearing for the safety of his family in Lafayette, jumped on a wagon traveling toward Lafayette with refugees. The wagon barely made it to the top of the hill at Oakbourne Plantation before the whole area behind it was covered with the swirling waters. As he stood safely at the top of the hill, Professor Stokes could hear hundreds of cattle in the adjoining woods struggling and mooing in their fright and efforts to survive. Professor Hughes, finding the bridge over the Ruth Canal submerged, drove his car over the higher railroad bridge and thus reached Lafayette safely ahead of the flood that soon spread over St. Martinville and intervening places.

Volunteers who went out in boats had trouble frequently in pursuading men to abandon their homes and seek safety. In some instances they had to be overpowered and forced into the boats. Most of those found in trees and housetops were glad to accept rescue efforts; and they were many. An occasional one however refused to leave unless he could bring along his chickens or a dog. Mr. Delio Pellerin in his red "bateau" brought in one load found clinging to a cabin roof. It consisted of two Negroes seventy three and seventy eight years of age, eight or ten chickens, their lone pig, a hound, and a pup. How they got the pig on the roof remains a mystery. By May 31, most of the refugees had been cared for and only a few came thereafter. The number at ten o'clock that morning was 19,426, representing 3936 families.

The task of caring for the large number of refugees proved to be a tremendous one for the local committee. Fortunately the National Red Cross sent in additional workers to direct and assist them. For instance on Sunday May 26 volunteer workers produced 18,600 sandwiches. On May 18, before all refugees had been received, the kitchens at the Greenville and fair ground camps prepared and served 3000 loaves of bread, 1400 pounds of meat, 400 pounds of rice, 400 pounds of beans, 150 gallons of milk, besides other foods. The bread was furnished locally and cattle purchased from refugees were slaughtered for meat. The Red Cross Production Unit under the direction of Mrs. Harold Demanade, with volunteers working in shifts of six hours at sewing machines, sorted and mended thousands of garments, donated to the refugees.

During the forty-eight hours ending at 7:00 PM Sunday May 27 her group prepared 2845 children's garments, 1495 for women and 2583 for use in hospitals. On the same day was received an order for several hundred sheets which her volunteers worked frantically to provide. On May 25 Captain F. B. Putney, in charge of Red Cross relief here approved bills for $85,000.00 and on June 14, others amountings to $160,000.00.

From the very beginning there was the problem of keeping up the morale of the refugees confined in the camps. For that purpose arrangements were made to hold regular religious services in the camps for both Catholics and Protestants. There was also organized a recreation committee under the chairmanship of Dean J. M. Smith of Southwestern. He was ably assisted by R. H. Bolyard of the faculty, Mr. H. E. Robinson of the Tulane University Y.M.C.A., and Mr. Frank J. Kennedy, sent by the Knights of Columbus. Paul Blanchet, Manager of the Royal Theatre, and W. H. Clark of the Jefferson Theatre, from time to time had refugees and their children as their guests. The committee arranged for the free movies in the dining hall at the fair grounds camp. A group consisting of Miss Vesta Richard, Miss Inez Neyland, Miss Annie Carter arranged for young girls a program including story telling, basket ball, and volley ball. A similar program was arranged for young men. Other groups in town presented amateur plays and musical programs. Among those who took part in them were Mrs. Eloi Girard, Mrs. Robert S. Barnett, Mrs. P. R. Dupleix, Miss Mary Louise Dugas, Miss Ida Katherine Hopkins, Miss Pansy Glover, Miss Rosabelle Whitfield, Mr. Spencer Barnett, Mr. Lloyd Whitfield, Mr. Leslie Norton, Mr. Hugh Billeaud, Mr. C. J. McNaspy, Jr. and Henry Voorhies, Jr. To keep some of the men busy there was organized under the direction of Professor Ashby Woodson of the Southwestern Department of Engineering a project of furniture making. The lumber companies furnished the wood and Professor Woodson the patterns. These were then sawed into the component parts in the wood shops at Southwestern and the Hopkins Lumber Company. These parts were then assembled at the camps. Some of the women assisted in painting the finished articles. In one week there were produced thirty benches, twenty tables, three wardrobes, and two cabinets.

As soon as all the refugees had been gathered into the camps all minds turned to the problems of reparation and rehabilitation. On Thursday May 27, a hurried meeting of citizens was called to consider the question. Speakers included Mayor E. G. St Julien, who had been elected to succeed Mayor Mouton, L. L. Judice, President of the Parish School Board, J. A. Roy, J. Allen Barnett, J. R. Jeanmard, President E. L. Stephens and I. B. Bendel. All agreed on the following resolution to be sent State Flood Director John M. Parker: "Resolved that the people of the stricken areas are entitled to full reparation and rehabilitation by the United States Government."

On May 31 the executive committee of the flood relief organization met, with T. L. Evans presiding in the absence of O. B. Hopkins. Present was A. Kaplan of Crowley who had been named in general charge of reparations and rehabilitation in the Parishes of St. Landry, Iberia, Lafayette, and St. Martin. Chairman Evans appointed a committee consisting of Mrs. F. E. Davis, J. Allen Barnett, J. R. Jeanmard and E. E. Soulier to name a rehabilitation committee for the Parish of Lafayette. This committee then named the following: J. A. Roy, President of the First National Bank, Chairman; Mrs. F. E. Davis, Chairman of the local Red Cross; J. C. Barry, President of the Bank of Lafayette and Trust Company; F. M. Bacque, Parish Farm Agent; Leonce J. Prejean, prominent farmer of Carencro; J. J. Fournet, President of the Lafayette Parish Police Jury; and District Judge W. W. Bailey of Abbeville. The first task of this committee, in conjunction with a similar one in St. Martin Parish was to make a survey of the losses and needs of flood victims in the two parishes. The names of this committee were sent to Governor O. H. Simpson, Col. W. H. Sullivan, Chairman of the State Reconstruction Committee, and T. J. MacCarty, Executive Secretary of the New Orleans Red Cross chapter.

On June 3 this committee met and made its report which was forwarded to Mr. M. K. Redford, Red Cross rehabilitation officer in Alexandria.

St. Martin Parish: — 170,000 acres of farm land flooded. The following crops to be planted as the water recedes: soy beans, rice, sweet potatoes, sorghum, cow peas, Irish potatoes, winter truck crops. Losses: 1500 head of work stock; 2400 farmers lost all implements; 2600 families lost all household goods. Recommended: $75,000. for seed; $225,000. to replace work stock; $25,000. to replace implements, $200,000. for six weeks rations; $168,000. to feed live stock; and a credit of $100,000. for immediate use by the rehabilitation committee.

Lafayette Parish: — 15,000 acres of farm land flooded; 7,500 acres to be planted as water recedes: — 3000 acres in soy beans; 700 acres in cotton; 700 acres in peanuts; 100 acres in Irish potatoes; 400 acres in fall beans; 1000 acres in corn; 500 acres in cabbage and fall truck crops; all the sweet potatoes possible. Losses: 100 farms lost all implements; small loss of work stock; 200 farms lost all household goods. Estimated need: $3,000, for work stock; $5,000 for seed; $2,000 for forage; $5,000 for food; and an initial credit of $12,000 for the Lafayette Committee.

It was on May 28 that the first word came that the waters were beginning to recede. On that day were evacuated the first two refugees, Noli Champagne and Alexandre Patin. Word of their leaving created such a restlessness in others who were anxious to leave that the camps had to be surrounded by high wire fences to prevent others from going without permission. By June 15, however, they were being evacuated at the rate of one hundred a day. Not until August 25 were all returned to their homes. As they left there remained the task of dismantling the camps and salvaging unused supplies. Lumber, wire, tents, blankets were used in restoring homes. On August 10 the disaster headquarters were moved to the Denbo-Nicholson building which stood on the land now occupied by the Washington Insurance Company at 214 Jefferson Street. The front offices were used for the Lafayette Rehabilitation Committee. The rest of the building was used for the storage of food, clothes, seed and surplus stock. There still remained in Lafayette Parish 250 to be supplied from these stores until fully rehabilitated.

As one looks back it is difficult to visualize the enormity of the task accomplished by the citizens of this community with the aid of the Red Cross. In a report to the Rotary Club on July 15 Chairman O. B. Hopkins stated that 815 volunteer cars and trucks had been used; and up to that time the Red Cross had already spent one million dollars here on care of the refugees. By July 29 the women's production group had received, processed, and distributed five hundred thousand garments valued at half a million dollars. In her report to the National Red Cross, Miss Gertrude McDowell, local Red Cross executive secretary, stated that a total of 19873 refugees had been registered, representing 4041 families. She estimated that, including refugees who were self sustaining, there had been 34,000 people in Lafayette besides the normal population of less than 15,000. Both Red Cross officials, and Secretary

Hoover, who visited Lafayette several times, had only the highest praise for the local committees and the hundreds of volunteers who were too numerous to name here.

While some of the refugees became restless at times they co-operated fully with the officials and volunteer workers, showing their appreciation in many ways. The following humble expression of one group's appreciation was left on the editor's desk of the Daily Advertiser on May 28: "We, the colored refugees, desire to thank our government and all other officials which have saved us from starvation. We have lost all we had earned in a lifetime, but we are thankful that we have good food and cleanliness. We are being handled by one of the best white boys that a mother could ever give to this world. He is C. J. Boudreaux. He gave up his job to come over and take charge of our kitchen at the Colored School, and we ask that the people let this man stay with us. We are willing to do anything for him because he is doing everything in his power to help us and we want him to know that we appreciate his management.

Yours truly,
The Colored Refugees."

CHAPTER XXII

SOCIAL ORGANIZATIONS

Fraternal

With the passing of the confusion which accompanied the period of civil war and reconstruction the people were able again to take up their commercial and social activities where they had dropped them at the war's beginning. Enough has been written already about the activities of such organizations as the Vigilance Committees and the Knights of the White Camellia. The new era was characterized chiefly by the organization of social and fraternal societies such as Masons, Woodmen of the World, Elks, Knights of Columbus, Knights of Honor, Catholic Knights of America, Knights of Labor and the Rotary Club. All the above societies have, or have had in the past, chapters in the Parish of Lafayette.

Probably the first of these organizations to establish a chapter in the parish was the Masonic Lodge, which received its charter on February 10, 1857. There is evidence, however, that there were a number of Masons in Vermilionville, prior to the granting of the charter, who no doubt met informally in a building known as the Masonic Lodge, which stood on the grounds now occupied by Mount Carmel Academy. This building was subsequently purchased by Father Megret for the school. The charter members of the lodge were M. E. Girard, C. H. Mouton, J. J. Caffery, Andre Martin, A. Bailey, Aimee Dufour, Claude Coulouvrat, N. Higginbotham, R. Dugas, and W. B. Erwin. Representing the Grand Lodge at the installation ceremonies was Thomas H. Lewis of the Opelousas chapter. Since the old meeting place had been sold to Father Mégret the newly organized chapter held meeting temporarily in the courthouse until a new home could be built. On August 15, 1857, Alexandre Mouton, Louisiana's ninth governor, and a member of Hope Lodge 145, gave to the lodge the site on which was built its first home. This donation was made official on June 29, 1861, when the senator appeared before William

Brandt, Clerk of Court, and donated town lot 84 in Vermilionville to members of the lodge. Michel E. Girard accepted the gift on behalf of the lodge membership, and Onézime Mouton and Andre Martin witnessed the transaction.

The first lodge building was a one story structure and during its time was used for many worthy purposes in addition to serving as a meeting place for the Masons. From 1861 to 1865 the lodge met in the courthouse in order to permit Reverend Thomas Rand to use the building as a school house. Many of Vermilionville's citizens of that time received instruction in this school. For a time also it was used by the Baptist congregation for Church and Sunday School purposes, as well as a meeting place for the Vermilionville Grange. After the Civil War a second story was added to the original building. This building served until 1916 when the membership became so large that it was necessary to consider larger quarters. In that year, therefore, a contract was let for the construction of the present building at a cost of $13,500. It was completed and dedicated by the officers of the Grand Lodge of Louisiana in 1917. Meantime the membership continued to grow, and numbered two hundred in 1923 and two hundred and thirty-five in 1935. In 1909 was organized a Royal Arch chapter with a membership of twenty-seven which had grown to one hundred and thirty-six in 1923. A council of Royal and Select Masters was founded in 1917 and in the same year a chapter of Knights Templars with a roll of twenty-three members.

The membership of these divisions has increased steadily. That of the Blue Lodge is now 435; of the Royal Arch Chapter, 186; the Royal and Select Masters, 166; and the Knight Templers, 209. There is also an Evangeline Shrine Club with 253 members.

On August 12, 1907, was organized a chapter of the Eastern Star with fifteen members. The charter was received the following year and Mrs. Rose Jagou chosen as first Grand Matron. The present membership is 255 and the Grand Matron is Mrs. W. E. Beadle, Sr.

Some years prior to 1900 a group of business and professional men organized a social club which older citizens remember as the Century Club. The promoters of this club were Dr. A. R. Trahan, C. M. Parkerson, Leo Judice, O. C. Mouton, S. R. Parkerson and others. Their first club rooms were located on the courthouse square where Judge Kaliste Saloom's office now stands. Later they moved to rooms in a building that stood on ground now used as a parking lot at 545 Jefferson Street. In 1904 they built the two story brick building at 534½ Jefferson Street, the second floor of which is now occupied by the Woodmen of the World and the lower floor by Bell's shoe store. The lower floor of this building was let for commercial purposes but the second was arranged for club uses. There was a dance hall, card rooms and other facilities. For many years this club was the center of Lafayette's social activities. Dances were held every Friday night and were very popular among the younger set. Every evening the card rooms were occupied by business men, who sought relaxation in their favorite card games. In 1917 however the club sold the building to the Woodmen of the World and then dissolved.

The idea of organizing an Elks lodge in Lafayette was conceived by Dr. F. E. Girard, who, in 1907, was a member of that order in New Iberia. In that year he and a few other lodge members who lived in Lafayette secured permission from the Grand Lodge to hold meetings. In 1908 he found twenty-three others who were anxious to join with him in the organization of a permanent Elks Lodge in Lafayette. The outcome of their efforts was that on July 15, 1908 a charter was duly issued to Lodge No. 1095 of the Benevolent and Protective Order of Elks. The meetings for the first year were held in a room over the old home of the Lafayette Building Association, which stood at 545 Jefferson Street, now a parking lot. The home was next moved to the second floor of the building now occupied by the Guaranty Bank and Trust Company, where it remained for two years. In 1911 the lodge occupied the large house owned by Dr. F. E. Girard on the corner of Congress and Buchanan Streets at the rear of the present Guaranty Bank. Two years later this property was purchased for a permanent home, which served until 1920. In that year, under the administration of the late Dr. R. D. Voorhies, the old home was moved and replaced with the large building that occupies that corner today. This new home contained on the first floor an office, parlor, swimming pool and dressing rooms. On the second floor were reception room, card rooms, and a large lodge room which was used frequently for dances. On the third floor was a gymnasium. This home, which was an ornament to the city, cost $85,000. When the movement for this home was started the membership was only one hundred and thirty-five; by 1923 it had reached six hundred and forty-one.

For several years the lodge home was the center for dances and many other social activities. At one time the Rotary Club held its dinner meetings there. In this manner the lodge continued to prosper until the period of World War I and the depression years that followed. Thereafter interest began to decline with the result that the membership fell off rapidly. Because of this lack of support, and the inability of the lodge to meet the payments on its bonded indebtedness, the lodge surrendered its beautiful home to the bond holders, who in turn sold the building for commercial purposes. Confronted with this misfortune the lodge was dissolved in 1930.

The same year that the Elks lodge received its charter there was organized in Lafayette a chapter of the Knights of Columbus. One of those most active in founding this order here was Mr. Charles Olivier Mouton who became the first Grand Knight. The original membership numbered sixty-two but by 1923 it had reached four hundred. For some time the Knights possessed no home of their own but in 1913 the present home was erected on Jefferson Street with funds generously advanced by Mr. C. O. Mouton. The membership has continued to grow and the original home has been remodeled and beautified.

In 1959, however, instead of the one original council of Knights, number 1286, there have been organized in the city three additional councils: The Father Teurlings Council, number 3202, Harold Calais, Grand Knight; Our Lady of Fatima Council, number 3480, Leroy Langois, Grand Knight. The combined membership of all four councils in June 1959 was twelve hundred.

SERVICE CLUBS

Perhaps the oldest of the service clubs in Lafayette is the Women's Club. This club had its inception in 1897 at a luncheon at which Miss Lizzie Parkerson, the late Mrs. D. L. Caffery, honored her sister-in-law after her marriage to Mr. Charles M. Parkerson. Having heard the guest describe the clubs in her home town of San Antonio, Texas, Mrs. Caffery was instrumental in getting together a number of ladies who decided to organize the Five O'Clock Tea Club. The organization meeting was held at the home of Mrs. T. M. Boissat who was elected the club's first president. This club later became the Lafayette Women's Club, which affiliated with the Louisiana Federation of Women's Clubs in 1901. Other charter members besides the president were Mrs. T. M. Blake, Mrs. Charles Caffery, Mrs. Louise G. Clegg, Mrs. A. B. Denbo, Miss Lea Gladu, Miss Eliza Hopkins and Mrs. W. A. LeRosen. Other members who took part in the early activities of the club were Mrs. F. E. Davis, Mrs. Baxter Clegg, Miss Fadra Holmes, Mrs. A. Hopkins, Mrs. J. A. Martin, Miss Hugh D. McLaurin, Miss Zelia Christian, Miss Edith Dupré, Miss Clye Mudd, Mrs. B. J. Pellerin, Miss Fannie Ramsey, Mrs. J. L. Kennedy, Miss Beverly Randolph (Mrs. E. L. Stephens), Mrs. J. E. Trahan.

During its long life the Women's Club has sponsored many worthy undertakings. One of the first projects was the holding of religious services in the city and parish jails at Christmas and Easter, after which packages of fruit, candy, and cigarettes were distributed to the prisoners. From 1897 to 1917 the club sponsored a lending library. In 1906 it established the first free scholarship at Southwestern to be awarded to a young man or woman residing in the Parish of Lafayette and not financially able to attend the college without assistance. The scholarship was later changed to a loan fund which has aided many needy students to receive a college education.

The first of the men's service clubs founded in Lafayette was the Rotary Club. The charter members of this club were: J. C. Barry, F. A. Baranco, J. P. Colomb, T. M. Callahan, F. E. Davis, Mike Donlon, A. B. Denbo, Dr. F. E. Girard, J. W. Harrington, O. B. Hopkins, Rt. Rev. Jules B. Jeanmard, P. Krauss, W. P. Mills, Robert L. Mouton, L. D. Nickerson, T. J. Reaux, Dr. M. E. Saucier, J. G. St. Julien, Mr. Upton and A. J. Wolff. The first president was J. C. Barry. Among the objectives of this club is the fostering of high ethical standards in all business transactions, and giving moral and financial support to all worthy enterprises that promise to advance the welfare of the community. To these ends the club has striven faithfully to gain support for the Chamber of Commerce, the Boy Scouts, the Mid-Winter Fair, and similar projects. One of its most notable achievements was the organization and maintenance of a fifty-piece boys' band. This band had its origin in the mind of Dr. M. E. Saucier while he served as club president in 1922. Under the direction of Rotarian Frank A. Baranco it did much to inspire a love of music not only in hundreds of boys, but in all South Louisiana. The Lafayette Rotary Club was organized August 20, 1920.

The second men's service club organized in Lafayette was the Kiwanis Club, organized for a brief existence in 1930. Due to the depression and the lack of support the club, after a year or so, gave up its charter. The present Kiwanis Club received its charter on

August 8, 1944. Among its first members were Henry Heymann, J. Sosthene Martin and D. S. Byrnside. In 1952 the membership numbered seventy-seven.

The Kiwanis Club has taken part in practically all community activities and fund raising campaigns. It took the lead in the organization of the Lafayette Health Council and the annual Football Jamboree. The club is perhaps best known for its aid to spastic paralytics and its sponsorship of National Kids Day.

Space does not permit a review of the history of all service clubs in the city. It is of interest, however, as evidence of the city's growth, to know that there are now in Lafayette two Rotary Clubs, two Kiwanis Clubs, two Optimist Clubs, an Exchange Club, Lions Club, Junior Chamber of Commerce, Moose, and Young Men's Business Club. Other fraternal, religious, youth, and social clubs now number over two hundred.

MARDI GRAS IN LAFAYETTE

Of all social functions in the history of Lafayette the one that has appealed to the greatest number and brought forth the greatest expressions of joy and enthusiasm is that which is held in celebration of Mardi Gras. Having been introduced into New Orleans in 1827 by a group of young Creole men who had observed the celebration in France, it soon spread to Lafayette, then Vermilionville, and other parts of Louisiana. In the early days, instead of parades and balls, masked and costumed groups on horseback rode from house to house in the village and country where a welcome awaited them. Having drunk, eaten, and made merry, they moved on to the next house where the celebration was repeated on and on through the day. Many of the older citizens can recall this type of celebration. In fact it is still kept up in the country except that the automobile has replaced the horse with its masked rider.

Just when the celebration was accompanied with a formal ball is uncertain. The first written record of such a ball was found in an old newspaper account dated February 13, 1869. The music was furnished by the Clements Band and the court house provided the ballroom. There were no king, queen and maids as there are today. It was said that every lady was a queen to her escort and he the king to his lady.

Additional information on the subject may be found by consulting the minutes of the Lafayette Parish Police Jury for the years

1870, 1871, and 1873. From these records it would seem that the Hyperion Club had been accustomed to celebrate Mardi Gras by holding its ball in the courtroom of the courthouse; for on September 5, 1870 the police jury in regular session passed the following resolution: "Resolved that the use of the courthouse for giving balls, concerts, shows, etc. is hereby prohibited."

The resolution of the police jury not to have the hall of justice desecrated by the holding of dances, shows, and concerts must have met with popular resistance, for on September 24, 1870, called no doubt as the result of pressure, a special meeting of that august body enacted the following: "Resolved that the resolution adopted at the last meeting prohibiting the giving of balls, etc. in the court house be and is hereby amended and modified to read as follows: 'That the President of the Police Jury and the Keeper of the Court House may allow Balls, Concerts, Shows, etc. upon the payment of fifteen dollars to the Keeper for the use of the Parish and to be paid into the treasury, and upon the condition that everything be cleaned and replaced in proper order.'"

All this was in the year 1870. The next year, 1871, Mardi Gras was to fall on February 21. As the big day approached the Police Jury again met in special session on February 4, 1871. At this meeting the Jury resolved that: "The resolution in force concerning the Court House be suspended in so far as to allow the use of the Court Room free of cost to the Hyperion Club of Vermilionville, for the purpose of giving balls on Mardi Gras and St. Joseph's day; provided that everything be properly cleaned and replaced."

Members of the jury present at this meeting were J. J. Caffery, president, A. J. Moss, clerk, and members M. G. Broussard, Landry, Hebert and R. LeBlanc. Absent were Messrs. Onesiphore Broussard and John Caruthers.

From St. Martinville we have evidence of the prevailing spirit of Mardi Gras.

I O F
PROCLAMATION

To our well-beloved buffoon, Knight of the Legion of Little Bells—Greetings.

With the aim of giving testimony of our love for our trusty, faithful subjects of the new province of the Têche, we have resolved to visit them shortly.

Consequently the 10th of next month we shall go to St. Martinville to receive their homage, and you are by these presents charged with the preparations necessary to our reception.

Given at New Orleans, at our imperial palace, under the great seal of the State, this January 12, 1877.

Rex Carnivalus

RISUS
Private Secretary.

* * * * * * *

By virtue of the preceding, we the buffoons, commandant of the Poste of the Attakapas, to receive appropriately His Majesty, we order the following:

February 10th there will be a great ball of fancy dress and masquerade at the Duchamp Hall, and we order that each one come to it in courtly costume. Secondly, at ten o'clock His Majesty will make his entrance in the ball followed by his staff and the cannon will announce an hour ahead the arrival of His Majesty.

No one will be admitted to the ball without an invitation countersigned by us and which he will have to give to the porter on entering.

To prevent their slipping in some enemy among us, we have named a committee of four faithful subjects of the King to examine the people arriving.

Any person desiring an invitation will have to apply by letter to the Knight Buffoon, General Delivery, at St. Martinville.

Done and commanded at St. Martinville this January 12th, 1877.

Buffoon,
Knight.

It was not until March 2, 1897 that Mardi Gras in Lafayette claimed the spotlight again. On that date was held the first Carnival celebration with its king, queen, dukes and maids who, in full regalia, paraded the streets in the afternoon before the ball that night. King Attakapas was no other than the famous "Bedon" (High Hat) George Armand Martin, physician, judge, lawmaker, planter, raconteur and genial gentleman. His queen, well known for her remarkable talents and beauty, was Miss Isaure McDaniel, a teacher of a private school, who was later married to Mr. J. E. Fletcher, making her home in Memphis, Tennessee.

Judge Martin had all the attributes of a king, pomp, dignity, and graciousness. He never appeared in public unless garbed in a Prince Albert coat and high silk hat. Roark Bradford in writing of him said: "Make no mistake, Judge G. A. Martin of Lafayette, Louisiana is a genial gentleman and scholar; a politician who has encouraged his opposition; a legislator whose record is written in the history of Louisiana; a physician whose ministrations to rich and poor alike, have won him thousands of friends . . . . and an Acadian whose pride of home and lands, combined with courage and audacity, is spread by report from Baltimore, Maryland to the Texas border."

The popular physician and judge is still remembered by many who can give examples of his wise decisions in court. There was the case of the two neighbors who laid claim to the same hen, and brought their dispute to the judge. After listening to the arguments the judge adjourned court until dusk. Having reassembled the litigants, with the hen as evidence, he proceeded to the neighborhood of the litigants and there released the hen in the middle of the street. The protesting hen shook herself, took a look around, and then made a bee line to the home of one of the claimants. The judge then declared: "The hen knows its own home; case dismissed."

It is doubtful if Mardi Gras in Lafayette, despite the pomp and glitter of recent Carnival balls, will ever have a king as dramatic and colorful as was its King Attakapas. That he understood well the importance of his position is evidenced in the proclamation which he issued to his loyal subjects:

King Attakapas,
The Royal Head of the
Mystic Knights of
Lafayette
Issues His Initial Proclamation
To the Loyal Subjects of His
Kingdom
Terra Firma, February 13th, 1897

To My Loyal and Beloved Subjects:

Being profoundly impressed with the spirit of progress now pervading the people of my Kingdom, and, having conviction that an occasional day of recreation and amusement is conducive to long life and happiness, I hereby decree by the absolute power vested in me, that Tuesday, March 2nd be and is hereby set aside as a day of mirth and merriment throughout my entire realm.

I command all loyal subjects to abandon all domestic and business cares on that occasion, and unite in making the event one of memorable enjoyment. It is my express wish that all stores and other places of business shall be closed from 1 o'clock to 5 o'clock, p.m. on the date named, in order that em-

Lombard's Hotel and Bar at the corner of West Main and Lafayette Streets was a popular place in the eighteen nineties. In front of the hotel holding the hands of his two children is Fidelle Lombard, the owner. The boy at his father's left was George, who died in France where he had gone to continue his education. The little girl, Horta, now deceased, became the wife of Daniel J. Mouton.

Below — "Little Willie's Bus." For many years in the early 1900's before the advent of taxis, Willie Lewis' bus carried passengers between the Gordon Hotel and the railway station. Between trains it parked in front of the hotel ready to carry others to different parts of town.

The Parish Jail about 1869.

The Recorder's Office was on the courthouse square at the corner of Lafayette and South Main. Built about 1860. From left to right: (1) "Fils" Hirsch (Leopold), grand uncle of Dr. Paul Salles, (2) Conrad Debaillon, (3) Crow Girard, (4) Arthur Greig, (5) Ovey Savoie, (6) Francois Comeaux, (7) Bruce Martin, (8) Phillip Martin, (9) "Parrain" (Alexandre) Comeaux.

City Hotel, built about 1845, at the north corner of Buchanan and West Main, now where the machine shops of the Lafayette Motor Co. are. Among the proprietors were the Abbots, the Voorhies, and the Chargois. Left to right: (1) Auguste Lisbony, (2) William Clegg, (3) George Cherre, (4) The Abbot family (center seven), (5) Baxter Clegg, (6) Treville Bernard, (7) Bruce Martin.

Below — The Orleans Hotel, built about 1880, was located on the west side of Lafayette Street about 150 feet from the corner of West Vermilion. This was the first store of Lazarus Levy from Russia who married Flora Plonsky. Their children were Rose, Hannah, Armand, Victor, Lena, William, and Mose. Later, this was the store of Mr. Armand Levy who, after several years, moved his business to South Washington opposite Bendel's store, later the Falk Mercantile Co. Mr. Victor Levy's residence was a few feet away from this hotel.

The Cottage Hotel at the corner of West Vermilion and Jefferson Street, facing West Vermilion was built about 1890; the residence of Mrs. Monroe Porter Young, the sister of Mrs. Leila (George) deClouet, both the daughters of Mrs. Adele Cornay. This home later was converted into a hotel for "drummers," (the traveling salesmen of the Victorian age). On the Jefferson Street side of this hotel was a long gallery where in the shade of the long summer afternoons "the drummers" enjoyed iced mint juleps and they read the Lafayette Gazette and wondered about the brown-eyed beauties as they strolled by on the plank walks.

On the porch from left to right: Viola Young (little girl on steps), Mr. Serret, Mrs. Serret, J. J. Davidson, Mrs. Monroe P. Young, Adele Young, her daughter later married Mr. Felix Mouton, the brother of Mr. Vavaseur Mouton, Mrs. Kelley, Willie Bonnet, Arthur Bonnet, married Mimi Cornay (Mrs. Young's sister).

Below — Begneaud Saloon about 1855 on north side of West Main and Lafayette on the corner opposite the courthouse. "Many social and political plots found their birth, and sometimes their death, here."

ployers and employees, alike, may enjoy to the utmost the brilliant street parade beginning at 2 o'clock, p.m.

I especially ordain that the Duke of Lafayette, the Duke of Carencro, the Duke of Broussard, the Duke of Scott, the Duke of Royville and the Duke of Duson, shall attend the King with their full retinue, in his triumphal march through the principal streets of Lafayette, my capital city."

> King Attakapas
> Lord of all he surveys
> Attest:
> Mossback
> Supreme Secretary

For many years after the reign of Judge Martin as King of the Mystic Knights of Lafayette the Carnival spirit seems to have subsided, as there is no record of a Mardi Gras ball until 1927. In that year Mrs. Harry L. Griffin, who had witnessed many of the Carnival parades and balls in New Orleans and whose father, Alexander Mouton, had been a charter member of the Krewe of Proteus, decided to renew the Carnival tradition in Lafayette. Accordingly she organized and staged the first high school ball in the city. This was patterned after those held in New Orleans, with king, queen, maids, pages and all typical panoply. The first king was Percy Primeaux and his queen was Daisy Romero.

Soon after Mrs. Griffin's plans were known she was approached by the late Paul Krauss and Gaston Hebert with the request that she direct the staging of a Carnival celebration and ball on a city-wide basis. The request was readily granted and soon committees were formed to select a theme, king, queen and maids; to arrange for the building of floats for a parade; and to devise a way of financing the celebration. The plans met with such wide-spread approval that business houses and individuals readily contributed substantial sums of money to finance the undertaking. The street parade with handsome floats, constructed by Mr. Louis A. Broussard and accompanied by several bands was a big success. Thousands of persons from city and country thronged the streets to view it. The ball that followed at night, with king, queen and their royal entourage was a brilliant social event. In this manner came into being the Southwest Louisiana Mardi Gras Association which, with its King Gabriel and Queen Evangeline has set the pattern for Carnival throughout this section of the state.

Below is a roster of those who have been honored with the titles of King and Queen of the Krewe of Gabriel. On Mardi Gras day the flags of past kings may be seen floating in front of their homes.

Date	King	Queen
1934	George Gardiner	Mabel Broussard
1935	Paul Salles	Esther Keller
1936	Emile Soulier	Dorothy Carlos
1937	Dr. L. O. Clark	Bella Nickerson
1938	Dr. O. P. Daly	Mary Huval
1939	Daniel J. Olivier	Rose Mary Doucet
1940	A. M. Bujard	Dorothy Daly
1941	Dr. F. H. Davis	Anna Belle Bernard
1942-1947	No celebration because of war	
1948	Joe Simon	Joanne McElligot
1949	W. W. Hawkins	Mary Virginia Hamilton
1950	Dr. James Comeaux	Patricia Dalferes
1951	cancelled because of war	
1952	Emanuel Ostrich	Diane Miller
1953	Forrest K. Dowty	Mary Alice Blanchet
1954	Horace Rickey	Nancy Jo Theriot
1955	R. J. Castille	Marie Elise Labbe
1956	Albert D. Miller	Martha Tolly Davis
1957	Jack Hayes	Barbara Burdin
1958	Paul Blanchet	Celia Anne Guilbeau
1959	Frem F. Boustany	Hilda Elizabeth McCullough

Meantime other carnival organizations have arisen in the city and parish. Beginning in 1945 the Quota Club of Lafayette, a business women's organization, presented a parade and brilliant pageant and ball. When this club disbanded in 1951 it was felt that the omission of this event would be a distinct loss to Lafayette. In response to popular demand, therefore, the membership of the Lafayette Town House agreed to continue this ball. For their krewe the Town House selected the name, "Troubadours," and for their king and queen, the romantic titles, Richard Coeur de Lion and Berengaria of Navarre. In 1955 a group of the younger men of the city organized a third carnival club to which they gave the name "Les Brigands de Lafitte."

Lafayette now has three major carnival organizations whose balls with the accompanying pageants have become so elaborate and dazzling that they are said to rival those held in New Orleans. In addition to these three, nearly every high school in city and parish now celebrates Mardi Gras with an elaborate pageant and ball in which all participants are garbed in costumes of ever-increasing beauty.

CENTENNIAL PAGEANT

Episodes from Lafayette Centennial Pageant presented at Southwestern Louisiana Institute stadium February 24, 1936, as reported in the Lafayette Advertiser.

Episode I   1699 Indian days; directed by Bernard Lang.
Episode II   1770 Arrival of the Acadians, directed by Miss Edith Dupre.
                 Interlude — an Acadian Folk Dance
                 "Sur le Pons d'Avegnoir"
Episode III   1821 Founding of first church, on present site of St. John's Cathedral. Directed by Right Reverend Monsignor A. F. Isenberg.
Episode IV   1836 March 11 — Founding of Lafayette, at that time Vermilionville, directed by Lionel Billeaud.
                 Scene I — At State Capitol, then in New Orleans, where Lafayette's first charter was signed by the governor.
                 Scene II — At the old courthouse here where the first town council met.
                 Interlude — Spanish Dance
Episode V   1858 Founding of the first Protestant Church, Presbyterian. Directed by Reverend R. H. Harper.
Episode VI   Early justice as administered by Viligance Committee — demonstrated by Mr. F. Xavier Mouton as administered in the court of the late Judge Campbell.
                 Interlude — Old fashioned waltz — dancing
                 "Blue Danube"
Episode VII   The founding of schools.
                 1846 Scene I — Establishment of first convent on present site of the Cathedral High School.
                 1847 Scene II — Founding of the first public school — at corner of Jefferson and Vermilion streets.
                 1900 Scene III — Beginning of Southwestern Louisiana Institute was depicted. Directed by Mrs. George P. Lesley.
Episode VIII   1700 to 1936 — Development of transportation. Following the Indians and white men, as they come in succession: a coach, a train represented by the motor train of Thibodeaux "40-8" of the American Legion, an old auto-

mobile, a late model car, a bus. Directed by Robert E. Chaplin.

Episode IX   Founding of Bank.

1800 Scene I — The rise of industry and commerce: pictured trappers selling pelts, a peddler displaying his goods, workmen cutting sugar cane and picking cotton, and other activities.

1891 Scene II — Founding of the city's first bank; the First National Bank. Directed by Mrs. P. B. Roy.

Interlude — Dance — by Miss Gertrude LeBlanc's dancing school — presenting "Tell Me Pretty Maiden" — a sextette number of the Gay Nineties.

Episode X   War Scenes.

Scene I — Acadian guards assembled for duty in the War Between the States.

Scene II — Soldiers leaving for World War Services.

Pageant closed with crowning of the Queen of the Centennial, directed by Mrs. J. J. Davidson, Jr. Here, Dr. Harry Lewis Griffin, head of the Centennial organization and author of its history from which this script of the Centennial was selected, together with Mayor Robert L. Mouton now ascend throne. The Queen's maids enter, followed by the Queen and her two trainbearers—little Ernest Jeanmard, Jr. and little J. Alfred Mouton, Jr.—and escorted by Dr. Merle Gaidry, Mayor Robert L. Mouton crowns the Queen. Her maids Misses Audrey Compton, Dorothy Roy, Thelma Williams, Lucille Roy, Dorothy Daly, Doris Knighten, Verna LeBlanc, Ellen Fletcher, Rose Mary Trahan, Mary Agnes Saloom, Bella Nickerson, and Lucille deBlanc. Their escorts: Paul de Laureal, Malcolm Fisher, Harry Saucier, Charles Compton, Burl Logan, Warren Butcher, Webb Smith, Ashton Mouton, Leslie Ball, Joe Reeves, N. D. Olivier. Mr. James J. Barry with co-ordinator of the pageant. This history of the first hundred years of Lafayette was reviewed by thousands of spectators in program at S.L.I. Stadium. Dr. Harry L. Griffin, historian. Presented in eleven episodes.

Chairmen of the pageant committees were:
1. Dean Harry L. Griffin, General chairman.
2. Bennett J. Voorhies, chairman of episodes.
3. Mrs. Joyce Hartzell Dalferes, Dances and Music.
4. George H. Gardiner — publicity.
5. Emile E. Soulier, Finance.
6. Miss Emily Huger, Stage and Properties.
7. Miss Agnes Brady, Costumes.
8. Mrs. J. J. Davidson, Jr. — selection of Queen and Maids.
9. Mr. F. Vavaseur Mouton, history and biography.
10. Mrs. Harry L. Griffin — parade and ball.

THE ONE HUNDREDTH BIRTHDAY OF LAFAYETTE PARISH

By Edith Garland Dupré

This is thy birthday, then, O Lafayette!
One hundred years ago it was that thou
First saw the light of civic glory dawn
On these thy prairies fair and forest pure,
Since then have come within thy portals wide,
Peace, Justice, Truth, and Fair Democracy,
And walking hand in hand with even gait,
Behold thy daughters three who bear the names
of Art, of Music and of Drama too,
Now, having shown thy worth unto all men,
Thou movest with thy train in bright array
To take the place on high reserved for thee.
See where America in all her pride
Stands ready wreath in hand to deck thy brow.

BIOGRAPHIES AND GENEALOGIES

GUSTAVE AURELIEN BREAUX

Colonel Breaux represented the best traditions of the old French stock of Louisiana. "Any honor that the Bar Association or the people of the State of Louisiana could give Colonel Breaux was bestowed upon him;" says Daisy Breaux, his step-daughter, Mrs. Clarence C. Calhoun, in her autobiography.

Gustave Breaux, a native of Lafayette Parish, was born December 5, 1828. He was head of the law firm of Breaux, Fenner, and Hall of New Orleans. In Lafayette, Colonel Breaux's office was on Buchanan Street in the rear of the present Knights of Columbus Hall. He died in 1910. Emilie Locke was his first wife. There were three children: Locke, a man of influence in New Orleans; Gustave, of Louisville, Kentucky; and Nina, who married into the Ballard family, also of Louisville. The members of the Breaux family will long be remembered on the Southwestern campus as the donors of the Breaux Collection of valuable books in the Stephen Memorial Library.

In the Catholic Cemetery in Lafayette in the rear of the Cathedral, the graves of Colonel Breaux and his second wife, Josephine Marr, born at Port Dover, Canada, daughter of Reverend Joseph Marr and Catherine Mathews Lowe, lie side by side. She died on March 29, 1919 in her seventieth year. Inscribed on the marble are these lines:

"The memory of her rare charm, of her gracious gifts, of her beautiful and generous nature prove a benediction and an inspiration to those who knew her and the daughter who survives her."

JOHN GREIG — OAKBOURNE PLANTATION

Oakbourne plantation was originally owned by the Greigs whose name formerly had been Gregory. They were from Perth, Scotland. John Greig, born in 1831, first settled in Vermilionville on St. John Street, a merchant and a banker. He had the first private bank in that town. It was located in the rear of what is now the Edward Martin property. Later John Greig moved to the country where he had a plantation of 1100 acres, including much of the present Oakbourne.

He had five children:
1. Arthur Greig, married to Louisianese Scranton. They were the parents of John Greig.
2. Sidney Greig, married to Melissa Moss. Their son was Don Greig.
3. Duncan Greig, married to Emily Moss.
4. Robert Greig, the school teacher, married to Maggie Jamison.
5. Martha, married to Dr. Francis Stirling Mudd.

One of the first three Greigs who came over from Scotland, James Greig, died of Asiatic cholera. His slaves buried him in the Protestant burying ground. Before this Catholics and Protestants were buried together at the rear of the Catholic Church. The grave stones are still there. The plot where he was buried is now the Protestant Cemetery at the intersection of Pin Hook Road and College Avenue. It was "cut out" of the property of Basil Crow. The late Miss Fannie Webb who gave the author much of this information and who was a granddaughter of John Greig showed him her grandfather's certificate to practice law, issued in 1846 by the State of Louisiana. It was signed by F. X. Martin, N. A. Bullard, E. Simon, A. Morphy.

When Don Greig's grandfather died, Oakbourne was sold by his heirs to Colonel Gustave Aurelien Breaux of Scott, Louisiana. At his death it was bought by the Baldwin Lumber Company. At this company's dissolution it was purchased by Mr. John Cameron Nickerson and Mr. Leo Judice.

JEAN MOUTON'S FAMILY

Linked inseparably with the history of Lafayette is the name Mouton. As already stated, among the earliest settlers of Lafayette Parish were the Acadians Jean and Marin Mouton. Jean, having been born in Halifax, was the son of Salvador Mouton, an Acadian exile, who was living in St. James Parish about 1756 and engaged in tilling the soil. In the archives of the church of St. Martinville one learns that he and his wife, Anne Bastarache had migrated to Louisiana from Acadia. They died shortly thereafter leaving three young children, Marin, our Jean, who had been born in Halifax, and a daughter, Celeste. Jean came to be known as

"Chapeau Mouton" to distinguish him from his brother Marin who wore a homespun cap. Jean first came into notice as a boatman on the Wichita and Arkansas Rivers, and a trader with the Indians. Afterward he settled in the Parish of Attakapas, having acquired land on the west bank of Bayou Carencro, about two miles above the point where Louisiana highway 167 crosses the bayou. A part of his old home still stands there in the midst of a magnificent grove of live oaks and magnolias.

While living on Bayou Carencro, Jean, about the year 1783, married Marie Marthe Bordat. Marthe was the daughter of Dr. Antoine Bordat, ex-surgeon of the French army, then living in New Orleans, and the widow, Mrs. Marguerite Martin, who had been driven from Nova Scotia at the time of the expulsion. It is said that the widow Martin with her children had fled Grand Pré to the forests where, for ten days she subsisted on nuts and berries. Having lost all hope of ever returning to her home, which, in the meantime had been burned, together with all the crops, she, after almost insufferable hardships, finally reached St. Louis and from there at last found refuge in New Orleans. There she later married Dr. Bordat. Being the issue of this marriage, Marthe was thus half Acadian and half French. To her and Jean Mouton were born twelve children: Jean Baptiste (fils), Joseph, Francois, Charles, Don Louis (pere), Alexandre, Antoine Emile, Césaire, Marie, Adelaide, Marthe, and Celeste. From the eight sons of this marriage have descended most of that numerous group in Southwest Louisiana who boast of the proud name, Mouton.

During the frequent visits of Father Barriere to his parishioners in the Attakapas District between the years 1795 and 1804 we find him recording the names of those whose homes he visited. Several miles south of Bayou Carencro was Grand Prairie, the name given to the area in which the city of Lafayette is located. Father Barriére records that on one of his visits there he found the large planation of Jean Mouton "L'Oncle dit Chapeau." Just when Jean moved to this last location is not known, but by the time he laid out the village of Vermilionville in 1824, he had become the owner of vast lands, including most of the present city of Lafayette.

Left an orphan, and without any formal education, except what he had gained from the prairies, the bayous, the crafty Indians, and clever traders, he had to fight his own way to success. Though deprived of the benefits of a "formal education." he gave to his children the courage and determination to attain goals today deemed impossible. His wife, Marie Marthe Bordat brought into the home the culture and refinement of France which she imparted to the family of twelve children, and by them handed down to future generations.

Because Jean Mouton was the founder of Lafayette and the donor of land for church and court house, it seems only fitting that some recognition be given to those descendants of this union with Marthe Bordat, who have gained distinction and brought credit to the community, state, and nation. A list of such descendants, prepared by the late Judge Julian Mouton is most revealing.

Jean Mouton, Jr., son of Jean Mouton, was the first representative of Lafayette Parish in the Louisiana legislature. Alexandre Mouton, son of Jean was a member and speaker of the Louisiana House of Representatives in 1831, United States Senator in 1837, Governor of Louisiana in 1843, President of the Vigilance Committee in 1858, President of the Louisiana Secession Convention in 1861, and on two other occasions delegate to the Democratic National Nominating Convention.

Charles Homer Mouton, a grandson of Jean Mouton, was a district judge of Lafayette and Vermilion Parishes, and Lieutenant Governor of Louisiana in 1856. Eraste Mouton, a grandson of Jean was a district judge of Lafayette and Vermilion Parishes; Edward Mouton, grandson of Jean, was also a district judge of Lafayette and Vermilion Parishes; James D. Mouton, another grandson, was district judge of Iberia and St. Martin Parishes.

Orther C. Mouton, great grandson of Jean Mouton was a district judge of Lafayette and Vermilion Parishes; Julian Mouton, another great grandson of Jean was for many years a judge of the state court of appeals; Fernand Mouton, a great, great grandson was lieutenant governor in 1916. Another great great grandson, Marc Mouton was lieutenant governor in 1944; and great great grandson Robert L. Mouton was a congressman in 1937.

There are other descendants of Jean Mouton through the female line, not bearing the name Mouton, whose achievements have brought honor to the founder of Vermilionville. Felix Voorhies, whose mother was Cidalise Mouton, a granddaughter of Jean Mouton, was district judge of St. Martin and Iberia Parishes; and Albert Voorhies, a brother of Felix, was a justice of the Louisiana Supreme Court, and in 1866 lieutenant governor.

James D. Simon, whose mother was Laurence Mouton, is a great

great grandson of Jean; he served for several years as district judge in St. Martin, Iberia and St. Mary Parishes, and is presently an associate justice on the state supreme court. The late Paul Deballlon, whose father was a district judge for Lafayette and Vermilion Parishes and whose mother was Louise Mouton, was a great great grandson of Jean, and at the time of his death had served for several years as district judge for the parishes of Acadia, Lafayette and Vermilion. James Domengeaux, another great great grandson, was congressman from this district in 1942.

From the above record one concludes that every judicial position in the history of Louisiana, as well as most of the top political offices of the state have at some time been held by a descendant of Jean Mouton and Marie Marthe Bordat.

In the military annals Jean Mouton's descendants have also gained recognition. Alfred Mouton, son of Governor Mouton and grandson of Jean, attained the rank of general in the Confederate Army and lost his life in the battle of Mansfield. Ambrose and Eraste Mouton served as captains in the Confederate Army. In the same army Sosthene Mouton was a major and William Mouton a colonel. All were grandsons of Jean; and Robert L. Mouton, a great great grandson was a captain of Marines in World War I.

When the above data was submitted by the late Judge Julian Mouton he commented: "This shows that however humble the origin of an American citizen may be, he may rise to important offices, judicial, political or miltary in this republic, the greatest republic of ancient or modern times." He also remarked: "The descendants of the Mouton family should always be grateful to the people of this City of Lafayette, their parish and state; and they should be absolutely true and loyal always to the principles of democratic institutions."

FAMILY OF JEAN MOUTON

Jean Mouton (the first) born about 1687 came from France to Nova Scotia prior *to* or *in* 1711, married in church of Port Royal in Nova Scotia.

Jean Mouton (fils)
    Louis — 39 years old 1770
        1. Frederic Mouton — married Anastasie Cormier of St. James Parish

2. Sylvestre Mouton — married Josette Comeaux of St. Landry Parish 1791
3. Emeranthe Mouton

Salvador Mouton—married Anne Bastarache in Halifax— 35 years old in 1770

1. Celeste Mouton — married Jean Guilbeau — no children
2. Marin Mouton — born in Louisiana, St. James Parish, married Marie Lambert probably on the German coast of Louisiana

Jean Mouton — born in Halifax — married Marthe Bordat, daughter of Dr. Antoine Bordat, ex-surgeon of the French army, in St. Martinville Catholic Church in 1783

Jean Mouton's home in "Grand Prairie" large plantation home south of St. Pierre — now Carencro — from Record of Father Barriere 1795-1804 recording names of homes he had visited.

LINE OF DESCENT
OF THE
FAMILY OF JEAN MOUTON

Salvador Mouton married Anne Bastarache or rather Bastarêche; the issues of the marriage were: Marin, Jean and a daughter by the name of Celeste, who married Jean Guilbeau and who died without issue. They were married in 1783.

Jean Mouton married Marie Marthe Bordat; the issues of that marriage were: Jean Batiste, Joseph, Francois, Charles, Don Louis, Alexandre, Emile, Césaire, Marie, Adelaide, Martha, Celeste. His children were all married and the following is a short EXPOSE of their marriages and their issues.

NOTA: Salvador Mouton and Anna Bastarache were both from Acadia. Jean, their son was born at Halifax.

1. Jean Batiste Mouton was married to Angele Martin; the issues were: Sosthene, Edmond, and Cidalise.

a. Sosthene Mouton married twice, first to Eugenie Latiolais; the issues were: Jean Sosthene, Sidney, Elodie, Angélina, Zilia, Ismêne and Auguste, and then to Cêlestine Vavasseur; the issues of that marriage were: Edmond, Emile, Emma, Estelle and Benjamin.

b. Edmond Mouton married Eulalie Voorhies; the issuses were:

Horace Adolphe, Felicia, Alice, Edward E., James E., Cecilia and Edgard.

c. Cidalise Mouton married Cornélius Voorhies; the issues of that marriage were: Edgard E., Albert, Alfred, Martin, Felix, Louis, Charles, Cornelie and Amélie.

2. Joseph Mouton married Cidalise Arceneaux; the issues of that marriage were: Louis, Emelia, and Coralie.

3. Francois Mouton married Clemence Dugas; the issue of that marriage was Eugenie.

4. Charles Mouton married twice, first to Doralie Dugat; the issue of that marriage was one son, Armas; and then to Julie Latiolais; the issue were: C. Homer, Orthaire, Eraste, John, Nisida, Martha, Lizima, Ophelia, Euchariste, Elina and Eugenie.

5. Don Louis Mouton was married to Lolette Cormier; the issues of that marriage were: Don Louis, Arsene and Euphemie.

C. Homer Mouton married twice, first to Celimene Dupre; the issue were: C. Kossuth, Louise Charlotte, Marie Julie, Julien Jubertie, Antoine Emile, Andrew Herron, Orther, Eugenie J., and he married the second time Emerite Olivier; the issues were: C. Maurice, J. Homer, Marie Lucie, S. Philip, Jerome, F. Thomas, Jeanne Francoise and Marie Marguerite.

Eraste Mouton married Corinne Loualier; the issues of that marriage were: Jean Jules, Charles Leon, Mathilde, Amelie, Pauline, Monique, Charles, Corinne, Emma, Joseph and Marthe.

Ophelia Mouton married Louis J. Mouton; the issues were: Clara, Cecile, Euhariste, Elina, Eugenie and Carmelite.

Lizima Mouton married William Mouton; the issue were: Césaire, Clarisse, Henriette and William.

Martha Mouton married Edgard Bienvenu; no issue.

Nisida Mouton married Timecourt Bienvenu; no issue.

6. Alexandre Mouton was married twice, first to Zilia Rousseau; the issues were: Jean Jacques Alex Alfred, Mathilde, Henriette Odeide, Cecilia Acadie; he then married the second time to Emma K. Gardner; the issues were: Anna Eliza, Charles Alexandre, Paul Joseph Julian, Marie, George Clinton and William Rufus King.

Jean Sothene Mouton married Henriette Odeide Mouton; the

issues were: Alexandre, Bordat, Olivier, Fred, Frank, Alida, Alice, Alfred, Sidney, Coralie, Aimeé and Rousseau.

Emile Mouton married Gadrate Rousseau; the issues were: Alcide, Rousseau, Ignace, Ambroise, Jean Jacques and Gadrate.

Césaire Mouton was married to Clarisse Guidry; only one son was born of that marriage, William.

Marie Mouton was married to Pierre Potier; the issues were: Adelaide, Pierre and Louis.

Adelaide Mouton was married twice, first to Joseph Malcheaux, and the second time, to Alexandre Dugat; she died without issue.

Celeste Mouton married to Joseph Guidry; the issues were: David, Thelismar, Stanislas, Felix, Horace, John and Marthe.

Marguerite Martin emigrated to Louisiana from the French colony of Acadia, now Nova Scotia, toward 1760. She was then the widow of Rene Robichot. She brought with her two daughters: Madeline who married J. Charles Hebert, and Genevieve who married Armand Dugat. She settled in the county of Attakapas and on the 31st of October 1767 she was married to Antoine Bordat, a surgeon; she had three daughters: Marie Marthe, who married Jean Mouton; Scholastie, who married Joseph Castille; and Modeste, who married David Guidry.

Madeline, wife of J. Charles Hebert had: Narcisse, Ursin, Valmont and two daughters, one married J. Guidry, the other Batiste A. Guidry.

Genevieve, wife of Armand Guidry had: Jean, Celestin, Maximilien and a daughter who married Pierre Cormier.

Scholastie, wife of Joseph Castille had: Joseph, Gervais, Zenon, Portalis, Emile and three daughters: one who married Jean Thibodeaux, one Duhamel, and afterwards Paul Briant, and one Derneville DeBlanc.

Modeste Bordat, who married David Guidry had five sons: Louis, Theville, Onezime, Narcisse, Joseph; and five daughters: Arsene, Emilie, Marcelite, Clarisse and Azelie.

Angele Martin, wife of Jean Baptiste Mouton, was the daughter of Petit Claude Martin and Marie Babin.

Joseph Mouton married Cidalise Arceneaux, daughter of Louis Arceneaux.

CONSTANTIN LIVERY STABLE

Built about 1875 by Ernest Constantin the stable faced the courthouse at the south corner of West Main and Buchanan.

Ernest Constantin, born in 1846, was the son of John Constantin and A. Richard, both natives of Lafayette.

John Constantin, a successful business man and stock raiser, was the owner of 300 acres in the parish besides much real estate in the town. He died in 1877.

Ernest Constantin in 1866 married Alice Begneaud who died in 1868 leaving a daughter, Marie, who married Couret. In 1870 Ernest married Eugenie Billeaud, who built a home at the southwest corner of Jefferson Street and West Main, which later and for many years was to be occupied by the Adam Judices. The lumber used in its construction was from the demolished Begneaud saloon.

Eugenie Billeaud's niece and adopted daughter, Aimeé Herbert, was married to Adam Judice of St. Martinville. His grandfather, Alceé Judice, established a private school near the Evangeline Oak in St. Martinville in which he used a French Grammar he had written.

Mr. Adam Judice's son was a major in the Chemical department of World War II.

Office of the Justice of the Peace built about 1880 was on the east side of Buchanan Street facing South Main. At the time of this picture, Theodore Alexander McFaddin, 1842-1916, the father of "Mr. Bob" McFaddin, was the Justice of the Peace. He was married to Sarah Eugenia Patterson, both of Greene County, Alabama.

Galbert Bienvenu and "Fils" (Abraham) Hirsch were his deputies. "Bidon (G. A.) Martin succeeded T. A. McFaddin who had willed the former his law library. The second from the end on right side is Bruce Martin, son of Martial Martin and grandson of Zepherin Martin.

Below — Results of a deer hunt at Avoca Island in 1925. Standing by is the late Earl S. Barnett, leader of the hunting party.

built 1868, was located at the corner of North Washington and West Vermilion Streets. John O. Mouton, born in 1846 on his father's plantation two miles from Lafayette, was the son of Onezime Mouton and Nathalie Dugat, a grandson of Jean and Marie Marthe Dugat. After attending St. Charles College in Grand Coteau, he enlisted in the 18th Regiment of the Confederate Army under Captain Alcibiades de Blanc of St. Martinville, serving as Major. He was mayor for four years, including the period of the yellow fever epidemic of 1878. An extensive property owner, John O. Mouton was successful in business enterprises. In 1883 he opened a store on Lincoln Avenue (now Jefferson Avenue "across the track") with N. P. Moss the manager. He married Alvina Boudreaux of Opelousas who died in 1925. Walter Mouton and Dr. J. Franklin Mouton were their two sons. In the picture Mrs. John O. Mouton is standing by the old hitching post. "Tine", (Philomine), her maid, on the gallery, lived with the family for many years.

Benjamin Falk's "General Merchandise" Store on the west side of South Washington Street between West Vermilion and Convent Street was built by its first owner, William Bendel, about 1865. William Bendel, born about 1836, was the husband of Mary Plonsky, the daughter of Leon Plonsky from Germany. Sam, Fannie, Issac, Rose, Henri and Louise were their children; Henri Bendel becoming a famous coutourier and designer. Mary Plonsky's second husband was Benjamin Falk, an employee of William Bendel. Their only child was Emma. "Falk's Opera House" was on the upper floor of the store — an auditorium for traveling troops of actors, local academic productions and entertainments. Charles Tolson, a relative of Dr. John Tolson, sang the part of Faust when a travelling troop produced the opera there about 1892.

The Lafayette Gazette Office, 1895. Founded by Homer Mouton, it was published first from the hall of the Homer Bailey School. The press was then moved to the second floor of Gus Lacoste's Hardware Store, now the Lafayette Hardware Store at the corner of 101 West Vermilion and Buchanan. Following this, the Gazette's next location was at 107 West Vermilion, the present offices of the new Lafayette Building and Loan Association. Graser's Tin Shop was on one side of the shop and the Telegraph Office of Miss Mary Littel on the other. Homer Mouton, born in 1870, died in 1904 of yellow fever. Then the offices were in the Deffez Building about where 416 Jefferson Street now is.

Below — A bakery, built about 1885, was on the N.E. corner of Jefferson and East Main opposite the new Post Office. Israel Falk, who was married to a Miss Monnier, was the original owner of this store. He was the brother of Benjamin Falk, a photographer.

Francois Mouton married Clemence Dugat, daughter of Pierre Dugat.

Charles Mouton married the first time, Doralie Dugat, daughter of Louis Dugat of Fausse Pointe; the second time Julie Latiolais, daughter of Joseph Latiolais.

Don Louis Mouton married Lolette Cormier, daughter of Jean Batiste Cormier and Pauline Martin.

Emile Mouton married Gadrate Rousseau, daughter of J. J. Rousseau and Celeste Dupre.

Césaire Mouton married Clarisse Guidry, daughter of David Guidry and Modeste Bordat.

(Note — *The above was presented to Alexandre Mouton by the late Felix Voorhies*)

ANDRE MARTIN — MAGNOLIA PLANTATION

Magnolia Plantation, the plantation of Andre Valerien Martin who had married Emelie Guidry, was adjacent to Oakbourne. Mr. Martin had acquired much of this land from a Mr. Sorrel who had come from France.

Clarisse was their daughter. She was married first to Rousseau Mouton, the son of Antoine Emile Mouton. Her second marriage was to William Campbell whose father was John Campbell of Scotland. At the time of her inheritance Magnolia Plantation consisted of a thousand acres.

De La Salle Normal School, the Immaculata Seminary and the Carmelite Monastery occupy the land which was formerly a part of Magnolia Plantation.

GOVERNOR ALEXANDRE MOUTON

Alexandre Mouton, the ninth Governor of the State of Louisiana and the first member of the Democratic party who occupied her executive chair — was born 1804, in Attakapas, on Bayou Carencro, the dividing line between that county and the county of Opelousas, at a place about ten miles from the present town of Vermilionville. He was graduated from Georgetown College, D. C. In 1825 young Mouton practiced law in partnership with Edward

Simon. In 1826, he served for three consecutive terms in the House of Representatives of the State Legislature, being Speaker of that body for two sessions.

The burning of the State House in New Orleans in 1828 — which at that time stood at the corner of Toulouse and Old Levee Streets — caused the Legislature during the remainder of that year's session and presumably in 1929, to meet at the old Ursuline Convent. The Legislature of 1830 sat at Donaldsonville.

In 1928, 1832, 1836, Alexander Mouton was also on the electoral ticket during the Presidential campaigns of 1828, 1932, 1836. In 1837, he was elected by the State Legislature to fill the unexpired term of Judge Porter in the U. S. Senate and was also chosen as his successor for the long term (six year). In 1843 he was elected Governor.

Leaving the executive chair, Governor Mouton again retired to private life, participating but very little in politics.

In 1852 he was chairman of the Great Southwestern Railroad Convention; he was also a delegate to the National Convention held at Cincinnati in 1856.

In 1858 he was selected President of the Vigilance Committee of the Attakapas country, which was organized to protect that section from the depredations of organized bands of marauders who set the laws at defiance.

In 1860 Alexander Mouton was a delegate to the National Convention held at Charleston, South Carolina, for the President of the United States. In 1861 he was the President of the Secession Convention in Baton Rouge which may be said to have terminated his public career, although he was a candidate for the Senate of the Confederate Congress afterwards.

Though Governor Mouton now evidently feels the weight of years, he still bears the indications that he has been, not only mentally but physically a remarkable man. Tall and commanding in figure, every feature of his countenance, especially his eyes (which are very attractive and fascinating) plainly expressed great courage and resolution; dignified and courteous in his manners, he plainly expressed great courage and resolution.

Governor Mouton was married in 1826 to Miss Zelia Rousseau, the grand-daughter of Governor Jacques Dupré, the richest stock-raiser in the county of Opelousas. Their children were Jean Jacques, Alexandre Alfred (Gen. Alfred Mouton) Mathilde, Henriette, Odeide, Cecilia, and 'Arcadie'. After the death of his first wife, the Governor married (while he was a senator) in Washington City in January 1842 Miss Emma Kitchell Gardner, daughter of Colonel Charles K. Gardner, an officer of the United States Army. The children of his second marriage were Anna Eliza, Charles Alexandre, Paul Joseph Julian, Marie, George Clinton, William Rufus King.

(From "Louisiana Biographies" dedicated to A. A. Ulman, Esq. of Bay St. Louis, Miss.)

THE VOORHIES FAMILY IN LOUISIANA

"The tradition in the Voorhies family in Louisiana is that our ancestor Cornelius Voorhies, Sr. was born in Kentucky." The urge of adventure caused him to migrate to the Parish of St. Landry where he met and married Aimée Gradenigo whose ancestors were from Venice, Italy. There were nine children. Among them was Cornelius, Jr. born in 1804. He was married to Cidalise Mouton in 1826—a direct descendant of Salvador Mouton, an exile who migrated from Nova Scotia in Louisiana in 1756. Cornelius became Justice of the Supreme Court in 1854, dying in 1859. Their children were Edgar, Albert, Alfred, Martin, Felix, Marie Cornelia, Marie Amelie, Charles, and Louis Voorhies.

Of these Albert, born in 1829 and Felix, 1939, gained the greater prominence.

Felix Voorhies, the author of "Acadian Reminiscences," was a brilliant lawyer. He was educated at St. Charles College, Grand Coteau. In 1861 he enlisted in the Confederate service. In 1874 he served in the state legislature, serving too as district judge of both St. Martin and Iberia Parishes for eight years. He devoted his leisure time to literature. In 1857 he was married to Modeste Potier, daughter of Charles Potier and Marcellite Broussard. The other son of Cornelius Voorhies, Jr. who gained wide prominence was Albert Voorhies. After studying at St. Charles College he subsequently went to Kentucky to study law. At that time his father was serving on the Louisiana Supreme bench. On his father's death in 1859 Albert succeeded him in office when only thirty, the youngest judge over to sit on that tribunal. Immediately after the war Albert Voorhies was elected Lieutenant Governor of the State. He prepared a revision of the Civil Code of Louisiana.

He died on January 20, 1913. Albert Voorhies was married to Leontine Durand, daughter of Charles Durand and Amelie le Blanc.

(Courtesy of Mr. Bennett Voorhies)

THE CROW—GIRARD FAMILIES

Among the Huguenots that fled France to escape religious persecution in the early nineteenth century were three Girard brothers. Having sailed from Bordeaux to North America their ship was wrecked off the coast of Cuba, only two surviving, Stephen and Michel Eloi. Stephen went to Philadelphia where he amassed a fortune in shipping. He never married and, leaving no direct heirs, is said to have left his fortune toward the establishment of Girard College.

The third brother Michel Eloi came to Vermilionville where he met Anastasie Mouton, daughter of Frederic Mouton, whom he married. With his bride he returned to France where he continued to live near Bordeaux. A son of this marriage, a second Michel Eloi, returned to Vermilionville in the land of his mother. There he studied law in the office of Basil Catryll Crow, and soon married Maxime Crow, daughter of his sponsor, who gave the young couple the land now embraced in the Girard and Elmhurst subdivisions of Lafayette. They built their home at the corner of College Avenue and Cherry Street, now occupied by the home of the late Ralph Voorhies. The children of this marriage were Percy M., Crow, Callie, and Felix E. Girard. Michel Eloi became widely known in legal circles and was a charter member of the Masonic Lodge in Vermilionville, serving as Grand Master of all the lodges in Louisiana.

Basil Crow was born in Kentucky in 1800. As a youth he heard the soldiers, returning from the Battle of New Orleans in 1815, give glowing descriptions of the Attakapas country. Desiring to settle there he asked his father for his share of the family estate. His wish was granted in gold. On his way to Louisiana he fell in with a band of Crow Indians bound for that state. Leaving the Indians at Alexandria, while they went on to the shell mounds at Lake Arthur, he followed the streams, including Bayou Têche, to Brashear City (now Morgan City). There he met a Miss Brashear, daughter of the founder of that settlement, and married her. The young couple then settled in Lafayette where he practiced law. In time he acquired most of the land on both sides of the Pin Hook Road between the Protestant Cemetery and the bridge. The cemetery was carved out of his land. His home stood on the north side of the road across from the Town House Motel. Basil Crow died in 1872 having become one of the prominent men of the Opelousas and Attakapas Districts.

GENERAL ALEXANDRE ETIENNE DeCLOUET

General Alexandre Etienne De Clouet was a descendant of one of the oldest and best families in Louisiana. His great grandfather, Alexandre de Clouet de Piedre, was born at Coteau-Canibresis, parish of St. Martin, France about the middle of the eighteenth century and emigrated to Louisiana where he married Louise de Favrot, 1771.

His son, Joseph Alexandre de Clouet, served under General Jackson at the Battle of New Orleans — a colonel. He left an only son, Etienne Chevalier de Clouet, who married Aspasie Fuselier, the daughter of Agricole Fuselier at one time commandant of the Poste des Attakapas. General de Clouet was born in 1812. Of his death the following account was taken from one of the Lafayette papers at that time — about 1890.

"Death of General de Clouet

It is with a reluctant hand that I have to chronicle the death of one of our esteemed and veteran citizens General Alexandre Etienne de Clouet, who fell a victim to crimson death at his country home, within the poetic woods of Lafayette, on the banks of St. Clair Bayou on Thursday, June 26th, 1890. His remains were laid away in the land of Evangeline (St. Martinville) on the banks of the beautiful and romantic Teche, by the gentle hands of the pallbearers; Major Jean Sosthene Mouton, Captain J. Edmond Mouton, Judge Conrad de Baillon of Lafayette, and Messrs. Louis Grevenberg, Auguste Duchamps, Charles Delhommer of St. Martinville; these were followed by the family and acquaintances to his last resting place.

By the death of the general, the whole parish is in mourning;

for his honor and integrity as a gentleman and law-abiding citizen has never been questioned."

(From a newspaper of the town of Lafayette, 1890.)

HONORABLE CHARLES HOMER MOUTON

"Hon. Charles Homer Mouton died at the residence of his daughter, Mrs. Conrad Debaillon in this city Saturday morning and was buried from St. John's Catholic Church at 11 o'clock yesterday morning. . . . . The large concourse of friends and relatives that followed him to his last resting place was a silent tribute to a long life well spent." *(From a Lafayette newspaper — March 18, 1912)*

Mr. Mouton was born in 1823. He was the son of Charles Mouton and Julie Latiolais and a grandson of Jean Mouton. He was a nephew of Governor Mouton and a first cousin of General Alfred Mouton. He received his education in private schools and at St. Charles College, where it is said the records show he was the first student matriculated at that institution. He read law under Judge Cornelius Voorhies of St. Martinville. He was appointed by the governor as district attorney of that judicial district composed of the Parishes of Lafayette, St. Landry and Calcasieu, covering that vast territory on horseback, for at that time there were no railroads. Subsequently he was elected a state senator. In 1846 he was elected Lieutenant Governor as the running mate of Governor Wickliffe. He was next elected to the office of district judge. He served as such during the war until the appeal for volunteers was made when he closed his court and reported to General Alfred Mouton for duty at the battle of Bisland, becoming aide-de-camp to General Mouton. In reconstruction days he headed the White League Movement in this parish.

In 1878 he moved to the parish of St. Martin and was elected district attorney for the parishes of St. Martin and Iberia. At the time of his death he was attorney for the Lafayette Parish police jury.

Mr. Mouton was married in 1848 to Miss Célémine Dupré, a granddaughter of Governor Dupré. By this marriage were Kossuth Mouton; Louise Mouton, wife of Judge Conrad Debaillon; Julie, wife of F. H. Thompson; Emile Mouton; Major Andrew Mouton of

Eunice; Judge Orther C. Mouton; Judge Julian Mouton of the Court of Appeals; and Josephine Eugénie Mouton, wife of J. C. Buchanan.

In 1867 he was married to Miss Emerite Olivier of St. Martinville. There were the following children: C. Maurice, J. Homer, Lucie, Philip S., Jerome, Frank T., and Marie.

JUDGE WILLIAM CAMPBELL (1853-1928)

William Campbell, the father of Judge Campbell, came over from Scotland with his father John. He was a sugar planter and was in partnership with Zepherin Doucet owning a store at 405 W. Main across the street from the present location of the First National Funeral Home. Mr. Zepherin Doucet's daughter, Leontine, married Frank Gardner Mouton and they were the parents of Lieutenant Governor Dr. Marc M. Mouton. Judge William Campbell, the son of the first William Campbell, was married first to Laura Couret then to Ellen Eastin. The Eastins were from Virginia, where Herbert had been on the staff of Andrew Jackson.

Judge Campbell was very prominent in civic affairs having held various offices — sheriff, mayor, district attorney. He was the district judge for the parishes of Lafayette, Acadia and Vermilion at the time of his death. Alice, his daughter, was married to Lieutenant Governor Dr. Marc M. Mouton.

ALEXANDRE MOUTON

To my son Alex;
My son, be this thy simple plan:
Serve God and love thy brother man;
Forget not in temptation's hour,
That sin lends sorrow double power;
Count life a stage upon thy way
And follow conscience come what may;
Alike with Heaven and earth sincere,
With hand, and brow, and bosom clear,
Fear God — and know no other fear.

This verse was written in exquisite script in the French Bible his mother presented to him upon his leaving his home, Beau

Sejour on Bayou Vermilion, to seek his fortune. Alexandre Mouton, born in 1853, author of the unpublished memoirs frequently quoted herein, was the eldest grandson and namesake of Governor Mouton. His long and eventful life was dominated by the spirit of these beautiful lines.

At the age of thirteen Alexandre went to New Orleans where he completed his studies in mechanical engineering. In 1876, at the time of the Centennial Exposition he was in Philadelphia building locomotives for the Pennsylvania Central Railroad. A few years later he was called to New Orleans to rebuild the United States Mint. In 1882 the Republic of Mexico employed him to build the Mexican mint in the City of Mexico. During his stay there he occupied a suite in the Royal Palace of Chapultepec while he constructed the mint in a wing of that famous monument. On completion of the mint, he supervised the coinage of one hundred ninety million pieces of money; gold, silver, and copper. While residing in the palace, he was presented with a number of historical relics which had been stored in the royal palace, among which was the opera hat of Maximillian. Because of his admiration of Maximillian, Mr. Mouton placed an extremely high value upon it. After completing his work at the mint, he served for some time as the superintendent of waterworks for the entire Republic of Mexico, an assignment that took him to every city and village in that country.

Upon his return to New Orleans in 1887, Mr. Mouton was engaged for several years as chief engineer in the New Orleans mint where he supervised the coinage. After a few years there he became interested in the modernization of sugar factories which were then being transformed from the open kettle process of evaporation to that of the vacuum pan. In this capacity he supervised the rebuilding of many of the older factories and the construction of new ones throughout the sugar bowl of Louisiana. In Lafayette he built his own new process syrup mill, producing a syrup which won first prize and a gold medal at the Louisiana Purchase Exposition in St. Louis. At the age of seventy-three he went to Ecuador under contract to supervise the building of a sugar factory in that country on the estate of Don Carlos Lynch. The Lynch estate, eighty-four miles square, was forty miles inland from Guayaquil. The factory cost over a million dollars and required over a year to build.

After his return from Ecuador Mr. Mouton used the leisure of his later years in wood carving. During the last year of his illness President Woodrow Wilson used a carved cane presented to him by Mr. Mouton.

In 1936, Dean Tevis, feature writer for the Beaumont Enterprise, interviewed Mr. Mouton and summed up the interview in these words:

"With a startling ability to etch clearly with words, he had drawn me across the years of eight decades — Portfiro Diaz — his grandfather Senator Mouton, Conklin, Blaine, Arthur, Hayes, and many another. His life was a long pageant of colorful events which had occurred from far Ecuador to Washington, D. C."

Alexandre Mouton was married in 1881 to Marie Coppens, daughter of General Coppens of Virginia. There were two sons born in Mexico City; Gaston Alexandre and Ralph Canedo, named for General E. Stanislaw Canedo, member of the Mexican Congress and a close friend of Mr. Mouton.

His first wife having died in Mexico in September, 1884 Alexandre Mouton married in 1888 Helen Barker Baillio, daughter of Gervais Baillio of Rosalie Plantation, Rapides Parish, and Elizabeth Morgan of Louisville, Kentucky; and a grandniece of Thomas Overton Moore, Civil War Governor of Louisiana. The grandfather of Gervais Baillio, Pierre Baillio, had come with his brothers from France to this country to settle on their land grant in Rapides Parish.

Of the two sons of Pierre Baillio, Harvard educated Gervais and Leonard; Gervais, married to Rebecca Leonard, originally from Massachusetts, was to become the father of the second Gervais. This second Gervais, while a student at Bardstown, Kentucky, met and married Elizabeth Morgan. Helen Barker Baillio was a daughter of this union.

By this marriage there were two daughters: Lucile Meredith Mouton who married in 1914 Harry Lewis Grifin of Clarksburg, West Virginia, later to become the first dean of the College of Liberal Arts of Southwestern Louisiana Institute, Lafayette, Louisiana; and Helen Muriel Mouton married in 1918 to a captain of the 57th Infantry U.S.A., Charles Wesley Ogden, son of Judge Charles Wesley Ogden of San Antonio, Texas, and in 1935 to Herbert Stanford Landell of Philadelphia, Pennsylvania.

DR. EDWIN LEWIS STEPHENS (1872-1938)

Dr. Stephens was born at Stephens Mill near Natchitoches, Louisiana, the son of Joseph Henry Stephens and Isabella Caroline Whitfield. In 1902 he married Beverly Randolph of New Orleans. Of this union were born three daughters, Beverly, now Mrs. Frederick Hard of Claremont, California; Caro, now Mrs. Crafton Harris of London; and Marjorie, now Mrs. Fritz Jochem of Alexandria, Virginia.

After receiving his elementary education in private schools he entered Keachi College in 1883 from which he was graduated in 1887. Having taken business courses during summer terms and learned telegraphy he interrupted his education to become a telegraph operator. In the fall of 1889, however, his father sent for him to come home to enter the State University at Baton Rouge. In order to validate his previous studies he successfully passed an entrance examination which admitted him to the sophomore class. As a cadet he attained the rank of first lieutenant and served as adjutant and secretary to the commandant. With the highest academic rank during the junior and senior years he received his B.A. degree from the university in 1892.

During the summer after his graduation he was principal of the public school at Provencal, Louisiana. That fall he accepted a position to teach at the Normal School at Natchitoches. While at the Normal he attended summer sessions at the Cook County Normal School, Rockford College and Harvard University. In 1896 he was appointed to the Helen G. Gould scholarship for two years at New York University from which he received the degree, Doctor of Pedagogy in 1899. In January 1900, while he was teaching Physics and Chemistry in the Boys' High School in New Orleans, he was elected first President of Southwestern Louisiana Industrial Institute.

By training and experience President Stephens was well equipped to administer the newly created Institute. At the very beginning he prepared a design for its future development. Patiently and intelligently he implemented his plan with the result that the school he started with sixth grade students became in 1921 a full four-year standard college granting the baccalaureate degree. Under his continued inspired and skillful guidance it soon thereafter became a fully accredited college with a curriculum, faculty and student body that gave it a high rank among colleges and universities of the United States.

Besides creating the design for a great college President Stephens, in 1935, gained international fame by founding a Society of Live Oaks. All members are trees. Each tree has a history and a name; each tree has a human guardian with power of attorney who protects it from whitewash and billposters. Members must be over one hundred years old and pay dues of twenty-five acorns each year at Christmas time. These acorns are planted in a plot on Southwestern's horticulture farm and the seedlings are distributed to alumni and lovers of trees. The president is the Locke Breaux Live Oak near Hahnville, Louisiana. In 1945 there were 119 members. The society's records are now kept in the library of the Louisiana State Museum.

JEFFERSON CAFFERY

In June, 1952, the Senate of Louisiana passed Resolution No. 18, entitled "A Resolution to honor Ambassador Jefferson Caffery, a Native of Louisiana, now Ambassador to Egypt and Dean of American Diplomats, reading: ". . . . Be it Resolved; That this Senate send Ambassador Jefferson Caffery a message conveying our heartfelt appreciation for the exemplary work he is doing in the field of international relations. . . ."

The person honored by the above resolution was born in Lafayette December 1, 1886, the son of Charles Duval and Mary Catherine (Parkerson) Caffery. There was one brother, James Parkerson, now deceased, and a sister Bessie, still living in Lafayette. On November 20, 1937 Mr. Caffery was married to Gertrude McCarthy.

After his graduation from Tulane University Mr. Caffery was admitted to the Bar of Louisiana in 1909. Two years later he began his diplomatic career as Secretary to the United States Legation at Caracas, Venezuela. Thereafter his rise in the service came rapidly. In 1913 after being assigned to the State Department, he was appointed Secretary of the Legation in Stockholm. In 1916 as Secretary to the Legation at Teheran, Persia, he was placed in charge of Turkish, German, British, and Italian interests in that country. Having been assigned to Paris in 1917 during and following World War I he represented the Department of State in many international conferences, heading the American Delegation to the International Conference at London in 1918. During the Paris Peace Conference of 1919 he had charge of protocol details for President Wilson during his attendance at the conference. In September of 1919, he was detailed to the Department of State to make travel and entertainment arrangements for the King and Queen of Belgium and the Prince of Wales during their visits to the United States.

On December 20, 1919 Mr. Caffery was advanced in rank and assigned Counsellor of the United States Embassy at Madrid, Spain. During the next five years he was counsellor of Embassies in Tokyo and Berlin and Charge d'Affairs in Athens, Greece. In Athens he cooperated with the Greek government and American Red Cross in assisting Greek refugees from Asia Minor in 1922. In Japan he was Chairman of American Red Cross relief activities in connection with the destructive earthquake of 1923.

On January 7, 1926 he received the reward coveted by all career men in the diplomatic service: Appointment to El Salvador with the rank of Envoy Extraordinary and Minister Plenipotentiary. During the next few years, he was given many assignments of honor and trust: 1930 with rank of Ambassador he represented President Hoover at the inauguration of President Olaya Herrera of Columbia; with similar rank he represented the president at the inauguration of the President of Cuba in 1936. During 1933 he served as Assistant Secretary of State. In 1933 he was assigned to Havana, Cuba as the personal representative of President Franklin D. Roosevelt with the rank of Ambassador, becoming Ambassador to that country the following year. His next assignment was Ambassador to Brazil in 1937. After the reconquest of France in the World War, he represented the United States with the personal rank of Ambassador to the de facto French Authority at Paris in 1944, becoming the regularly appointed Ambassador the same year. On December 16, 1948 he became Ambassador to Egypt, a position he held until his retirement February 28, 1955, having served as chief of mission for over twenty-nine years.

In addition to his duties as an officer in the diplomatic service Mr. Caffery has represented his country in many other capacities. In 1933 he was Assistant Secretary of State. With the rank of Ambassador, he has represented several presidents at the inauguration of other heads of states. As a representative of the United States he signed Peace Treaties with Italy, Hungary, Roumania, and Bulgaria in Paris at the end of World War II. In 1950 and 1953 he presided over two conferences at Cairo on problems of the Middle East. For the United States since 1926, he has signed more than forty additional treaties and international agreements with foreign countries. In 1948 he was Acting Deputy United States representative on the United National Security Council.

In recognition of his distinguished services to his country Mr. Caffery has been the recipient of many honors. He is a member of the Foreign Service Association and Sons of the American Revolution. In 1950 he received the State Department's Distinguished Service Award. Among academic honors are: LL.D. from Catholic University of America, 1941; Ph.D. (honorary) University of Brazil, 1943; LL.D., University of Lyon, France, 1947; LL.D., Seattle University, Seattle, Washington; Doctor of Juridical Science, Holy Cross College, Worcester, Massachusetts; Catholic Action Medal 1944; Bellarmine Medal from Bellarmine College, Louisville, Kentucky; the President's Medal from Cansius College, Buffalo, New York; and the Laetare Medal from the University of Notre Dame, Indiana.

Other honors include: Member of the Brazilian Bar Association, 1940; Medal of the City of Metz, France, 1947; Croyen d'honneur of Dijon, France, 1947; of Fontaineblue, 1948; and of Ville d'Estaing, 1949. While in Cairo, Egypt, he was made Honorary Member of the Bedouin Howeitat Tribe of Jordan, Egypt and Saudi Arabia, 1950; and of Bedouin Basil Tribe of Fayoum, Egypt, 1952.

Mr. Caffery is now living in Rome. However he is in constant touch with the American Embassy there. Since his retirement he has been called upon to represent President Eisenhower at the inauguration of the Pakistan Republic and its first President, Karachi. In 1956 he was consultant to the United States Special Committee to study Foreign Aid Programs in France, Italy, Spain, Portugal, and the United Kingdom. He has been recently appointed a private Chamberlain to the Pope and made a Knight of Malta.

REVEREND CHARLES BURTON MOUTON

Reverend Charles Burton Mouton, J.C.D., son of F. Xavier Mouton and Mildred Louise Bechet, born on June 5, 1926.

Ordained priest June 11, 1949 and received his Doctorate in

Theology from the Angelicum in Rome in 1951. He received his Doctorate in Canon Law from the Lateran University, J.C.D. in Rome in 1957 and completed a two-year course in Diplomacy at the Pontifical Ecclesiastical Academy in Rome in June 1958.

He served for several months at the Vatican in the English Department of the Secretariat of State during the Pontificate of the late Pope Pius XII.

Father Mouton, who has been for some time past attaché at the Apostolic Internunciature in New Delhi, India, has recently received from the Holy Father the distinguished appointment as Papal Chamberlin with the title Very Reverend Monsignor. Monsignor Mouton is now Secretary at the Apostolic Internunciature.

CONFEDERATE VETERANS

Genealogical data of the Confederate veterans who were photographed at the plantation home of Major Jean Sosthene Mouton, Beau Séjour on Vermilion, in 1888. (See illustration)

N.B. As complete as possible from available records.

Seated, left to right:

JUDGE ALLEN

CHRISTIAN STEINER

Christian Steiner, 1822-1908
  married Caroline Campbell, 1839-1923

Children
1. Christine married John Whittington, Alcide Alleman
2. Agnes married Joe Sellers
3. Caroline married Aculie Hernandez
4. Verna married Albert Hernandez
5. Loretta married Marcellus Verot
6. Effie married Joe Rogers; Joe Verhalg—Holland
7. Franklin married Margaret Sellers
8. Wilhelm married Margaret David
9. Leonce married Cecile Hernandez
Christian Birg—Alice Nugent, an adopted nephew.

WILLIAM CLEGG

William Clegg, Macksville, N. C., 1842-1916
  Mary E. Collins, Raleigh, N. C., 1839

Children
William Clegg, Jr., 1868 m. Helen Eugenia Gifford
Baxter Clegg, 1869, m. Louise Torian Givens

Charles Judson Clegg, 1871-1882
Collins Clegg, 1872-1873
Oliver Clegg, 1874-1875
Maury Clegg, 1875
Philip Clegg, 1881, m. Louise Alma Wilson

Mr. Ware
Pierre Bernard

One daughter Felicien, married Edras Breaux in Carencro.

Martial Martin

Mother, Caroline Daigle, 1807-1902.
Father, Charles Zepherin Martin, 1802-1863.
Grandparents, Andre Martin and Gertrude Sonnier, who had one of the first land grants.
First wife, Nydia Taylor, died during Civil War. One son, Bruce Martin, died 1920.
Second marriage, Byna Harmon.

Children

Annette, married Maurice Francez
Elizabeth, married Philobert Broussard
Katharine, married Joseph P. Arceneaux
Marie, married John Chiasson
Felix Riggs, married Celemene Breaux
Fernest, married Cecile Breaux
Lena, married Benjamin Fontenot
Sophie Martin, died at nineteen years of age.

Jean Sosthene Mouton

Jean Sosthene Mouton, 1824-1896.
Henriette Odeide Mouton, 1834-1912.
"Married on the plantation of her father on the 21st of January, 1852, by the Rev. A. D. Mégret, cure of the parish of Lafayette."

Children

1. Alexandre married Helen Baillio
2. Antoine Bordat not married
3. Charles Olivier married Mathilde Mouton, Leonie Labasse
4. Frederic married Martha de Blanc, Marie Barry
5. Alida "died on our plantation—11 yrs."
6. Frank Gardner married Leontine Doucet
7. Alice married Edward G. Voorhies
8. Alfred married Alix Judice
9. Sidney married Gadrat Mouton
10. Coralie not married
11. Marie Aimee "Entered religious order of Sacred Heart"
12. Rousseau Valerien

Sidney Greig (brother Arthur Greig)
Son of John Greig

Sidney Greig, 1838-1920.
Married   1. Melissa Moss
               2. Miss Landry from Broussard

Children

1. Helen — Mrs. Romero
2. Louise

3. Adelaide — Mrs. Romero
4. Burt
5. Harry
6. Don — Rosaline Landry — Span. American War 1874-1956

WILLIAM B. TORIAN

William B. Torian — Halifax County, Virginia (in cavalry — Civil War) 1939-1926.
Married to Livinia Redding — 1844-1931.

<table>
<tr><td colspan="3">Children</td></tr>
<tr><td>1. Walter Scott</td><td>married</td><td>Daisy Love</td></tr>
<tr><td>2. Thomas Wilson</td><td></td><td>Belle Love</td></tr>
<tr><td>3. Mattie Glenn</td><td></td><td></td></tr>
<tr><td>4. Pickney Bethell</td><td></td><td>Ray Davis</td></tr>
<tr><td>5. Virginia Walters</td><td></td><td>William Carrigan</td></tr>
<tr><td>6. Sallie Louise</td><td></td><td>Pickens Bennett</td></tr>
<tr><td>7. Edwin Walters</td><td></td><td>died at age of 18</td></tr>
<tr><td>8. Agnes</td><td></td><td>died at age of 4</td></tr>
<tr><td>9. Mary Lavinia</td><td></td><td>Archie Morgan</td></tr>
<tr><td>10. Emma Redding</td><td></td><td>J. P. Jackson</td></tr>
<tr><td>11. John Givens</td><td></td><td>Celeste Ophelia Stelly</td></tr>
</table>

Standing, left to right:

SAMUEL JAMES MONTGOMERY

Samuel James Montgomery, 1829-1909. He was married to Anastasia Breaux who was born in 1847 and died in 1896.

Children

Robert Donat Montgomery, born 1869, married to Alma Prather. Robert Montgomery deceased.
Ella May Montgomery, born 1872. Married to George Doucet. Ella M. Montgomery deceased.
Samuel Richard Montgomery, born 1874, deceased, was married to Jennie Davis.
George Breaux Montgomery, 1876, deceased, was married to Arsene Duhon.
James William Montgomery, born 1878, deceased, was married to Emma Boring.
Charles Adrien Montgomery, born 1880, deceased.
Willis, or William, Albert Montgomery, born 1882, deceased, was married to Florence S. Shackford.
John M. Montgomery, born 1885, deceased, was married to Nora Feray.
Francis Sterling Montgomery, born 1888. Married Iona Adcock or Adcox.
Effie Montgomery, born 1889, has not married.

ARTHUR GREIG

Arthur Greig was married to Louisianese Scranton, born 1843; died 1886, the daughter of Dr. George Scranton and Natalie Breaux. There was one son, John, who died very early in life.

ALEXANDRE COMEAUX

Alexandre Comeaux married Amelie Granger.
Children
Galbert
Sidney married to Paula Landry
Kossuth
Edna
Edmae

The Third Lafayette Parish Courthouse. Built in 1859 by Paxton and Templeton this colonial structure served judges and lawyers until 1927. The bell in the tower summoned lawyers to the court sessions.

Lafayette's First Episcopal Church, erected in 1901 at the
corner of Jefferson and Garfield Streets on a lot donated by

Statue to Governor Mouton. Erected by the Jewish congregation
of Lafayette in appreciation of his having donated the land for

The mausoleum of Governor Jacques Dupre and his wife in the cemetery in Opelousas, Louisiana. Jacques Dupre was Governor of Louisiana in 1830.

Ici Repose

Jacques Dupre

decede de 14 Septembre 1846

Age de 74 ans

Theotisle Roy

epouse de

Jacques Dupre

nee le 22 Juliette 1775

Decede

le 17 Septembre 1854

STATUE OF GENERAL MOUTON AT LAFAYETTE

"In the annals of time no breed has produced nobler specimens of manhood than . . . General Alfred Mouton (and Leclerc Fuselier, an aide on the staff of General Taylor) and while descendants of the French colonists remain on the soil of Louisiana, their names should be revered as are those of Hampden and Sidney of England."

—*"Destruction and Reconstruction"* — Richard Taylor, Lieutenant General Confederate Army.

Piece cut out of the much beloved battle flag of our gallant 18th Louisiana Regiment following the death of General Alfred Mouton at the Battle of Mansfield, April 1864.

"Furl that Banner! True 'tis gory,
Yet 'tis wreathed round with glory,
And 'twill live in song and story
Though its folds are in the dust.
For its fame and brightest pages,
Penned by poets and by sages,
Shall go sounding down the ages—
Furl its folds though now we must.

—*"The Conquered Banner"* by Father Ryan

TIBUS DUGAS (No Information)

LUCIEN ST. JULIEN

Lucien St. Julien, 1840-1928, married (1st) Elzina Broussard from Loreauville and (2nd) Marie Pelessier who left France at age of 11.

Children

Louis St. Julien, legally adopted by Lucien St. Julien and Marie Pelessier, married Regina Melancon from Rayne.

LOUIS GUSTAVE BREAUX

Mr. Louis Gustave Breaux, Civil War, 1861-1865. Settled on land from U. S. Government in 1836 acquired by grandfather Aurelie Breaux. He was deputy sheriff of Lafayette Parish during Issac Broussard's administration. He gave to Lafayette Parish School Board one square arpent of land in Scott, Louisiana, for its first public school.

LEONIDAS CREIGHTON

Leonidas Creighton, 1838-1900. Wife, Mathilde Ducharme, died at age of 92.

Children	married	
Euphemie Creighton		Mrs. I. N. Fields
Lydia Creighton		Mrs. Ben Downey
Mathilde Creighton		Mrs. W. A. Sweeney
Edna Creighton		Mrs. A. F. Da Costa
Willie Creighton		Alice Erigoni
John Creighton		Ara Rabb
Clifton Creighton		Hycinth Neveu
Eula Creighton		

JOSEPH ALBERT CHARGOIS

Ada Castille
Born: 4-6-1856
Died: 2-11-1893

Joseph Albert Chargois
Born: 1-30-1848
Died: 1-27-1940

Children

Agnes Chargois, born 11-15-1875
Richard Chargois, born 2-17-1877; died 11-15-1948; was married to Florence Ditch Chargois, born 11-2-1893.
Albert Edwin Chargois, born 12-7-1879; died 5-1-1956; was married to Agnes Mouton Chargois, born 10-19-1887; died 2-16-1944.
Edward Eugene Chargois, born 11-14-1881; died 11-15-1953.
Martha Julia Chargois King, born 6-28-1885; married to Arlington Sherman King, born 6-28-1883.
Joseph Castille Chargois, born 5-11-1888; married to Marie Louise Judice Chargois, born 5-10-1898.

AUGUSTE LISBONY

Auguste Lisbony, with Col. Gustave Aurelien Breaux, was one of the founders of the Confederate Veterans' Reunions in Lafayette Parish. He married Annie Schlinkwine. Lisbony family was from Spain. (The family was from Germany)

Children

1. Mary married Joseph le Blanc.
2. Joseph married - - - - - Ledet.
3. John married Massie Lunsford.
4. Olivier died an infant.

John Charles Buchanan

John Charles Buchanan was born July 23, 1841 and died April 7, 1909.
Josephine Eugenie Mouton was born February 11, 1863.

Children

Ann Spotswood Buchanan
Mary Buchanan married John Henry Fitzgerald
John Spotswood
Charles Buchanan married Marietta Hedges
Sarah Buchanan married Paul Salles
Josephine Buchanan
Catharine Buchanan married Thomas Erwin Noland
Thomas Eli Buchanan
Virginia Buchanan married Daniel Jerome Olivier
Sophie Williams Buchanan married Theo Hart Israel
Gertrude Helen Buchanan married Frank Wylie Stewart

Douglas Robert Cochrane

Douglas Robert Cochrane, 1841-1905.
Elmire Martin, 1841-1915; granddaughter of Andre Martin

Children

1. Robert Cochrane married Rose Vienet
2. Joseph Gradney Cochrane married Laure Bernard
3. Edmond Douglas Cochrane married Madeline Doucet
4. Charles Albert Cochrane
5. Coralie Cohrane married Placide Breaux
6. Cecelia Cochrane married C. C. Higginbotham
7. Elmire Cochrane married Eugene Reynaud

Henry Joseph Church

Henry Joseph Church from Ireland; wife, Lucinda Rabb.

Children

1. **Francis** — Mrs. Pulver
2. **Carmelite**, Mrs. Eddie Aucoin
3. **Ellen**, Mrs. Al Wiggins
4. **Roma**
5. **Albert**
6. **Ira**
7. **Dave** Church 1881-1956, Spanish-American War; married (1) Susan Bienvenu, (2) Mary Gaudet.

Dave Church is one of the small boys; these are his ancestors.

APPENDIX

OLD RECORDS OF THE POSTE DES OPELOUSAS

The post was named after the Opelousas Indians who had their camp on the site of the present city of Opelousas. The name is said to mean "black leg" or "black foot." The District of Opelousas extended to the Texas border and included the present parishes of St. Landry, Evangeline, Acadia, Jefferson Davis, Allen, and Calcasieu.

1720	In old records, mention of trading posts at Attakapas and Opelousas is made as early as 1720. In that year Governor Perrier was requested to send licensed traders to those districts. A few licenses were issued.
1735	Bienville was requested to send traders to the same territories.
1764	Louis Pellerin, an officer of colonial troops stationed at the post, was granted a concession of 126 acres by 63 arpents at the Opelousas Poste in order to establish a settlement there. This grant is considered to be the beginning of the town of Opelousas.
1765	The Bishop of Quebec, who had jurisdiction over Louisiana, granted permission for the celebration of Mass, baptisms, and marriages in the home of Jacques Guillaume Cortableau, who previously had obtained a grant to a large tract of land on the bayou which bears his name. This home thus served as the first church in the Opelousas district.
1765	Names of early settlers living in the Opelousas district at this time were: Louis Pellerin, Antoine and Pierre Mallet, Vanentin Moreau, Etienne Robert de la Morandiere, Francois Lemelle, Antoine Langlois, Louis Fontenot, Joseph Cormier, Augustin Soileau and Chretien.
1774	The first church in the territory was built at Church Landing, now Washington, with Father Valentin, a Capuchin priest from the Province of Champagne, France, as first pastor. The church was named "La Iglesia Paroqual de Immaculada Conception del Puesto de Opelousas."
1786	On December 30, 1786, was executed a marriage contract between M. Veiolan Rousseau and Demoiselle Marie Gradenigo. The future bride contributed seven slaves worth 5000 piastres; a home at Natchitoches on four arpents of land worth 1500; twenty-five arpents of land at Vermilion in the Attakapas post worth 2000; for a total of 8500 piastres. The future husband contributed a Negro named Sophie, aged six years, worth 400 piastres and furnishings worth 2000, for a total of 2400 piastres.
1796	The Catholic Church was moved from Church Landing to the Poste Opelousas and rebuilt on the present site by Michel Prudhomme, who donated the land, measuring three arpents front by forty deep, and all the lumber needed for the church and for fencing the church yard and the cemetery. The act of donation was dated October 16, 1796 and was executed in the presence of Martin Duralde, Captain of Militia and Civil and Military Commander of the Poste. The rebuilt church was renamed St. Landry's Church.

1797	Recorded in the St. Landry Catholic Church is the baptism of Etienne de la Morandier, son of Etienne de la Morandier and Marguerite Grandenigo. He was the ancestor of many present day residents of St. Landry Parish.
1803	Opelousas was made the seat of the County of Opelousas.
1810	The District was officially named St. Landry Parish.
1814	On September 15 Father Michel Bernard Barriere recorded in marriage book I, page 256, that, after publication of banns for three successive Sundays he had solemnly married James Resin Bowie, native of Tennessee and Miss Margaret Nevil, native of Georgia. In addition to the bride, groom and priest, the book was signed by James Nevil, Mary Nevil, Arthemise Montgomery, Baptiste Jeansonne, Vital Estilette, and Don Joachim Ortega.
1821	Opelousas was formerly incorporated by legislative act, and included all land within half a mile of the court house.

NOTES CONCERNING THE POSTE DES ATTAKAPAS FROM OLD RECORDS

1715-1744	St. Dennis, Commandant at Natchitoches, set up trading posts at Attakapas and Opelousas and maintained a licensed merchant in each place to trade with the Indians.
1754	Robin, who visited the Attakapas district in 1804-5, reported that, about 1754, a man named Masse, who belonged to a rich family of Grenoble, France, settled there and brought with him some twenty Negroes. He also mentions two "Dauphinois" named Sorel and Berard who became prosperous owners of great herds of cattle.
1760	Gabriel Fuselier de la Claire became the first Commandant of Attakapas after it became a military post. He was probably one of the first settlers in the district. He also served as Commandant of the post at Opelousas.
1765	Commissioner Aubry reported he sent 230 destitute Acadians to the Attakapas District.
1765	Archives of Catholic Church in St. Martinville on May 10 record the baptism, shortly after the arrival of the Acadians, of a baby girl born to Olivier Thibaudaut and his wife Magdeline Broussard, by Father Jean Francois, a Capuchin Franciscan missionary, who later added that the baby died on May 16.
1765	The church records show that on November 25, the same priest officiated at the burial of the leader of the colony, "Beausoleil Broussard."
1756-1765	First Dom Pierre Didier, a Benedictine monk, attached to the Capuchin mission, and then Capuchin Valentin visited the Poste des Attakapas from Natchitoches, Point Coupee, and Opelousas.
1765	With the arrival of the Acadians Father Jean Francois was appointed resident priest. He built a small frame church on land donated by Captain Dauterive.
1769	The new Spanish Governor Alexander O'Reilly transformed the trading centers of Attakapas and Opelousas into military stations,

	with a commandant exercising the powers of a military ruler and justice of the peace.
1779	Approximately 300 Spanish emigrants from the Canary Islands settled near Spanish Lake (New Iberia).
1775-1787	Chevalier Alexandre DeClouet served as Commandant of the Districts of Opelousas and Attakapas.
1787	District of Opelousas separated from that of Attakapas and DeClouet left in charge of the latter.
1779	Approximately 600 militiamen from the Attakapas, Opelousas, and Pointe Coupee districts answered the call of Spanish Governor Bernardo de Galvez to join him in capturing the British forts in the lower Mississippi Valley as a contribution to the American Revolution.
1793-1794	An Irish secular priest, Father George Murphy, and his assistant were the first to mention St. Martin as patron of the Church. Other rectors had designatd the parish in their records as St. Joseph and St. Bernard, but St. Martin des Attakapas prevailed in the end.
1795	Father Michael Bernard Barriere, a priest refugee from the French Revolution, began a fruitful ministry at St. Martin's Church.
1797	A document signed by Governor de Lemos, now in the archives of the St. Martinville courthouse, outlines instructions for the Commandant in accepting and settling prospective colonists.

1. Bachelors must prove success in farming for four years, before securing title to homesteads, unless married into the family of some honorable planter in which case they could secure the land sooner.
2. Protestant preachers were not to be given land.
3. Catholics were preferred but non-Catholics "of great personality" were occasionally accepted.
4. Two hundred acres to be granted to all approved settlers, with fifty for each child, and twenty more for each slave owned.
5. At least ten acres must be cultivated within a year.

1803	Louis Charles DeBlanc was the last Commandant.
	This descendant of an old Provencal family was born in Natchitoches on April 8, 1753, the son of the second Commandant of that fort and of the daughter of its founder, the Chevalier de Saint Dennis. After holding offices under Governor Claiborne, he died in 1825 and was buried in the old church-yard in St. Martinville, leaving twelve children and a reputation for being one of the Acadians' noblest and most generous friends.
1805	The first grand jury in the County Attakapas was held in the Poste des Attakapas, with the famous traveller and author, Robin, as a member. The new law had not yet declared whether penalties were to be inflicted according to the Spanish, French, English, or American code. Neither jurors nor witnesses could understand English and the court officials could not understand French or Spanish. The result was that the grand jury finally

	gave up and admitted it could not make any report. The judge agreed.
1805	Governor Claiborne visited the Poste des Attakapas and fell in love with a beautiful young lady, daughter of a rich *habitant*, serving as temporary post commander.
1805	The old Attakapas District becomes the County of Attakapas, with a county judge and county sheriff.
1807	County Attakapas becomes the Parish of Attakapas. The offices of county judge and sheriff were abolished and in their place were created a parish judge and several justices of the peace. Governor Claiborne appointed as first Judge of the Parish of Attakapas the Honorable James White and as justices of the peace Messrs. Dominique Prevost, David Rees, L. C. deBlanc, Alexandre deClouet and his son Olivie, Joseph Sorrel, and Fusilier.
1806	Governor Claiborne married the beautiful lady with whom he fell in love during his first visit to the Attakapas district. She was Mademoiselle Clarissa Duralde, daughter of Martin Milony Duralde and his wife, Marie Perrault Duralde. Mr. Duralde, a native of Biscaya, Spain, served as Deputy Commandant during the last month of the Spanish regime. In a letter to President Jefferson, November 12, 1806, Governor Claiborne wrote: "On my next visit to the United States I anticipate the pleasure of introducing to your acquaintance Mrs. Claiborne; — She is a native of Louisiana, born and educated in the Prairies of Opelousas, and unites to other qualities, which to me were interesting, those of a sincere Attachment to the Government of the United States, and to the American Character; — This little Stranger solicits that her most effectionate *wishes* for your health and happiness, may accompany *those* of your faithful friend William C. C. Claiborne."
1811	The County of Attakapas divided into two parishes, to be called the Parish of St. Martin and the Parish of St. Mary.
1812	The Poste des Attakapas incorporated under the name St. Martinville, after the fourth century French Bishop and Saint who was the patron of its church.
1819	On February 26, 1918 the legislature approved a charter of the "Attakapas Steam Company" for the operation of steam boats from the Teche and Vermilion Bayous to the Mississippi. On May 3, 1820 this company registered a "steamboat" named *Teche*, of 295 tons, hailing from Attakapas, and described as having "one deck, one mast, square stern, billethead, hurricane house on deck."
1823	St. Martin Parish divided by the creation of Lafayette Parish.

EARLY LAND GRANTS

The early settlers of the Attakapas and Opelousas districts acquired their lands originally in four different ways: 1. by purchase from the Attakapas Indians; 2. by grant from the French or Spanish governor evidenced by a patent; 3. by order of survey issued by the governor; 4. by occupation later confirmed by the government. Below is a record of a few of such acquisitions.

From the Indians

1801   Before Mr. Duralde, judge or commandant, Celestine de Tortue, Attakapas Chief, sold to John Lyon 224 arpents situated in the District Attakapas.

1802   Before Mr. DeBlanc, judge or commandant, Tacoble Tortue, Attakapas Indian, sold to Thomas Nicholson 3360 arpents in the District of Attakapas.

1803   Before Mr. H. LaChaise, judge or commandant, Celestine le Tortue, Attakapas Chief, sold to D. Guidry and J. Mouton 4960 arpents located in the District of Opelousas.

1802   Before Mr. DeBlanc, commandant, Bernard, Attakapas Chief, sold to Marin Mouton 4351 arpents in the District of Attakapas.

By Grant Evidenced by Patent

1772   Louis d Unzaga, Governor of Louisiana issued to Joseph Broussard a patent for land six arpents front on the west side of Bayou Teche, in a triangle closing at a depth of thirty arpents, and six arpents front by forty in depth on the east side of said bayou in the District of Attakapas.

1776   Governor Louis de Unzaga issued to Firmin Giroird a patent for land ten arpents front by forty-two deep on Bayou Tortue in the

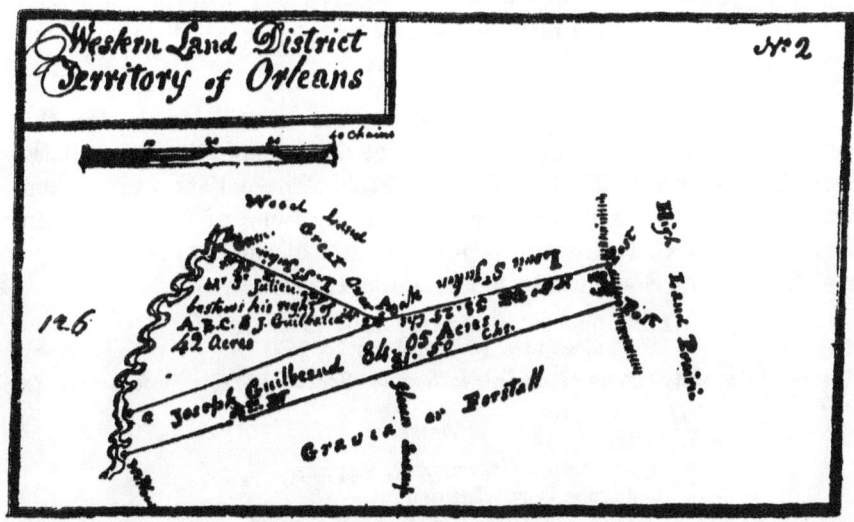

Early survey map of land sold by Louis St. Julien to Joseph Guilbeau. Of interest are the boundary posts consisting of trees and wooden posts which have long since disappeared, making present day tracing of boundaries very difficult. Turtle Bayou runs back of the Lafayette airport and east past Broussard. (Courtesy of the St. Julien family)

	Cote Gelee section front by forty-two deep on Bayou Tortue in the Cote Gelee section of the District of Attakapas.
1777	Governor Bernardo de Galyvez issued to Francois Broussard a patent for land ten arpents front by forty-two deep on Bayou Tortue in the District of Attakapas.
1781	Bernard de Galvez, Governor of Louiisana, issued to Joseph Hebert a patent for eight hundred arpents, ten arpents front by forty deep, on both sides of Bayou Petite Anse in the Attakapas District.

By Order of Survey and Assignment

1775	Governor Louis de Unzaga directed Alexandre de Clouet, Commandant of the Attakapas and Opelousas District, to deliver to Bernard Dauterive a tract of land fronting one league on both sides of Bayou Teche to a depth of half a league on the east side, and to Bayou Tortue on the west side. A league is eighty-four arpents. A few years later a patent was issued for this land, on which is now located the entire town of St. Martinville.
1787	Estivan Miro, Governor of Louisiana, ordered a survey of two hundred arpents of land situated in Prairie Sorrel in the Attakapas District in favor of Jean Baptiste Landry. The title was later confirmed by a commission of the United State Government.

By Occupation and Cultivation

1814	Claude Broussard claimed 640 arpents on the west side of Bayou Vermilion in the County of Attakapas. Evidence that the claimant had inhabited and cultivated the land for twenty-five or thirty years prior to 1814. The claimant was sixty-five years old and had a family of nineteen children. The claim was approved by a commission of the United States Government.

ATTAKAPAS MILITIA

Below are two lists of Attakapas District militiamen for the years 1774 and 1777; and three lists of Opelousas District militiamen for the years 1776, 1777, and 1788. These lists were taken from the Spanish records collected for the Sons of the American Revolution by C. R. Churchill, now on film at the Stephens Memorial Library at Southwestern Louisiana Institute.

NAMES OF THE ATTAKAPAS MILITIA COMPANY
Taken at a review, June 20, 1774

(From the archives general de Indies Seville, Spain. Papeles Procedentes de Cuba 161)

Officers

Augustine Grevemberg, Captain
Jaques Sorel, Lieutenant
Jean Baptiste Grevemberg, Ensign

Sergeants	*Corporals*
Louis Armand	Jaques Fortin
Joseph Bordat	Claude Martin

Soldiers

Rene Trahan
Oliver Trahan
Francois Grevemberg
Louis Roge
Vincent Barra
Francois Boutet
Paul Bonain
Barthalemy Grevembert
Michel Maus
Charles Hevert
Jean Lake
Simon LeBlanc
Joseph Willis
Philipe Boutet
Francois Broussard
Pierre Broussard
Andre Fangue
Luis V'lien
Oliver Tibaudau
Simon Broussard
Michel Bernard
Pierre Naizai
Antoine Boutet
Paul Trahan
Bonaventura Martin
Jean Baptiste Broussard
Maturin Broussard
Joseph Babien
Philippe Vilse
Baptiste Lalonde
Baptiste Porche
Amand Broussard
Charles Babin
Rene le Blanc
Baptiste Prevot
Louis Sandric
Antoine Bonain
Jaques Elfe
Baptiste la Baure
Anselme Tibodau

Gregoire Pellerin
Joseph Prevost
Charles Quainbidau
Armand Tobaudau
Oliver Trahan
Jean Louis Bonain
Joseph Landry
Claude Broussard
Effreme Robico
Jean Trahan
Joseph Hebert
Silvain Broussard
Martin Pokhe
Jean Dugas
Michel Parche
Germain Trahan
Francois Soudrie
Firmin Landry
Baptiste Boutet
Joseph Broussard
Pierre Dugas
Francois Prevot
Joseph Broussard
Baptiste Semer
Jean Gilliesbau
Jean Baptiste Hebert
Joseph Prevot
Michel Doucet
Pierre Borel
Gaspard Berthelemy
Joseph Carlin
Pierre Gaillard
Charles Dougat
Paul Tibodau
Joseph Martin
Charles Gilliebau
Joseph Doucet
Antanase Trahan
Martin Soudric
Santurnine Landry

Total 88 hommes

Excused on account of illness
    Jean Berard Sindric
    Louis Grevembert estropie
    Francis Allain — 60 ans

I certify this is a true report of the review of June 20, 1774.

                                            Le Chevelier De Clouet

MEMBERS OF THE OPELOUSAS MILITIA COMPANY
April 15, 1776 at Company Review

(Archives General de Indies, Seville, Spain. Papeles Procedentes de Cuba. 161)

Officers
don Esteven Roberto de la Morandier, Captain
Mr. Le Melle, Lieutenant
Mr. Noel Soileau, Ensign
Mr. Donato Bello, Major

Sergeants
Mr. Mondan
Mr. Casse
Mr. St. Germain

Corporals
Baptiste Fonteneau
Amable Bertrand
Henry Fonteneau

Soldiers

Louis Fonteneau
Laurento Baillio
Michel Brignac
Jaques Brig....o..
Pierre Fonteneau
Baptiste Guillorie
Antoine Langlois
Blaise LeJeune
Oliver Sounier
Laurent Dupre
Joseph Guillorie
Pierre Primeau
Charle Jeansone
Blotted Jeansonne
Jean Savoie
Jaque Fontenot
Auguste Soileau
Francois Pitre
Pierre Yoberto
Francois Frenan
George Steley
Michel Prudhomme
Victor Richard
Fablen Richard
Jean Chevalier
Pierre Thibeaudet
Francois Botin
Lange Brougue
Antoine Belard
Silvain Launier
Baptiste Doucette
Charbonneau
Charlie Vigee
Flourantin Pouvier

Francois Veillon
Jaque Dupree
Dominique Caillaux
Francois Cavel
Claude Guillorie
Pierre Richard
Pierre Trahan
Joseph Boutin
Joseph Story
Pierre Frugier
Blaise Brasse
Jean Baptiste Soileau
Joseph Fonteneau
Le Gran Louis
Michel Cormier
Jean Jean Sou(m?)
Joseph Silvester
Joseph Sausier
Louis Broussard
Jaques Mistre
Charles Bourussu
Christophe Plaise
Michel Janise
Francois Campeau
Baptiste LaFleur
Louis Fonteneau
Louis Jotre
Jaque De Borde
Jean Ortotanto
Louis Guillorie
Joseph Guenard
Francois Fregier
Jaque Grouque
Jaque Melayan

Romain de la Fosse
Pierre Seasioe
Reneau Lamarque
Joseph Cormier
Jaque Lafleure
Jaque Derosier
Baptiste Seausier
Paul Jeansonne
Joseph Vaible
Charle Commeau
Antoine Counard

Jean Deborde
Jean Baptiste Stilly
Jean Jeansonne
Michel Cormier
Francois Frugier
Joseph Chevaller
Joseph La Miranda
Martin Carmarsague
Francois LeBleu
Jaques Gagnard

Exempt by the state because of age or sickness
   Messrs.:

Vidrine
LaSaude
La Tiolet
Mane
Philip Langlois
Lolier
Philipe Fonteneau
Paul Boutin
Petit Langlois
Carrier
Marcantelle
Saint Mout
Louis Billet
Honore Trahan
Joseph Bourque
Joseph Caron
Vincent Pinet

Pierre Frugier
Pierre Panelle
Patin
Bois Dorez
Cretien
Pierre Guiderie
Jean LaFleure
Joseph Maureau
Juan Louis Fonteneau
John Tison
Berthelemy LeBleu
Francois Rivore
Allesandre Verosin
Joseph Vaible
Gui Blanchard
Pierre Fonteneau
Joseph Fonteneau

Sergeants	3
Corporals	3
Soldiers	87
Exempt	34
Total	127

I certify that the above is a true record of the review of April 15, 1776.
                                    Le Chevalier DeClouet

NAMES OF THE OPELOUSAS MILITIA COMPANY
Recorded June 8, 1777 at a Company Review
(Archives General de Indies, Seville Spain. Papeles Procedentes de Cuba. 161)

Officers
Don Esteven Roberto de la Morandier, Captain
Mr. Le Melle, Lieutenant
Mr. Noel Soileau, Ensign
Mr. Donato Bello, Major

Sergeants   *Corporals*
Mondon   Bte Guillorie
Frederick   Amable Bertrant
St. Germain   Enry Fontenot

Soldiers

Constant Lamirande   Jean Debordes
Michael Janisse   Pierre Jobert
Jaques Jolbre   Simon Fonteneau
Michel Brignac   Louis Belvue Guillorie
Joseph Sonnieu   Michel Prudhome
Blaise LeJeune   Charlie Gransonne
Josua Carete   Joseph Drowain
Augustin Soileau   Joseph Silvestre
Michel Cormin   Francois Bossie
Pierre Cariere   Baptiste Stillie
Francois Frenot   Charles Bourasen
Augustin Fonteneau   Antoine Langlois
Endre Marche   Florentin Poiret
Abello Arbre   Maturin Tesson
Victor Richard   Joseph Maurau
Cleman Fainelle   Joseph Poiret
Jaque Croque   Francois Debrander
Jean Poiret   Martin Camarine
Pierre Fruge   Francois Quare
Joseph Jansonne   Jaque Fontenau
Jean Boullon   Michel Carierre
Pierre Primau   Laurent Dupre
Jean Jeansonne   Joseph Fontenau
Jean Savoie   Joseph Guillorie
Joseph Vable   Joan Ortolant
Pierre Savoye   Claude Guillorie
Antoine Bellard   Pierre Richard
Silvin Saunier   Joseph Guonard
Jean Baptiste Barre   Francois Fruge
Baptiste Sauseier   Fabion Richard
Cristofe Paytre   Joseph Thery
Jaque Mirke   Thomas Priestman
Jean Paul   Romain de la Fance
Charlie Vige   Daniel Jeansonne
Pierre Doucette   Joseph Grange
Jean Baptiste le Jeune Jaques Lafleur
Jean Comau   Pierre Trahan
Francois Veillon   Joseph Boutin
Louis Fonteneau   Jacob Genet
Louis Jetrue   Michel Peitre
Pierre Fontenau   Jaques Metelle
Antoine Patin   Blaise Brasse
Francois Baree   Renard Tamague
Francois Pitre   Charles Comau

Antoine Connard
Jorge Stelie
Baptiste Douscette
Francois Campau
Philipe Fontenau

Joseph Lamarande
Jean Lettre
Jaque Dupre
Jaque Deborde
Simon Fontenau

Officers	4
Sergeants	3
Corporals	3
Soldiers	99
Total officers and soldiers	109

I certify this to be a true review of the Opelousas company of Militia as of June 8, 1777.

(No signature)

NAMES OF ATTAKAPAS MILITIA COMPANY
Recorded at a Review May 1, 1777

(From the Archives General de Indies Seville, Spain. Papeles Procedentes de Cuba. 161.)

Officers

Mr. Augustine Grevemberg, Captain
Mr. Jaques Sorel, Lieutenant
Mr. Jean Baptiste Grevemberg, Ensign
Mr. Louis Ducrest, Major

Sergeants
Jaques Fostin
Pierre Broussard
Joseph Carlin

Corporals
Jean Huval
Joseph Landry
Michel Maux

Soldiers

Francois Grevemberg
Antoine Boutte
Silvin Broussard
Joseph Prevot
Louis Roge
Anselmo Martin
Claude Dusnt
Pierre Dougat
Joseph Wiste
Antoine Barret
Rene Broussard
Simon LeBlanc
Simon Broussard
Jean Mountin (Mouton)
Jean Hebert
Mathurin Hebert
Vincente Barrat
Paul Bonin

Baptiste Prevot
Antoine Bonin
Baptiste Cormier
Baptiste LaLonde
Oliver Thibodaux
Jean Louis Bonin
Jean Labbe
Firmin Robichot
Jean Delterseo
Francole Marent
Marvin Prejean
Pierre LeBlanc
Firmin Breaux
Amant Thibodaut
Jean Baptiste Broussard
Joseph Castil
Jaques L'epines
Jean Dougat

Francois Preret	Pierre Gaillard
Joseph Doucet	Marvin Mouton
Claude Broussard	Joseph Hebert
Michel Bernard	Jean Guillabaut
Francois Ozene	Philippe Bouttee
Francois Moutte	Ament Landry
Philippe Wirte	Joseph Babin
Bartholemew Grevemberg	Charles Duant
Baptiste Boutte	Bonaventure Martin
Baptiste Lebauve	Anselme Tribodaux
Joseph Hebert	Jean Henry
Francois Guillebaut	Germain Trahant
Sinturim Landry	John Baptiste Harbert
Pierre Doucet	Jean Baptiste Simarre
Charles Guillebaut	Francois Broussard
Pierre Nize	Jean Berard
Michel Doucet	Joseph Broussard
Francois Sudrique	Paul Trahant
Renez LeBlanc	Augustin Boudrot
Joseph Prevot	Amant Broussard
Augustin Broussard	Victor Blanchard

Officers	4
Sergeants	3
Corporals	3
Soldiers	79
Total	89

I certify this is a true record of the Attakapas Review.

             Le Chevalier De Clouet

MEMBERS OF THE OPELOUSAS MILITIA, 1788

(Archives General de Indies, Seville, Spain. Papeles Procedentes de Cuba. 161)

Compania de Milicia Urbana del Partide de Opelousas, 1788.

Names	Nationality	Age
Don Santiago Cortableau (captain)	Creole	48
Jayme Patin (lieutenant)	Creole	33
Soldiers		
Franco Mercantel	Italian	38
Juan Zeringue	Creole	36
Francisco Manc	Swiss	48
Joseph Laurent	Creole	49
Antonio Pilet	Creole	47
Antonio Langlois	Creole	19
Carlos la Case	Canadian	32
Joseph Chevalier	Creole	24
Carlos Comau	Canadian	30

The 1959 Southwest Louisiana Mardi Gras. King Gabriel — Frem Boustany. Queen Evangeline — Hilda Elizabeth McCullough. Pages to the King (left to right): Edmond Reggie, Jr., and Francis F. Boustany, Jr. Pages ot the Queen (left to right): Charles Peck Gahn and Ronald Joseph Palmer.

A MARDI GRAS BALL IN LAFAYETTE

Dr. Edwin Lewis Stephens, President of Southwestern Louisiana Institute, standing by a member of his famous Live Oak Society. (1937)

IOF

PROCLAMATION.

A NOTRE BIEN AIMÉ POLICHINELLE, CHEVALIER DE LA LÉGION DES GRELOTS.—SALUT.

Dans le but de témoigner notre amour à vos fidèles sujets de la nouvelle province du Teche, nous avons résolu de les visiter prochainement. En conséquence, le 10 du mois prochain, nous nous rendrons à St. Martinville, pour recevoir leurs hommages, et vous êtes, par ces présentes, chargé des préparatifs nécessaires pour notre réception.

Donné à la Nlle. Orléans à notre palais impérial, sous le grand Sceau de l'État, ce 1er Janvier 1877

BISUS   REX CARNIVALIS
Secrétaire intime.

En vertu de ce qui précède, Nous Polichinelle, commandant du Poste des Attakapas, font recevoir convenablement sa majesté, ordonnons ce qui suit:

Le 10 Février, il y aura un grand bal paré et masqué à la Salle Duchamp, et maintenons à chacun d'y venir en costume de cour. Je à dix heures, sa majesté fera son entrée dans le bal suivi de son état major, et le canon annoncera un quart d'heure auparavant, l'arrivée, de sa majesté.

Personne ne sera admis au bal, sans que invitation contresignée par nous, et qu'il aura à donner au portier en entrant.

Pour empêcher qu'il se glisse quelque ennemi parmi nous, avons nommé un comité de quatre fidèles sujets du roi pour garantir les arrivants.

Toute personne désirant une invitation, aura à adresser sa lettre au Chevalier Polichinelle (poste restante à St. Martinville.

Fait et ordonné à St. Martinville ce 12 Janvier 1877.

POLICHINELLE,
Chevalier.

Lafayette's Three Catholic Churches

Below — The interior of the Catholic Church about 1883

Residence Building of the Academy of the Sacred Heart at Grand Coteau, founded in 1821. Many young women at Lafayette Parish were educated there.

Mount Carmel Convent in 1873

Noel Soileau	Creole	25
Juan Soileau	Creole	20
Augustin Soileau	Creole	18
Petro Mallet	Creole	26
Miguel Comau	Acadian	35
Pedro Richard	Acadian	40
Silvano Soigne	Acadian	32
Phelipe Langlois	Creole	36
Andres Mondon	French	34
Pedro Tobidau	Acadian	45
Michel Cormier	Acadian	26
Olivero Sonnier	Acadian	19
Joseph Bourg	Acadian	18
Joseph Cormier	Acadian	30
Francisco Cabe	Creole	25
Victor Richard	Acadian	22
(torn) Mulle	Creole	22
(torn) dre Barre	Creole	25
(torn) Bulli	English	29
(torn) Charante	Creole	30
(torn) usas Olier	French	35
Henrique Fontenoy	Creole	26
Pedro Jobert	French	36
Pedro Doucet	Creole	25
Juan Doucet	Creole	17
Francisco Pitre	Acadian	23
Antonio Bellerose	French	21
Mighel Brinac	Creole	27
Joseph Cretien	Canadian	40
Nicolas la Fonte	French	40
Luis de Rosier	French	30
Joseph Careau	Canadian	32
Joseph La Mirande	Creole	18
Bartholome le Bleu	Creole	46
Jean Terson	French	40
Donato Bello	Italian	37
Andres David	French	21
Juan Saucier	Creole	28
Luis Richard	Creole	31
Phelipe du Plechin	Creole	42
Gregorio Guillori	Creole	58
Joseph Guillorie	Creole	16
Luis Guillorie	Creole	15
Padre Fontenot	Creole	37
Amador Beltran	Canadian	31
Carlos Janson	Acadian	23
Antonio Boisdore	Creole	33
Francisco Vellont	Creole	20
Juan Tige	French	48
Franco Botin	French	35

Carlos LaBeau	French	36
Joseph Penel	French	44
N. Rivar	Canadian	45
Santiago laFleur	Creole	30
Joseph LaFleur	Creole	30
Joseph Vigra	Canadian	40
Andres deBrando	French	50
Juan LaFleur	Creole	28

The above list is not dated and is unsigned. It was probably prepared by Captain Cortableau and the date is probably 1788.

EARLY CHURCH RECORDS

Taken from the old records in the archives of the Church of St. Martin in St. Martinville:

June 15, 1756 Baptized and married "la meme jour" with the consent of the master, Mr. Masse, with the permission of Father Baudoin, Vicar General of Louisiana, I have married Jean D'Ige, negresse, who is also of the group of Mr. Masse of the Attakapas area.
    Signed Didier, pretre

June 19, 1765 I, a capuchin priest, baptized Augustin Surret, son of Pierre Surret and Marie Thibodeaux. Parraine is Augustin Grevemberg; Marraine is Catherine Thibodeau. Cure of the Acadian people, Jean Francois.

Scholastique Borda, born on 18th February, 1770 of Antoine Borda, surgeon of Poste des Attakapas, and Marguerite Martin. Parrain is Jean B. Grevembert, who in his absence was represented by Armande Broussard. Marraine is Magdelen Broussard.
    Witnessed by Antoine Borda

Baptised in the Church of the Attakapas on July 17th, 1772, the pastor being absent, Modeste born January 24, 1772, of the marriage of Antoine Bordat and Marguerite Martin; parrain Michel Doucette; marraine Magdalene Robichaud.

1773, 17th of April, I a Capuchin priest, pastor of Pointe Coupee, who was in the Attakapas country, which has no priest or pastor, baptized conditionally Frederick and Eugenie. Le premiere, born on 10th September, year 1770. The second born 8th of March, 1772. Both of the legitimate marriage of Gregoire Pelerin and Cecile Prejean.

1775, 12th of January, born of the legitimate marriage, one daughter of Jean Labbe and Marie Francois Barras, baptized on 24th November 1776, named Euphrosine. Parraine, Vincent Barras. Marraine, Leurine Barras.
    Signed: Louis Marie, Capuchin

Marie Louise Hiacinthe de Clouet born 8th April 1776, legitimate daughter of Monsieur Chevalier de Clouet, Captain of the Infantry and commandant for the King of the Poste Attakapas and Poste Opelousas, and Louise Favrot. Parraine, Leon Francoise Le Dee. Marraine, Mademoiselle Hiancinthe DeGruy. Baptised on the 25th of August 1777. Parish of St. Bernard of the Attakapas.

1771, 30th of April, married after publication of one ban, Gabriel Fuselier de la Claire, native of this parish, son of Pierre Fuselier, who is Captain of the Militia and commandant for the King and judge for the quarters of Attakapas and Opelousas, and Dame Leudivine Chaufouran to Helene Soileau, native of Natchez and daughter of Noel Soileau "grandemagarin pour le Roi" and of the poste of Natchez, and Marie Josef Richaume. They were dispensed. Signed by Capuchin priets, pere Irenee; also signed by F. de la Claire, Helene Soileau, Jacques Courtableau, Marie Richaume, Donato Bellau, Noel Soileau, J. L. Zeringue and J. B. Soileau. Pere Irenee gave the couple the nuptial benediction in the presence of these witnesses.

This entry in the Register is followed by the baptism of their child in 1772, Helene Fuselier.

(Boutte, ancestors of Jean Lafitte)

On July 12, 1778, after publication of two bans, the two brothers, M. M. Boutte with the two sisters of de Gruis in the presence of witnesses. Signed Louis, Cure.

1779, 11th of Jan. "I, the undersigned pastor of the parish 'de L'Ascension' a Lafourche, Chetimachas, after the publication of three bans for the marriage and after having received mutual consent of and marriage according to ceremonies in the Church of the Attakapas, Antoine Bonain, son of Antoine Bonain and Marie Peltier, a native of Mobile, to Mademoiselle Magdeline Prevot, native of Pointe Coupee who resided two months in this parish of St. Joseph of the Attakapas."

       Witnessed by Bonaventure Martin
             Francoise Asset
             Jean Guillebaut

Signed by Pere Ange de Reveilla, Cure

MARRIAGE CERTIFICATE

  St. Martin Church, St. Martinville, La.
The Records of This Church
Certify, under date of June 23, 1788
to the marriage of Jean Mouton
legitimate son of Salvador Mouton
and Anne Bastarache
to Marthe Borda
legitimate daughter of Antoine Bordat
and Marguerite Martin
  Said Record is signed by Rev. Gioffrotin
Witnesses: Joseph Landry
    Jean Hebert
    Jean Guillbeau
True copy of Record #114 Bk. 1782-84
    Rev. Msgr. Henri Hamel
    By Kenneth Bienvenu
    Date August 17, 1959
 (Seal of
St. Martin's Church
St. Martinville, La.)

EARLY RECORDS *de l'église St. Jean Evangeliste du Vermilion*

L'église St. Jean was dedicated in 1821 and until then was only a mission of St. Martinville. That same year it was detached from St. Martinville and put under the jurisdiction of the church at Grand Coteau. The following year the land on which the chapel stood, containing five and a half arpents, was given for church purposes by Jean Mouton "because of his love and devotion to the Church." The same year Vermilionville with its surrounding territory was erected into a separate parish with its own pastor. Father Barriere was the first pastor. Many of these records are signed by him. In 1824 he sailed for Bordeaux where he died eight days after his arrival in France. His successor was the Rev. Lawrence Peyretti.

In the archives of St. John's Cathedral are carefully guarded these earliest records of the church, then St. Jean, Evangeliste.

As a basis of selection legibility has been the prime consideration, time having dimmed the exquisite script.

The first listed records in each division have been copied in their entirety. Those following, in most instances, record only the names of the persons concerned.

BAPTIMES
1822-1824
Register I — Folio I

Marie Adelle Arconneau	Dans mil huit cent vingt-deux le quatorze novembre j'ai baptise Marie Adele nee le huit septembre derniere fille huit legitime de Francois Arconneau de Marie Mouton parrains seraient Sosthene Arconneau et Marcellite Mouton en foi de Quoi Mg. Bern'd Barriere, cure de St. John.
Josephine Broussard	L'an mil huit cent vingt-deux le vingt-six j'ai baptise Josephine nee le dix neuf mai dernier fille legitime de Joseph Broussard a Sosthene Boudreau parrain Onezime Mouton a Scholastique Dur-en (Durand?) en foi de quoi Monsignor Bern'd Barriere cure de St. Jean.
Alexandre a Charles Guedri	L'an mil huit cent vingt-trois le quinze juin j'ai baptise Alexandre nee le trois fevrier dernier fils legitime de Charles Guidry et de Marie Bernard, parrain Francois Printanuir et Marcellite Bernard, en fois de quoi Mons. Barriere, cure de St. Jean.
Louis Mouton	L'an mil huit cent vingt-trois j'ai baptise Louis nee le dernier novembre dernier fils legitime de Don Louis Mouton et le Marie Cormier parrain Francois Mouton D'angelle Martin epouse de Jean Mouton fils-en foi

	de quoi Mons. Bern'd Barriere, cure de St. Jean.
Onezime Mouton	L'an mil huit cent vingt - le vingt neuf - j'ai baptise Onésime née le vingt huit - dernier fils légitime d'Augustin Mouton et Francoise Baudoin, parrain Florian Mouton et Ceraphie Trahan; en foi de quoi. Mons. Bern'd Barriere cure de St. Jean.
Josephine Broussard	Joseph Broussard, père
	? Boudreau, mère
Julie Celestin Duga	Celestine Dugas, père
	Julie Chiasson, mère
Onesime Gautrau	Jerome Gautrau, père
	Marie Dugas, mère
Anne Morgan	Salomon Morgan, père
	Anne Folk, mère
Jean Florentin Bourk	Jean Florentin Bourk
	Josephine Thibaud
Celestin le Blanc	Eloi LeBlanc
	Marie Arthemise Langlinais
Onezime Mouton	Onesime Mouton
	D'aspasie Hebert
Marie Urasie Toups	Anbroise Toups
	Marie Baudoin
Adeline Suire	Andrée Suire
	Marie Dartez
Cleonide Grange	Cleonide Grangé
	Charles Grangé
Simeon Hebert	François Hebert
	Domitille Grange
Celestine LeBlanc Lachausseé	Edward le Blanc
	Marie St. Julien
Pierre Montemar	Jean Baptiste Saunier
	Clemenié Bro
Eugene Maux	Arthamise Maux
	Emelie Mercier
Felicite Nerau	Jean Baptiste Nerau
	Marie Arthemise Caruther
Marie Roussel	Pierre Roussel - de Nantes
	Marie Anne Clow - de St. Charles sur Miss.
Theogine Landry	Joseph Landry
	Lise Labauve
Adelaide Kilkris	St. Julien Kilcris
	Marguerite Pivotau
Charles Holloe	Issac Holloe
	Adélaide Berard
Adelle Boule	Louis Boule
	Adelaide Bernard
Marie-Adelle Arsonneau	Francois Arsonneau
	Marie Mouton

Emilien Sellers	Matthieu Sellers
	Marie Rosine Ocoing (Aucoin?)
Marie Comau	Edouard Comau
	Marguerite Grangé
Antoine Guidri	Antoine Guidri
	Madellaine Poitiers
Les Saints Primo	d'Seraphime Baudoin
	Catherine Checkenaydre
Toussaints Checchenaidre	Toussaint Checchenaidre
	Arthemise Frederic
Alexandrea Charles	Charles Guidry
	Marie Bernard
Eloise Labauve	Placide Labauve
	Anne Thibaudau
Marguerite Cleonice Trahan	Xavier Benoit
	Marguerite Trahan
Rosemond Benoit	Augustin Benoit
	Anastie Babinaud
James Robert Martin	James Robert Martine
	Marie Colmen
Louis Hubert Broussard	Edouard Broussard
	Pelagie Du Bois (shepherd of the wood)
Les Saints Quebedo	Nicholas Quebedo
	Marguerite Landry
Arthemise Brasseux	Joseph Brasseux
	Marie Dugas

MARRIAGES

December 1824 - - October 1829

Folio IV

Mariages parvoisse de St. Jean du Vermilion registre de marriages pour la paroisse du Vermilion commence le troit decembre de l'annee de notre Seigneur 1824-1829.

The records in the folio are complete — signed by the witnesses and by Pere Laurent Peyretti, curé de St. Jean Evangeliste.

1824 Hebert Eastin, natif Louisville, Kentucky, avec Marie Euphrosine Arceneaux, fille de Alexandre Arceneaux et Dame Helen Carmouche.

    Michel Girard, native of France, son Michel Girard and Marie Landreneaux, both of France to Anastasie Mouton daughter of Frederic Mouton and Anatasie Cormier, "du fleuve" (of the river) St. James Parish

    Francois Boudreau avec Demoiselle Marguerite Simon

    Francois Hebert avec Pelagie D'Artese

    Louis Broussard avec Anastasie Landry

    Don Martin Pellerin avec Marie Zoe St. Julien

    Olivier Blanchette avec Carmelite Boudreau

    Madame Marie Cormier avec Don Louis Mouton

Jean Babinot avec Hortance Perry
Baptiste Guidry avec Marguerite Dugat
Herbert Eastin avec Euphrosine Arceneaux
Valery LeBlanc avec Carmelite Trahan
Alexandre Sellers avec Marguerite Duhon
Vallery Cormier avec Marguerite Hebert
Don Louis Thibodeaux avec Marguerite Landry
Joseph Hebert avec Marie Denise Bourg
Joseph Thibodeaux avec Marie Louise Cormier
.... Renery, native of Liverpool, avec Marie Theotiste Stelly
Simon Onezime Giroir avec Adeline Deroin
Pierre Lapointe avec Marguerite Meaux

1826 Eugene Pellerin avec Cleonide St. Julien
Girard Chiasson avec Aspasie Guidry
Joseph Guidry, son of David Guidry and Dame Modeste Borda avec Celeste Mouton, daughter of Jean Mouton and Marie Marthe Bordat from Europe
Cornelius Voorhies, fils de Cornelius Voorhies and Dame Aimee Gradenigo, avec Cidalise Mouton, fille de Jean Mouton and Dame Marie Angelique Martin, signed by H. Mouton, André Martin, E. Lamorandier
David Kellogg avec Madame Nanette Martin
Alexandre Langlinais avec Adelaide Montet
Jean Primeaux avec Marie Celeste Mirre
Joseph Guilbeau avec Clotilde Landry
Zepherin Dubois avec Dame Adelaide Dugat
Norbert Comeaux avec Clarice Comeaux

1827 Pierre LeBlanc avec Adeline Broussard
Augustin Guidry avec Marie Leontine Guilbeau
Treville Broussard avec Anne Cidalise Broussard
Elise Messonnier avec Louise Thibodeaux
Pierre Guidry avec Julienne Saunnier
Joseph Dugat (fils) avec Marguerite Arminionne Hebert
Charley Thibodeaux avec Magdeline Constantin
Louis Stiven avec Mlle. Marie Baudoin
Onezime Broussard avec Carmelite Thibodeaux
Antoine Guidry avec Clementine Guidry
Aurilien Broussard avec Marguerite Seller

1828 Dominique Brousset of Toulouse, France, avec Elizabeth Valleau
Marceline Dugat avec Melanie Boudreaux
Raphael Smith of Grand Coteau avec Clemence Guilbeau
Pierre Alexis Lagneau avec Marguerite Benoit
Napoleon Lalande avec Susanne Fabre
Edmond Mouton avec Eulalie Voorhies
Louis Chiasson avec Suzanne Dugat
Charley Granger avec Madame Anastasie Giroir

1829 Alexandre Cormier avec Suzanne Ledoux
Joseph Evariste Broussard avec Scholastique Giroir
Archelle Brau avec Marie Carmelle Mirre
Joachem Miler avec Modeste Léger

      Antoine Denise Trahan avec Marguerite Hebert
      Joseph Ursine Lalande avec Marie Sixnayder
1837 John Creighton, son of Matthew Creighton avec Polly Jacobs
      Euphemie Mouton, daughter Don Louis Mouton avec Marie Cormier

ENTERREMENTS

1822, 1824 to 1831

Folio VII

"Registre des enterrements meus pour la paroisse du Vermilion commence le seize décembre — année de notre Seigneur 1824 par Laurent Peyretti, curé de St. Jean Evangeliste du Vermilion état de la Louisiane le 16 decembre mil huit cent vingt-quatre.

1822	Don Louis Bordat agee 22 yrs	père, Jean Mouton mère, Marie Marthe Bordat
	Josephine Cleonide Bro 13 ans	père, Baptiste Bro mère, Marie Anne Girouard
	Enfant de Valerin Martin et Cleonide Dugas	père's père, Valerin Martin mère, Cleonide Dugas
	Silvanie Girouard 11 ans	père, Simon Girouard mère, Adelaide Broussard
	Don Louis Mouton 2 ans	père, Jean Mouton mère, Marthe Borda
	Marguerite Doucet Lebreton 50 ans	
	Jn. Bte. Treville Girouard Quatre ans	père, Jean Baptiste Girouard mère, Josephine de Rouen
	Petit Jean Trahan de la Grosse Ile 33 ans	père, Joseph Trahan mère, Francoise Pitre
	Jeanne LeBlanc	père, Joseph LeBlanc mère, Marie Broussard
	Adelaide Duhon morte de courte maladie	daughter of Marie et Pierre Saul Montet
	Mad'elle Marie Prejean cinquarte huit — morte de longue maladie	fille de Charles Prejean et Marguerite Richard
	Thomas Caruthers 33 ans	
	Pierre Caramouche 88 ans	père, Francois Caramouche
	Pierre A. Bazile Landri 45 ans	père, Pierre Landry mère, daughter of Joseph Dugas

	Alexis Beaulieu 1 ans	père, Benjamin Beaulieu
	L'enfant de 2 jours	père, Charles Mouton mère, jeune fille Latiolais
	Clemille Bernard 5 yrs	père, Francois Bernard mère, Demoiselle Caramouche
Dec. 1822	Enfant Charles Mouton "oublie dans le temps"	père, Charles Mouton Dame Julie Latiolais
1823	Marguerite Martin ve Bordat	L'an mil huit cent vingt-trois le douze janvier a ete inhume dans le cemetiere de cette parroise le corps de Marguerite Martin agee de cent quatre — epouse de Monsieur Bordat en foi de quoi Mg. Bernard Barriere cure de St. Jean.
1824	L'an mil huit cent vigt-quatre et la seize — decembre a ete cure de la paroisse de St. Jean Vermilion inhume dans le cemitiere — Eglise le corps Leufroy Lapointe fils legitime de Mr. Pierre Lapointe et de Dame Elene Landry des pere et mere decede hier chez Charles St. Germaine a deux heurs apres âgé de vingt et un ans — en foi de quoi j'ai signé L — curé de St. Jean.	
1824	Marie fille	père, Alexandre Guidry mère, et Carmelite Broussard dit Beaul Soleil

1826

Luifroy Lapointe	Marcelite Bernard
Marie Marthe Mouton (epouse de Pierre Dugat)	Julien Pierre Brau
	Melanie Landry
Olivia Bernard	
	Julie Guilbeau
Alexandre Cormier	
	Ozemine Louviere
Emilien LeBlanc	
	Marie Dominille Labove
David Carother	
	Melanie Hebert

1827

Josephine Cormier	Natalie Brau
Leufroy Trahan	Francois Mouton
Suzanne Granger	époux de Clemence Dugat
Martin Broussard	Alidon Broussard

1828

Simon LeBlanc

Marguerite Romaire

épouse Nicolay Balleau

Charley Redoux

Anastasie LeBlanc

Elizabeth Valleau

épouse Dominique Broussard et petite fille de Onezime Landry

1829

Adelaide Boulet

Jean Demas Bernard

Narcisse Saunier

Augustin Boudreaux

Julienne Guidry

Caroline Boudreaux
(fille Jean Boudreaux et Dame Marguerite Mouton)

Alexandre Antoine Mouton (fils Antoine Emile Mouton and Dame Marie Gadrat Rousseau)

Claire Armante Arceneaux

Enfant Charley Guidry (fils Charley Guidry et Caroline Landry)

1830

Simon Benoit

Celeste Comeaux

Aurelien Bernard

Hilaire Giroir

Alexandre Guidry (fils Augustin Guidry et Dame Marie Leontine Guilbeau)

Hilliare Trahan

Celime Broussard

Jean Charley Hebert

1831 Francoise Angelique Zenaidee Mouton (fille de Sosthene Mouton et de Dame Eugenie Latiolais)
Marie Marthe Bordat — épouse Jean Mouton pere décédé hier âgée environs soisante sept ans

1834 Jean Mouton, père — husband Marie Marthe Bordat (deceased) décédé le meme jour à quatre heure du matin âgée d'environs 79 ans

1835 Zelia Rousseau — epouse d' Alexandre Mouton âgée "environs" 25 years (aged about 25 years)
Eugenie Latiolais — wife Sosthene Martin âgée 35 ans
Martin Demaret Brashear, son of Thomas B. Brashear and Maria Crow

1838 Alphonsine Bailey, daughter of William Bailey and Vallerie Neveu aged six years

1839 Clarisse Guidry, wife Césaire Mouton aged 26 years

1842 Michel Eloi Mouton, son Eloi Mouton and Carmelite Domingue
Joseph Baillet — "Professeur," décédé hier chez Mr. Charles Mouton a l'âge de 72 years

1843 Eastin Martin, son of Albert Eastin and Marie Arceneaux aged 12 years

1861 "Dame Emile" Mouton (née Gadrat Rousseau) wife Antoine Emile Mouton, son of Jean Mouton, pere, aged 45 years.

In St. John's Cemetery, Lafayette, Louisiana are two graves side by side. The following is a true copy (to the best of my ability) made from tracings. August, 1959.   Virginia B. Olivier

ICI REPOSE
JEAN MOUTON
Décédé le 22 Novembre 1834
Agé de 80 ans

———

SES ENFANS
par respect pour sa memoire lui ont levé
cette pierre

Ici repose
MARIE MARTHE BORDAT,
épouse de Jean Mouton
décédé le 7 Septembre 1831
agée de 65 ans.

L'example de ses vertus est le plus
bel héritage qu'elle ait laissé à ses enfans
comme Epouse et comme mère elle fut
sans reproche.

———

Translation:

Here lies
JEAN MOUTON
Died the 22 November 1834
At the age of 80 years

———

His children
through respect for his memory have raised this stone

Here lies
MARIE MARTHE BORDAT
wife of Jean Mouton
died the 7 September 1831
at the age of 65 years

The examples of her rightousness is the grandest heritage that she left her children. As wife and as mother she was without reproach.

BAPTIMES
1822
Folio II

Personnes de Couleur

Celestine, Suzanne a Charles Dugas	L'an mil huit cent vingt-deux j'ai baptise Celestine mulatresse du vingt-deux janvier mil huit cent vingt et un naturelle de Suzanne negrette a Charley Dugas. Les parrains ont été Jean Bte Trahan et Marie Gautro, en foi de quoi. Barriere — curé

FUNERALS OF SLAVES
1825 - 1842
Folio IX

un petit slave de "Jean Mouton"	L'an mil huit cent vingt-six le douze decembre a ete par nous soussigne de la paroisse Lafayette, Vermilionville inhume dans le cemetiere de cette e'glise le corps d'un petit enslave a "Jean Mouton" decede hier age de deux ans. sig. Father Barriere

The following deaths are recorded in the manner as above.
The names of Jean Mouton pere and Andre Martin appear very frequently as possessors of slaves.

Rosalie — slave of Pierre Giroir
Celeste — slave of Valerien Martin
Petit Negre, slave of Jean Bernard, pere
Pelagie, negress-libre
Catherine, enslave de Francois Arceneaux
Henry, enslave de Madame Martin
Jean, enslave de Charles Mouton
Un petit, slave a Jean Mouton pere
Lise, enslave de Pierre Dugat
Henry, enslave de Alexandre Mouton
Ermance, enslave de Madame ve Andre Martin
Celeste, enslave de Pierre Giroir
Un petite, enslave de Baptiste Jaunier
Un petite, enslave de Sosthene Mouton
Henrietta, enslave de Mr. Basile Crow
Enfant, enslave a Zepherin Martin
Enfant, enslave a Treville Bernard
Jacques, enslave a Jean Guilbeau
Augustin, enslave de Francois Carmouche

Un Petit, slave de Joseph Landry
Un petit, enslave de Francois Mouton
Un petit, enslave de Alexandre Guidry
Agathe, enslave de Charles Mouton
Slave de Olivier Boudreaux
Slave de Wm. Brashear
Slave de Andre Prejean
Slave de Marin Martin
Slave de David Kellog Markham
Clarisse, slave de C. Voorhies fils 1838
Draussin, slave de Antoine Delhomme, 1838
Celeste, slave de Vallery Veillon
Celeste, slave de Pierre Cormier
Celeste, slave de Charley Comeaux, 1839
Ondoyne (Antoine?) slave de Andre Martin
Louis, slave de Lucien Bourg
Un Petit, enslave Desire Judice
Un Petit, enslave Andre Prejean
Celanie, enslave Me - ve Carlite Duhon
Un petit, enslave Pierre Dugat
Un petit, enslave Placide Labave
Un Petit, enslave Moise Hebert
Eugene, enslave Pierre Richard
Un petit, enslave de Charley Brau
Marie, enslave de Dominique Babinot
Francois, enslave de Pierre Saunier

CENSUS REPORTS OF ST. MARTIN AND
LAFAYETTE PARISHES

A. Third Census 1810, Louisiana Attakapas (St. Martin) Parish December 10, 1810, before the Parish was divided.

Part 1. Settlements of Carencro west of the Vermilion River to its junction with Bayou Tortue and from thence on both sides of said Vermilion River to the sea shore and the settlement of Cote Gelee west of Bayou Tortue. By Ransom Eastin.

Free white males		Free white Females	
to 10	308	to 10	242
16	117	16	122
26	39	26	97
45	159	45	120
45+	80	45+	69
	753		650

Free persons of color except Indians—41. Slaves—652. Total for this enumeration, 2096.

Part 2. The number of persons in that part of the county or parish of Attakapas situated below the Attakapas Church on both sides of the River Teche, including the petite anse/ac Tasse and bayou Salle. Taken by Peter Regnier, assistant to the secretary of the Territory of Orleans.

Free white males		Free white Females	
to 10	337	to 10	254
16	109	16	95
26	190	26	145
45	244	45	115
45+	54	45+	44
	934		653

Free people not taxed—150; slaves 1532.
Total for this enumeration, 3269.
Grand total for entire Attakapas County (parish) 5365.

Note: The small numbers in age group above forty-five is significant.

B. Census of 1820 showing the population of St. Mary Parish, detached from St. Martin in 1811, and of St. Martin Parish which in 1820 still included the parishes of Iberia, Lafayette and Vermilion. Enumerator, Henry E. T. Trigemann.

	St. Mary	St. Martin
Free white males	532	2436
Free white females	432	2247
Included above:		
Foreigners not naturalized	43	362
Engaged in Agriculture	28	118
Engaged in Commerce	300	1343
Engaged in Manufacturing	19	148
Slaves — males	907	2001
Slaves — females	830	1893
Free colored persons — males	122	282
Free colored persons — female	56	194
All other persons, except Indians, not taxed	7	26
Totals	2886	9078

C. Census of 1830. First census of Lafayette Parish after its creation in 1823. Enumerator, Hubert Chargois, Assistant to the Marshal of the Western District of Louisiana.

Free white males		Free white females	
under 5	374	under 5	340
5 to 10	248	5 to 10	248
10 to 15	186	10 to 15	203
15 to 20	204	15 to 20	153
20 to 30	312	20 to 30	252
30 to 40	197	30 to 40	141
40 to 50	101	40 to 50	55
50 to 60	52	50 to 60	49
60 to 70	23	60 to 70	18
70 to 80	9	70 to 80	5

80 to 90	0	80 to 90	4
90 to 100	3	90 to 100	0
100, etc.	0	100, etc.	0
Totals	1709		1468
Slaves, male	1210	Slaves, female	1157
Free colored males	60	Free colored females	49

Total number of individuals 5653

White persons included above:
  Deaf and dumb   6
  Blind   1
  Unnaturalized aliens   26

Slaves and colored included above:
  Deaf and dumb   0
  Blind   2

D. Census of 1840, Lafayette Parish: Signed November 17, 1840: by Anaclet Richard, and witnessed by C. H. Mouton and O. Mouton.

    Free white persons   4580
    Slaves   3246

    Total individuals   7826

Universities or colleges	0	Number of students	0
Academies and grammar schools	1	Number of scholars	5
Primary and common schools	12	Number of scholars	96

Number of scholars at public charge   4

E. Census of 1850. Lafayette Parish. Enumerator, A. Toulouse, Assistant Marshal.

    Free inhabitants   3552
    Slaves   3289

    Total individuals   6841
    Number of slave owners   266

Note: The drop in population from that of 1840 was due to the cutting off of Vermilion Parish in 1844.

F. Census of 1860, Lafayette Parish. Enumerator, James H. Stokes, Assistant Marshal.

    Free whites   4319
    Free colored   228
    Slaves   4387

    Total individuals   8934
    Foreign born included above   269

G. Census of Lafayette Parish, 1870. Enumerator, Ed. P. Goodwin, Assistant Marshal.

    Individuals outside Vermilionville   9612
    Individuals in Vermilionville   777

    Total inhabitants   10,389

H. Census of 1880, Lafayette Parish. Enumerators: Jules J. Mouton, A. C. Kennedy, W. H. Cunningham, R. B. Martin, J .J. Caffery.

White persons	7670
Black persons	4574
Mulatto persons	988
Total inhabitants	13,232

I. Census of 1890, Lafayette Parish   15966
   Census of 1900   22825
   Census of 1910   28733
   Census of 1920   30841
   Census of 1930   38827
   Census of 1940   43941
   Census of 1950   57743

View of beautiful cypress lake taken from the Student Union Building on the Southwestern campus.

CHARTER MEMBERS — Five members of the first faculty at Southwestern Louisiana Institute relax in the garden on Oct. 25, 1928. They were present for the opening of school in 1901. (Left to right), they are Mrs. Samuel Wood Brown, the former Gertrude Mayfield; Miss Edith Garland Dupre; President Stephens; and Mrs. E. L. Stephens, Beverly Randolph. (Photo courtesy Dupre)

Southwestern's Cadet Corps of 1906. Deployed on Jefferson Street

PARTIAL LIST OF NAMES AND BRANDS OF SOME OF
THE EARLIEST CATTLEMEN IN THE ATTAKAPAS
DISTRICT, WHICH UP TO 1611 INCLUDED THE
PARISHES OF ST. MARTIN, ST. MARY, IBERIA,
LAFAYETTE, AND VERMILION.

Taken from the Brand Book for the Attakapas and Opelousas Districts 1739 to 1888.

Date	Owner of Brand		
1739	Louis Grevemberg Grevemberg, Bartheleny	Sold to Baptiste Bernard	F B ID
1748	Ozene, Pere		N
1748	Ozene, fils		ID
1748	Ozene, Jaques Fcois pere		OZ
1748	Ozene, Francois		SL
1758	Sorrel, Joseph		AS
1760	Alexandre		Ꞁ
1760	Litette		↳
1761	Tellier, George		Я
1761	Bernard, Michel		71
1762	Argroso		
1762	Argraw		7+
1762	Provost, Nicolas		Ж
1764	Broussard, Simon (partly torn off)		S
1764	Patin, Dame Toinan		PA
1764	Bonin, Antne pere		BA
1766	Guidry, Charles		▢

Date	Owner of Brand		
1766	Vve, Claude	⋎	
1766	Mire, Placide		T
1766	Semer, Baptiste	o-o	
1766	Trahan, Rene		R
1767	Broussard, Francois	BR	
1767	Thibodeau, Olivier		OT
1767	Broussard, Jean Baptiste	∽	
1767	Berard, Jean Pere		⊕
1767	Beauseleil, Francois	BR	
1767	Broussard, Jn. Bte.		∽
1767	Broussard, Jean, pere	OT	
1767	Thibodeau, Nicolas		H
1768	Boute, Pere	R	
1769	Broussard, Valery Claude		ZR
1769	Broussard, Claude	72	
1769	Landry, Firmin		5B
1769	Trahan, Michel	⋎	
1769	Trahan, German Broussard, Claude—trans'd to Treville Grange 27 May 1840.		⊞
1787	De Aguilar, Bernard	B	
1787	De Aguilar, Tubin		A (torn)

Date	Owner of Brand	Brand
1760	Alexndre	AS
1780	Arunauy, Pierre	Torn off
1789	Arunauy, Pierre fils	
1789	Arunauy, Alexandre, Transfer to Numa Breaux 27th of May 1859	
1789	Arunauy, Cyprien	
1789	Aucoin, Claude	V
1789	Alston, William	WA
1814	Amoit, Genevieve, Transfer Andre Mallet 4th Sept. 1850	XC
1815	Arseneaux, Pierre Bienvenue	
1815	Pierre, fils, Arseneaux	
1815	Argrove, Celeste fille de Dreyes Argrove	
1817	Arail, Manna	M
1819	Obechez, Benjamin	Jd
1821	Ardain, Lise	
1821	Artache, Isadore	
1822	Aubert, Donis	
1822	Alexandre, nigre libre	A
1811	Babinot, Julien, Vendu a Constantine fils 12 Juin 1937	8T
1793	Brqu, Francois	B
1801	Bernard, Adelaide	P
1793	Bernard, Lefroy	KI

MAYORS OF LAFAYETTE

Note: From 1836 to 1869 Vermilionville had no mayor, only a presiding officer, elected by the five member Council. The Charter of 1869 provided for a Council of seven and an elective mayor. There is no record that the Secretary of State issued their commissions until 1885.

Name	Years Served
Alphonse Neveu	1869-70
W. O. Smith	1870-71
Wm. Brandt	1871-72
W. O. Smith	1872-73
August Monnier	1873-75
John O. Mouton	1875-76
G. C. Salles	1876-77
John O. Mouton	1877-79
John Clegg	1879-81
M. P. Young	1881-84

Name	Date Commissioned
W. B. Bailey	May 9, 1885
William Campbell	May 13, 1891
A. J. Moss	May 6, 1895
Charles D. Caffery	May 19, 1891
William Campbell	May 10, 1899
Charles D. Caffery	May 29, 1900
Charles O. Mouton	May 4, 1905
Dr. G. A. Martin	May 13, 1909
Dr. A. R. Trahan	May 12, 1911
Dr. G. A. Martin	May 16, 1913
Robert L. Mouton	May 5, 1919
J. Gilbert St. Julien	May 12, 1927
Robert L. Mouton	May 14, 1931
J. Maxime Roy	May 14, 1936
Claude C. Colomb	May 2, 1944
Ashton J. Mouton	May 21, 1948
Jerome E. Domengaux	May 8, 1956

JUDGES—CIRCUIT COURT OF APPEAL*

Name	Date Commissioned
Joseph M. Moore	January 26, 1880
Alfred B. Irion	January 26, 1880
Robert S. Perry	June 6, 1888
John Clegg	(?) 1888
W. F. Blackman	(?) 1894
Julien Mouton	(?) 1898
J. Hugo Dore	March 2, 1935
Albert Tate, Jr.	December 3, 1954

*No records on this position prior to 1880.

DISTRICT ATTORNEYS

(Complete as far as records are available)

Name	Date Commissioned
Cornelius Voorhies	February 15, 1843
James D. Hallam	January 20, 1845
P. D. Hardy	January 31, 1852
William Mouton	December 18, 1855
James M. Moore	May 26, 1846 (withdrew)
John H. Overton	May 30, 1846
C. H. Mouton	February 25, 1848
James M. Moore	May 26, 1848
E. D. Estilette	May 20, 1866
George W. Hudspeth	July 14, 1868
William C. Crow	January 31, 1873
J. A. Chargois	June 6, 1873
*M. F. Rigues	March 25, 1874
Joseph A. Chargois	December 24, 1874
Robert C. Smedes	March 22, 1884
M. T. Gordy, Jr.	(?) 1894
William Campbell	May 18, 1900
J. J. Robira	December 4, 1908
C. B. De Bellevue	December 6, 1912
Percy T. Ogden	December 8, 1916
James A. Gremillion	December 5, 1924
C. B. De Bellevue	December 4, 1936
N. S. Hoffpauir	December 4, 1942
Richard J. Putnam	December 3, 1948
Bertrand DeBlanc	December 3, 1954

*Listed as "Parish Attorney or District Attorney pro tem"

DISTRICT JUDGES

(Complete as far as records are available)

Name	Date Commissioned
William B. Lewis	May 26, 1846
John H. Overton	February 5, 1948
Lucius T. Dupré	June 7, 1853
Adolphe Bailey	March 20, 1866
James M. Porter	July 14, 1868
John E. King	December 28, 1870
Eraste Mouton	December 13, 1872
John Clegg	December 15, 1881
Orther C. Mouton	June 10, 1890
W. W. Edwards	(?) 1890
A. C. Allen	(?) 1894
P. S. Pugh	December 5, 1904
William Campbell	December 4, 1908
W. W. Bailey	December 14, 1920

DISTRICT JUDGES (Continued)

Paul Debaillon — September 14, 1931
N. Smith Hoffpauir — (?) 1948
Edward Meaux — December 3, 1948
A. Wilmot Dalfres — September 11, 1950
Frank W. Summers — July 30, 1952
Richard J. Putnam — December 3, 1954

PARISH JUDGES

A. J. Moss — July 14, 1868
M. F. Rigues — December 19, 1876

CITY JUDGES OF LAFAYETTE

R. W. Elliott — 1910-1916
G. A. Martin — 1916-1932
A. W. Dalferes — 1932-1950
Allen J. Lacobe (de facto) — 1950-1953
Kaliste J. Saloom, Jr. — 1953-to present

CORONERS, LAFAYETTE PARISH

Name	Date Commissioned
Charles Peck	March 3, 1846
John A. Rigues	December 30, 1847
James McMullen	December 31, 1855
Desiré Judice	May 21, 1866
L. Duhon	July 14, 1868
H. M. Bailey	December 31, 1870
J. R. Batchelor	December 26, 1872
Francis L. Mudd	March 26, 1873
Alphonse Gladu	December 13, 1874
George Scranton (resigned)	January 5, 1880
Dr. T. O. Bernard (failed to qualify)	October 6, 1880
Dr. Homer T. Guidry	October 10, 1882
Alphonse Gladu	(?) 1888
A. R. Trahan	(?) 1893
Dr. J. F. Mouton	May 31, 1900
Dr. L. A. Prejean	May 25, 1908
Dr. J. O. Duhon	May 31, 1912
M. M. Mouton	May 29, 1924
J. O. Duhon	April 19, 1932
M. E. Boustany	May 23, 1952
Henry C. Voorhies	May 18, 1956

LAFAYETTE PARISH—SHERIFFS

(Complete as far as records are available)

Name	Date Commissioned
Edmond Mouton	February 15, 1843
Horace F. Voorhies	January 20, 1846

Phineas E. Smith	June 26, 1865
Gerard Landry	May 21, 1866
Hazard Eastin	December 16, 1872
Edgar Mouton	January 5, 1880
William Campbell	June 15, 1885
Isaac Broussard	January 5, 1888
Louis LaCoste	May 24, 1904
F. M. Latiolais	June 2, 1916
J. Dassas Trahan	May 29, 1924
Jack Doucet	April 19, 1932
J. C. Chargois	May 22, 1936
Gaston P. Hebert	May 17, 1940
Walter S. Comeaux	May 21, 1948
Mayo B. Harson	May 23, 1952

LIST OF PARISH SUPERINTENDENTS OF EDUCATION

Parish school records in Lafayette Parish are incomplete. The administration of the parish schools, prior to the appointment of a superintendent is described below. A list of superintendents follows:

1823-1845	The police jury from time to time appointed a school committee which rarely functioned.
1845	The state constitution authorized the appointment of parish superintendents of schools.
1847	Legislative enabling act put the above provision in effect. No record of appointments.
1852	Office of parish superintendent abolished and his duties transferred to the parish treasurer.
1855-1870	No record available.
1871-1884	Schools administered by Board of Directors.
1871	The board consisted of: L. E. Salles, President; Dr. Thomas B. Hopkins, Treasurer; M. G. Broussard, Secretary; Alfred Peck; A. Fortune Richard; Calvin Moss; Gustave St. Julien.
1872	The Parish School Board consisted of: W. H. Williams, President; L. E. Salles, Treasurer; A. H. Monnier; W. B. Bailey; M. G. Broussard.
1877	The School Board consisted of: Dr. Thomas B. Hopkins, President; William Clegg, Secretary-Treasurer; Michael Lyons; Oneziphore Broussard; Narcisse Mouton (colored); Joseph Boudreaux; N. D. Young; Charles T. Padillo (colored).
1884	Parish Superintendents again authorized by the state. Since then the following have held the office:
1884-1886	A. E. Martin
1886-1896	T. E. Tall
1896-1898	F. C. Latiolais
1898-1901	O. P. Guilbeau
1901-1907	L. J. Alleman
1907-1908	V. L. Roy, Joint superintendent of Lafayette and Avoyelles Parishes.
1908-1909	W. J. Avery

LIST OF PARISH SUPERINTENDENTS OF EDUCATION (Continued)

1909-1912 E. L. Wright
1912-1918 L. J. Alleman
1918-1922 A. W. Bittle
1922-1942 J. W. Faulk
1942-1946 Odon Hebert
1946-1948 A. A. McBride
1948-1957 J. C. Landry
1957 to
Present   Robert L. Browne

LAFAYETTE PARISH CASUALTIES IN RECENT WARS

World War I, Killed or Died in the Service

Isadore Alpha
Leon Chester Breaux
Gustave Celestine
Sully Bourque
Angelas Broussard
Jean B. Broussard
Joseph Francois
Cleophas Foreman
Willie Griffin
Louis Guidry
August Hebert
Edwin A. Hoffpauir
Eli Maleveaux
Louis Stanley Martin

Reuben Broussard
Ernest Burke
Rhul W. Burleigh
Sidney Campbell
Alexander M. Cockerell
Leonard Demas
John Mathews
Kentroy Nichols
Noah Savoy
Ulysse R. Servat
George Smith
Abel Claude Trahan
Sidney Whitmeyer

World War II Casualties — Lafayette Parish

List I. Killed in action, Died of wounds, Died of injuries, Missing persons:

Wilson Preston Arnaune
Curley Babineaux
Dave H. Bailey, Jr.
Curman J. Begnaud
Adley V. Benoit
Clement J. Bernard
James W. Bernard
Lee Roy Bernard
John L. Bernard
Robert J. Boudreaux, Jr.
A. B. John Breaux
Antoine Breaux
Bennet J. Breaux
Lawrence Breaux
Rene Breaux
Shirley Broussard
Albert B. Cantrelle

John E. Hunley
Lucien Johnson
Gabriel Knight
Claude J. Landry
Cyril J. B. Landry
Wilfred Landry
Claude O. Langlinais
Pierre Langlinais
Sidney Gerald Larriviere
Andrew Lormand
Woodrow LeBlanc
Joseph Lormand, Sr.
Gauthier Melancon
Numa E. Martin
Rixby J. LeBlanc
Joseph L. Mestayer
James K. Michot

Sam E. Carothers
Alexander P. Choplin
Donald C. Dailey
Louis Felix Ducrest
Silas J. Dufrene
Albert P. Elliott, Jr.
Elay J. Fung
Louis P. Flandry
Alfred E. Gahn
Jerry W. Goodsell
Charles D. Gueriniere
Clifford Guidry
Jerry Maurice Guidry
Joseph W. Guidry
Richard J. Guidry
Edgar J. Guilbeaux
Harold O. Harrison
Ellis John Hebert
Clifton J. Himel
Clarence J. Himel
Ewell J. Sonnier
Rynette Arthur Spell
Richard A. Stayton
Leigh E. Stewart
Elinor R. Stutes
Lee Roy Joseph Stutes
Ellsworth J. Thibodeaux

Antoine J. Miller
Merlin J. Miller
Robert Allen Meaux
Gussie A. Monte
Ralph J. Monte
Cecil W. Morgan
John Mouton
Ovey Mouton
Charles M. Nini
Louis J. Pellerin
Weston F. Poche
Preston L. G. Prejean
Norman Frederick Randolph
Toussaint L. J. Richard
Sexton Richard
Weston Rogers
Raoul Simon
Udley J. Simon
Alton Smith
Paul L. Smith
Joseph H. Thibodeaux
Avers J. Trahan
John Trahan
Lennest Trahan
Octa Trahan
Benjamin Voss

List II. Died in non-battle:
Nelson Anderson
Horace Adkins
Alfred J. Benoit
Stanley Benoit
Louis Boudreaux
Nicholas Boutte
Rheul P. Broussard
Theo Broussard
John R. Chaisson
Clarence Coleman
Francis X. Comeaux
Remy Delahoussaye
David Deroussel
Earl J. Flandry
George C. Fontenot
Jonas Francis
Bryan R. Gilliam

Francis W. Guidroz
Olin Guidry
Rex W. Hamilton
Elie Hebert
Lawrence Jacket
Ambrose Kilchrist
Wilbert W. Loston
William A. Moores
Caffery Mouton
Floyd J. Mouton
Jerome E. Mouton
Wavard J. Myers
Oleus Robichaux
Antoine Sinegal
Ulysse Sonnier
Russell Byrne Voorhies

KOREAN CASUALTIES—LAFAYETTE PARISH
Killed or Missing in Action

Lifford J. Daigle
Edward Broussard, Jr.

Charles R. Parkerson
John Corcoran

KOREAN CASUALTIES—LAFAYETTE PARISH (Continued)

Rayford J. Comeaux
George Broussard
Joseph H. Thibodeaux
Felix Boudreaux
Hayward J. Roy
Ernest J. Jacques
Raymond Joseph Patin
Ralph A. Pecot, Jr.
Andrew Benoit
Bernard Houston
Murphy Gabriel
Melvin Dugas
Moise Melancon, Jr.
Clarence J. Jones
Ferman Cormier
Alex C. Dorsey
Percy Allemand
Paul E. St. Julien
Joseph B. Joe
Paul V. Brouchet

COMPARATIVE STATISTICS, CITY OF LAFAYETTE

	1942	Dec. 31, 1958
Population	19,210	Est. 50,300
Building & Loan Resources	$3,500,000	$45,563,329
Bank Resources	$6,000,000	$65,208,788
Retail Sales	$8,000,000	$65,932,000
Postal Receipts	86,373	$ 583,586
Effective Buying Income	$9,600,000	$92,782,000
Gas Meters	2,900	16,388
Electric Meters	3,961	12,825
Telephones	3,400	25,942
Dwelling Units	5,059	12,908

Resources of Lafayette Banks and Bulding and Loan Associations
December 31, 1958

American Bank and Trust Co.
Capital Stock ....$ 500,000.00
Surplus ....$ 175,000,00
Undivided Profits ....$ 109,953.00
Total Resources ....$ 9,963,599.76

First National Bank
Capital Stock ....$ 750,000.00
Surplus ....$ 1,250,000.00
Undivided Profits and
  Capital Reserve ....$ 497,954.11
Total Resources $31,514,389.10

Guaranty Bank and Trust Co.
Capital Stock................$ 600,000.00
Surplus ....$ 600,000.00
Undivided Profits and
  Reserves ....$ 755,585.93
Total Resources $23,695,920.44

Home Building Association
Total Assets $19,240,590.96

Lafayette Building Association
Total Assets $25,698,224.33

PARTIAL LIST OF LAFAYETTE'S CIVIC, FRATERNAL, AND OTHER ORGANIZATIONS

American Assoc. of Univ. Women
Area Oil Wives' Club
Attakapas Area Tuberculosis Assoc.
Bayou Girl Scout Council
Business and Professional Women
Lafayette Chapter for Retarded Children
Lafayette Charity Hospital Guild
Lafayette Community Concerts Assoc.

Catholic Daughters of America
Cedars Club of Lafayette
Daughters of the American
    Revolution
Desk and Derrick Club
Disabled American Veterans
Evangeline Area Boy Scouts
Exchange Club
Hobo Volunteer Firemen
Hub City Rifle and Pistol Club
Junior Chamber of Commerce
Kiwanis Club
Knife and Fork Club
Knights of Columbus
Krewe of Gabriel
Ladies Auxiliary of the Lafayette
    Parish Medical Society
Ladies Auxiliary of the Third
    District Dental Society
Ministerial Association
Moose Lodge
Oakbourne Country Club
Parent Teachers Association
Petroleum Club of Lafayette
Rotary Club
S. L. I. Faculty Wives
Lafayette District Nurses Assoc.
Lions Club
Lafayette Little Theatre
Lafayette Parish Bar Association
Lafayette Parish Chapter of the
    American Red Cross
Lafayette Museum Association
Lafayette Parish Chapter of the
    National Foundation of Infantile
    Paralysis
Lafayette Parish Medical Society
Lafayette Parish Crippled Children
    Unit
Lafayette Parish Unit of the
    American Cancer Society
League of Women Voters
L'Heure de Musique
Les Vingt Quatre
Mid-Winter Fair Association
Service League of Lafayette
Sons of the American Revolution
Veterans of Foreign Wars
Womans Club
United Givers Fund
Young Men's Business Club
Masonic Lodge

FIRST GRADUATES OF S.L.I. — 1903
Annie T. Bell, Academic
Maxime Beraud, Academic
Rhena Boudreaux, Academic
Harold Demanade, Academic
Alma L. Gilley, Academic
William Parkerson Mills, Academic
Henry de Koven Smedes, Academic
Pothier J. Voorhies, Academic
Jacques Domengeaux, Manual Training
Edith Trahan, Domestic Science
Ula Coronna, Stenography
Munger T. Ball, Commerce
Valsin Benoit, Jr., Commerce
Mentor Chiasson, Commerce
Earl Hatfield, Commerce
Perry T. Singleton, Commerce
D. Clarence Smith, Commerce
Frederick Voorhies, Commerce

ACKNOWLEDGEMENTS and SOURCES OF INFORMATION

First to my wife, Lucile Meredith Mouton Griffin, for her interested and helpful assistance in collecting material and pictures and reading the manuscript; to Dr. Elmer D. Johnson, Director of Stephens Memorial Library and Miss Pearl Mary Segura, Reference Librarian for help in tracing down difficult to find information; to the family of the late Judge Paul Debaillion for access to Judge Deballion's collection of documents, manuscripts and notes on local history.

For information on families, local history and traditions my gratitude to:

The Rt. Rev. Msgr. Albert J. Bacque
Mr. Allen Breaux
Mrs. Paul Breaux
Calvin and Inez Blue
Miss Daisy Broussard
Mrs. J. C. Chargois
Miss Philomene Campbell
Mrs. Bessie Caffery
Miss Eula Creighton
Mrs. William Couret
Mrs. Margaret Ponder DeBlanc
Mr. Charles Debaillon
Mr. Leon Delhomme
Mrs. Louis Delhomme
Mrs. Henri L. Ducrocq
Miss Edith Dupre
Mr. T. W. Faulk
Mrs. Eloi Girard
Mr. Eloi Girard
Mrs. John Givens
Mrs. Don Greig

Mrs. C. E. Hamilton
Mrs. Irene Whitfield Holmes
Mrs. Helen M. Mouton Landell
Mrs. W. A. LeRosen
Mrs. Mose Levy
Miss Alida Martin
Mrs. Joseph Martin
Mr. A. A. McBride
Mr. J. Alfred Mouton
Mr. William H. Mouton
Mr. Xavier Mouton
Mrs. Marc M. Mouton
Miss Marie Reynaud
Dr. George B. Roberts
Mrs. Paul Salles
Mrs. J. G. St. Julien
Mr. John G. Torian
Mr. Bennett J. Voorhies
Mr. P. J. Voorhies
Mrs. Fred Voorhies and
many others

BOOKS

Barde, Alexandre—*Histoire de Comites de Vigilance aux Attakapas, Saint-Jean-Baptiste (Louisiana)* Imp. du Meschacebe et de l'avant Coureur; 1861.

Cable, George Washington—*Bonaventure*, New York, 1888.

Carleton, R. L.—*Local Government and Administration in Louisiana*, Baton Rouge, 1935.

Catlin, George—*North American Indians*, 2 vols. Philadelphia, 1913.

Chambers, Henry Edward—*A History of Louisiana*, Chicago, 1925.

Coughey, John Walton—*Bernardo de Galvez in Louisiana 1775-1783.* Berkley, University of California Press, 1934.

Fortier, Alcee—*History of Louisiana,* 4 vols. New York 1903.

French, B. F.—*Historical Collections,* 1846.

Gayarre, Charles Etienne Arthur—*History of Louisiana,* 4 vols. New Orleans, 1885.

Goodspeed Publishing Company—*Biographical and Hishtorical Memoirs of Louisiana,* Chicago, 1892.

Halliburton, Thomas C.—*Historical and Statistical Account of Nova Scotia,* 1829.

Harris, T. H.—*The Story of Public Education in Louisiana.* Baton Rouge, 1924.

Marchand, Sidney Albert—*Acadian Exiles in the Golden Coast.* Donaldsonville, 1943.

Martin, Francois-Xavier—*The History of Louisiana From the Earliest Period.* New Orleans, 1927-29.

Perrin, William Henry—*Southwest Louisiana, Biographical and Historical.* New Orleans, 1892.

Read, William A.—*Louisiana French.* Baton Rouge, 1931. *Place Names of Indian Origin.* Baton Rouge, 1927. *Louisiana French.* Baton Rouge, 1931.

Robin, C. C.—*Voyages dans l'interieur de la Louisiane,* 1802-1806.

Scott, Robert N.—*War of the Rebellion,* Official Records of the Union and Confederate Armies; Series I, Vol. XXXIV pp. 560-572. Washington, Government Printing Office, 1891.

Swanton, John R.—*Indian Tribes of the Lower Mississippi Valley.* Bureau of American Eithnology, Smithsonian Institution, 1911.

Taylor, Richard—*Destruction and Reconstruction.* D. Appleton and Co. New York, 1879.

Voorhies, Bennett J.—*The Lafayette Bar Association and Early History of Lafayette Parish.* Lafayette, 1950.

Voorhies, Felix—*Acadian Reminences.* Boston, 1907.

PERIODICALS, NEWSPAPERS, PAMPHLETS, UNPUBLISHED NOTES AND MEMOIRS, AND PARISH AND CHURCH RECORDS

Archives in the Opelousas Courthouse and Catholic Church.

Archives in the St. Martinville Courthouse.

Archives in the St. Martinville Catholic Church.

Biographical Sketches of U. S. Congressmen and Senators, Library of Congress, Washington, D. C.

Brand Book for the Attakapas and Opelousas Districts, 1739-1888.

Calhoun, Robert Dabney—The Origin and Early Development of County-Parish Government in Louisiana; Louisiana Historical Quarterly, Vol. XVIII.

Churchill, C. Robert—Transcript of Spanish Records in Seville, Collected for the Sons of the American Revolution; on film in the Southwestern Louisiana Institute Library.

Claiborne, William C. C.—Official Letter Books of the State Department of Archives and History, Jackson, Mississippi, 1917, 6 vols.

Deballlon, Paul—Extensive Collection of unpublished notes, essays and documents relation to the history and families of the City and Parish of Lafayette.

Gardner, Emma Kitchell—Second Wife of Governor Alexandre Mouton; Scrap Book, now owned by a granddaughter, Mrs. Paul Breaux.

Kelley, Mimie—Acadian South Louisiana; Journal of Geography, March, 1934.

Lafayette Advertiser, Files of.

Lafayette Progress, Files of.

Lafayette Parish Clerk of Court, Records of.

Lafayette Parish School Board, Minutes of.

Lafayette Parish Police Jury, Minutes of.

Lafayette Chamber of Commerce, Industrial Survey of Lafayette, 1956.

Mouton, Alexandre, Scrap Book.

Mouton, Alexandre, Unpublished Memoirs, 1853-1936.

Opelousas "Daily World," Some History of St. Landry Parish from the 1690's. Opelousas 1955.

Souvay, C. M.—Rummages through old Parish Records; St. Louis Catholic Review, Vol. II.

Southern Pacific Bulletin, October, 1952. Houston, Texas.

Southwestern Louisiana Institute; Catalogues of 1901-1938.

State of Louisiana, Department of Conservation; Twentieth Biennial Report, Baton Rouge, 1952.

St. John the Evangelist Catholic Church, Records of births, marriages and burials.

State of Louisiana, Department of Public Works; Resources and Facilities of Lafayette Parish. 1955.

Survey of Federal Archives—*Louisiana*. Ship registers and enrollments of New Orleans. Louisiana State University, 1941-1942. 6 vols.

Swanton, John R.—Indian Tribes of the Lower Mississippi Valley. U. S. Government Printing Office, 1911.

Times-Picayune, Files of. New Orleans, Louisiana.

United States Census Reports, 1810-1950.

Voorhies, Felix, Unpublished essays, plays and papers relating to Southwest Louisiana.

Works Progress Administration, Inventories of Parish Archives of Louisiana, Prepared by the Historical Records Survey.

Wooster, Ralph, The Louisiana Secession Convention. Louisiana Historical Quarterly, Vol. 34, pg. 103. April, 1951.

PROGRESS

By Edith Garland Dupré

P-roceed, O muse, to yield us one more theme,
R-elating how in all the coming years
O-'er Lafayette shall Progress wave her wand
G-ive us the Vision of a future bright
R-ich with the spoils of time and God's best gifts;
E-xact from each of us his toll of love,
S-o that the passing days may serve to bring
S-ome glory still undreamed of by our State.

THE END

"Monsieur Beaucaire" by Booth Tarkington, presented in the auditorium of Southwestern Louisiana Institute in 1902 under the supervision of Miss Edith Dupre and Miss Beverly Randolph, later Mrs. (Dr.) E. L. Stephens.

From Left to Right:
1. Aimee Thibodeaux
2. P. J. Voorhies m. Lucy Comeaux
3. Lena Bass
4. Ferdinand Siadous
5. Gertrude Lane
6. Herbert McNaspy
7. Eleanor Compton
8. Joseph Authemot
9. Mathilde Richard
10. Edith Trahan
11. William D. Sutter
12. Marcelle Blot
13. Robert Dutsch
14. Mary Dutsch
15. Willis Roy
16. Adeline Turner
17. James Grevenberg

Portraits at the top of picture:
(Left) Mrs. Maxime Girard
(Right) Robert Martin

Southwestern's first Football Team. The coach, Professor Ashby Woodson, is not shown. Standing (left to right) Breaux or Boudreaux, Fernand Siadous, Aldwin Talbot, Joseph Authemont, William (Bill) Sutter, Marshall Boudreaux. Top row (seated) P. J. Voorhies, Marcus Padgett, Aubert Talbot. Second row (seated): Harry D. Smedes, Mentor Chiasson, Cy McNaspy, Henry Domengeaux, Herbert McNaspy. Front, Felix Breaux.

FLOOD OF 1927

Top — Refugees on the road from Lafayette to Breaux Bridge.
Center — Pin Hook Bridge near Lafayette swept away.
Bottom — Saw Mill plant of Baldwin Lumber Co. under water.

INDEX

This index does not include the names found in the various lists given in the Appendix. For instance, the members of the militia companies are listed in the appendix and are not found in this index.

A

Academy of the Sacred Heart—93
Acadia Parish—3
Acadians—4, 12, 13, 14, 131
Acadian Reminiscenses—131
Adams, J. H.—82
Advertiser, Lafayette—65, 114
Alleman, L. J.—97
Allen, Judge—206
Alpha, Hazel—119
Alpha, James A.—118, 119
American Bank & Trust Co.—110
Anderson, Louis—150
Angelle, Robert—110
Antoine, C. C.—70
Arceneaux—15
Arceneaux, Ovnac—72
Arceneaux, Paulin—66
Arceneaux, Pierre—15
Assembly of God Church—84
Atchafalaya Bay—3
Atchafalaya River—3
Attakapas Region—3, 12, 13, 22
Attakapas, Indians—9, 10, 11
Attakapas, Militia—218, 226
Attakapas, Records of Old Poste—214
Attakapas, Sanitarium—128
Aubry, Acting Governor—13, 14, 214
Aucoin, Rev. Mother St. Paul—94
Audubon—Birds of America—19.
Avoyelles, District—3

B

Bacque, F. M.—165
Bailey, Abijah—53, 117
Bailey, Colombus—117
Bailey, H. M.—66
Bailey, Polk—143
Bailey, William—117
Bailey, W. B.—37, 52
Bailey, Judge W. W.—165
Baillio, Helen Barker—201
Baillio, Pierre—201
Ball, Leslie—180
Balin, Gustave—140
Ballard, Nina Breaux—185
Baldwin Lumber Co.—111
"Bamboula"—46
Banks, Gen.—142
Baptist Church—82
Barah, Mammy—41
Barde, Alexander—80
Barnett, Allen, Earl, Robert—111
Barriére, Father Michael Bernard—76, 77, 79, 214, 215
Barry, J. C.—110
Battle of New Orleans—70
Baumgartner, John—39, 41
Bayou Carencro—15
Bayou Têche—3, 5, 7
Bayou Queue Tortue—135
Bayou Vermilion—7, 15
Beadle, Mrs. W. E.—169
Beau Bassin—4
Beau Sejour—43

Bechet, Mildred Louise—205
Begneaud, Martin—139, 140
Begneaud, Toledano—69
Bendel, I. B.—164
Benton, Hemp—140
Beraud—15
Beraud, Honoré—41
Beraud, Thomas—24
Beraud, W. D.—47
Berde, E. L.—112
Bernard, Anastasie—125
Bernard, Anabelle—178
Bernard, Gerasin—44, 125
Bernard, Jean—86
Bernard, Joseph—24, 86
Bernard, Mrs. Sarah—70
Bernard, Traville—72
Bertrand, Vincent—94
Betsy—131, 136
Blanche, Mary Alice—178
Bibliography—252, 255
Bienville Code—76, 147
Bienville, Governor—21, 213
Bigot, Governor—14
Billeaud, Martial—78, 106
Biossat, T. Moore—60, 107, 111
Biossat, Jewelry Store—60
Bittle, A. W.—XI
Blanc, Archbishop—80, 116
Blanc Brothers—139
Blanchet, Col. A. D.—68
Blanchet, Paul—110, 178
Black, Capt. A. L.—82
Bodemuller, Mrs. H. R.—83
Bonaparte, Napoleon—51
Bond Election—62
Bond, H. C.—XI
Bordat, Dr. Antoine—122
Bordat, Marie Marthe—122
Boustany, Alfred F.—110
Boustany, Frem F.—178
Boudreaux, Col. A. A.—69, 139
Bourgeois, Dr. Ralph—127
Bowie, James Resin—214
Bouvier, Marjorie—54
Brands of Cattle—241, 242, 243
Brandt, W.—37, 137
Brashear, Marin—108
Brashear, Hon. Thomas B.—24, 94
Breaux—15
Breaux, Anatalie—124
Breaux, Dr. Edgar P.—127
Breaux, Francis—98
Breaux, Col. Gustave Aurelian—106, 124, 140, 141
Breaux, Joseph—98
Breaux, Louis Gustave—209
Breaux, Mrs. Paul—55
Breaux, Paul—150
Breaux, Rosamond—72
Briant, Judge Paul—77
Broussard,—15
Broussard, Alexander—15
Broussard, Izidor—39
Broussard, Sheriff Isaac—140
Broussard, Louis A.—177
Broussard, Desiré—74
Broussard, Town of—73
Broussard, Aledon—34, 74
Broussard, Beausoliel—214
Broussard, Gourhept—17

Broussard, Horace—26
Broussard, Isaac—26
Broussard, Mabel—178
Broussard, M. G.—68
Broussard, Magdeline—214
Broussard, Mrs. I. A.—82
Broussard, Valsin—73
Broussard, Victor—15
Brown, C. C.—109
Brown News Restaurant—61
Buchanan, Capt. John Charles—126, 210
Buchanan, Sarah Philomene—126
Bujard, A. M.—178
Burdin, Barbara—178
Burdin, Dr. J. J.—110, 127
Burguieres, Leufroy—46
Burkett, Dr. A. R.—75
Busuire, Chas. de—122
Butcher, Warren—180
Butcher, William—41

C

Cable, George—20
Cade, Robert—88, 93, 108
Caffery, Ambassador—208
Caffery, Chas. D.—60, 107, 111, 208
Caffery, Jeff—44
Calcasieu Indians—9
Calais, Harold—171
Callahan, Thomas M.—112, 119
Calhoun, Mrs. Clarence—185
Camellia Broadcasting Co.—121
Campbell, William—173
Canada,—13
Carencro—72
Carmouche, Father Francis—24, 77
Carnival Kings & Queens—178
Carlos, Dorothy—68
Carter, Rev. Edward—82
Castille, R. J.—178
Cattle Brands—241, 243
Cayret, V.—74
Celestine La Tortue—9
Century Club—43, 60
Census Reports—237, 240
Chamber of Commerce—111
Chaplin, R. E. Lieut.—160
Chargois Bros.—61
Chargois, Chief A. E.—160
Chargois, Joseph Albert—95, 209
Chargois, Hubert—24
Chargois House—47
Chargois, Richard—51
Chaix, Aristide—52
Carter, Inez—164
Chevis, Dr. John W.—81
Chinese Restaurant—74
Choctaw Indians—7
Chopin, Louis—154
Christian Bros. School—49
Christian Science Church—83
Church, Henry Joseph—210
Church of Christ—84
Church of St. Jean, Early Records—228, 237
Church of St. Martin, Early Records—226, 227
Civil War Companies—143
Clark, Daniel—148

— 257 —

Clark, Dr. L. Oran—125, 127, 178
Claiborne, Gov. C. C.—22, 216
Clegg—15
Clegg, John—37, 66
Clegg, William—49, 58, 108, 206
Clegg, Mrs. Louise G.—171
Cline, Dr. I. M.—153
Cobb, Elizabeth—124
Cochrane, Douglas Robert—210
Code Justinian—136
Code Napoleon—136
Code Noir—147
Colomb, J. P.—38, 110
Columbia Broadcasting Co.—121
Comeaux, Baptiste—86
Comeaux, Dr. James—178
Comeaux, Demas—37
Comeaux, Telesmar—143
Committee, Vigilance—135
Compton, Audrey—180
Compton, Charles—180
Confederate Veterans—206
Constitution of 1845—25
Constantin Livery Stable—59
Coppens, Marie—201
Cormier, Pierre—72
Corona, B. N.—110
Coroners—246
Courtableau, Bayou—87
Cote Blanche Bay—3
Cote Geleé—4, 132
Couget, Dr. (dentist)—126
Couret, Laura—199
Couret, Mrs. William—45, 125
Courier of Opelousas—135
Cousins, E. A.—78
Creighton—15
Creighton, Col. John Republican —19, 41, 66
Creighton, Leonidas—209
Creighton, Dr. Matthew—122
Crow, Basil C.—44, 86, 93, 108
Crow, Maxime—53
Crow, Girard—196
Crow, Madame Maria Crow—94
Crozat, Anthony—147
Cumberland Telephone Co.—120
Cuny, Father—78
Cunningham, Dr. Wm. H.—66
Cushman, John—75
Cushman, Milton—75

D

D'Abadie, Journal of—13
Dalferes, Mrs. Joyce Hartzell —181
Dalferes, Patricia—178
Daigre's Variety Store—60
Daly, Dr. O. P.—178, 180
Dauterive—15
Dauterive, Capt.—15
Davidson, J.—118
Davidson, J. J.—109
Davis, Mrs. F. E.—155
Davis, Martha Tolly—178
Davis, Dr. F. H.—127, 178
DeBlanc—15
De Baillon, Charles—58
De Baillon, Judge Conrad—26, 88, 109, 140
De Baillon, Dan—139
De Baillon, Judge Paul—53, 77, 117
De Blanc, Capt. Alcibiades—
De Blanc, George A.—26
De Blanc, L. P.—156
De Blanc, Louis Charles—215
De Clouet—15
De Clouet, General Alexandre—88, 197

De Favrot, Louise—197
De la Houssaye—15
De La Clair—15
De St. Laurent, Madame—93
De Vaugine, Capt.—140
DeHamel, Dr.—126
De Laureal, Dr. George R.—125
De Laureal, Paul—180
Del Homme, Alexandre—66
Demande, Felix—26, 109, 111
Demaret, Martin—108
"Democrat" of St. Martinville —135
Demouly Dr.—126
Denais, Baptiste—74
Denais, Jean—74
Denbo, A. B.—106, 110
Dennister, E. C.—149
Derbigny, C.—37
Derbonne, Dr.—126
Des Ormeaux, Dr. Nugier—45
Dinsmore, John, Jr.—33
District Attorneys—245
Dolores, Mother Superior—95
Domengeaux, Louis—46
Donlon, Mike—156
Doremus, Dr.—126
Doty, P. B.—112
Doucet—15
Doucet, George—59
Doucet, Leo—108
Doucet, Rosemary—178
Doucet, Zepherin—199
Dowty, Horace—178
Drossarts, Bishop—95
Du Bourg, Bishop—77
Dubuisson, E. B.—141
Ducrocq, Dr. Henri L.—124
Dugas, Jean—15
Dugas, Joachim—68
Dugas, Tibus—209
Dugas, Waldo—126
Duhon, Dr. J. O.—126
Duplex, Mrs. Nina—125
Duplex, Mrs. P. R.—164
Dupré, Célémine—198
Dupré, Edith—XII, 64, 181
Dupre, Gov. Jacques—46, 194
Dupré, H. Garland—141
Dupré, Lucius Garland—141
Duralde—10
Duralde, Clarissa—26
Duralde, Martin Milony—23
Durhon, Father—79
Dyer, A. L.—73

E

Eastin, Herbert—145
Eastin, Willam—143
Eastern Air Lines—116
Echo of Vermilionville—135
Elk's Lodge—170
Episcopal Church—83
Erwin, Maxime—47, 56
Erwin, William—47
Evangeline, Heroine—12
Evangeline Broadcasting Co.—120
Evangeline Hotel—42, 44
Evans, T. L.—155

F

Fabacher, Joseph—106
Fabre, Marcel—70
Falk, B.—83
Falk Opera House—58
Falk's Store—59
Faulk, J. W.—149
Figaro, Achille—150
Fisher, Malcolm—180
Five O'Clock Tea—171
Flanders, Benjamin—88

Fletcher, Ellen—180
Fletcher, Joel Lafayette—112
Flood Relief Committees—156, 164, 166
Foltier, Father E. Jules—95, 98
Foote, Irving P.—103
Foreman, J. Y.—81
Foreman, Nathan—66
Forge, Father—77, 95
Forguet, Julien—33
Fontainebleau, Treaty of—13
Fournet, J. J.—165
Fournet, O. A.—118
Foster, Gov. Murphy J.—65, 99, 117, 141
France—13, 123
Francez, Dr. Romain—73, 123 125
Franklin—5
Frazar, Lether E.—99
Francois, Father Jean—214
French Opera House—20
French Royalists—15
Fuselier-de-la-Claire—8
Fuselier, Gabriel, Commandant —148

G

Gaidry, Dr. Merle—180
Galvez, Gov.—8
Gardner, Emma Kitchell—42
Gardner, General Frank—142
Gardiner, George—178
Garland, R.—108
Gatchet, Dr.—9
Gauthier, Dr. V.—80
General Gardner Ave.—143
Gerac—15
Gerac, Pierre—109
Girard, Crow—99, 109
Girard, Eloi—108
Girard, Dr. Felix E.—26, 38, 125, 128
Girard, Mrs. Maxim A.—99
Girard, Michel Eloi—53, 58
Girard, Dr. Percy M.—47, 48, 123, 125
Giroir, Firmin—27
Giroir, John—68
Glaudu, Miss Lea—171
Glaudi, Miss A. R.—128
Glover, Pansy—164
Goldsmith, Julius—112
Gordon Hotel—111
Grand Lake—5
Grand Prairie—122
Grandenigo, Demoiselle Marie —23
Gradenigo, Aimeé—195
Graduates of Southwestern La. Inst. 1908—142
Grangé, Louis—41
Gregnon, E. I.—108
Gregnon, E. J.—116
Greig, Arthur—208
Greig, Mrs. H. G.—82
Greig, John—23, 93, 155
Greig, Martha—123
Greig, Robert—93
Greig, Sidney—207
Grimstaff, Burton—119
Guidry—15
Guidry, Alex. M.—66
Guidry, Emelie—193
Guidry, Homer—62
Guilbeau, Jean—24
Guilbeau, Celia Anne—178
Guilbeau, Joseph—15
Guilbeau, P. D.—68
Guilheod, Lucien—93
Gulf of Mexico—2
Guillot, Father—78

H

Haas—83
Hamilton, Mary Virginia—178
Hamilton, Dr. C. E.—127
Hardee, General—142
Harper, Rev. R. H.—179
Hathorne, William—24
Hawkins, Mrs. W. W.—118
Hawkins, W. W.—178
Hayes, Mrs. A. C.—81
Hayes, Jack—178
Hayes, Mr. & Mrs. J. T.—82
Hayes, Rutherford B.—70
Hays, Caroline—125
Health Unit—129
Hebert, Charles—68
Hebert, Louis—28
Hebert, Gaston—177
Hebert, Ursin—108
Herchershine—97
Herpin, J. C.—38
Heymann, Maurice—114
Hobo Fire Co.—58
Hodges, Elmo—112
Hoggasett Telephone Co.—120
Holmes, Rev. R. H.—83
Hohorst, H. H.—26
Holy Rosary Convent—151
Hoover, Herbert—154
Higginbotham, Jim—39, 41, 81
Hopkins, F. K.—82
Hopkins, Ida Katherine—164
Hopkins, O. B.—82, 155
Hopkins, Eliza—171
Hopkins, Mr. & Mrs. T. B.—84
Hopkins, Dr. Thomas Benjamin—123
Huff, W. D.—110
Huron Plantation—73
Hutchinson, J. P.—15, 110
Huval, Joe—110
Huval, Mary—178

I

Iberia Parish—3
Ile Copal—19, 42, 51, 52, 57, 144
"Impartial"—117
Incorporation, Act of—34
"Independent"—117
Ingalls, Gen.—142
Island of Lacasine—9
Isenberg, Monsig.—79

J

Jagou, Mrs. Rose—169
Jamerson, Eliza—82
Jamison, H., Jr.—66
Jeanmard, Bishop—78, 79
Jeanmard, Ernest, Jr.—180
Jeanmard, J. R.—111, 112
Jeanmard, J. F.—110
Jefferson Theatre—58, 111
Jewish Congregation—83
Joe Plonsky's Store—59
Johnston, A. R.—110
Judice, Alcide—74, 97, 109, 111
Judice, Mrs. Alix—57
Judice, Leo L.—46, 112, 162
Judges, City—246
Judges, Circuit Court—244
Judges, District—245, 246
Judges, Parish—246

K

Kahn, Sig—60
Kellogg, William P.—65, 66, 70, 71
Keller, Esther—178
Kendrick, Rev. J. L.—82
Kennedy, Mary Willis—124
Kennedy, Mrs. Mary E.—82
Kennedy, Dr. John Bailey—124
Kennedy, John L.—139

Kiam, Edmond—83
King Attakapas—175
Kinemo, Chief—8
Knighten, Doris—180
Knights of Columbus—171
Krauss, Paul—177
Krauss, Mrs. Paul—51
Krewe of Gabriel—177
K. V. O. L.—121

L

Labbé, Adrian—70
Labbé, Alceé—37
La Chaise, H.—217
Lacoste, Antoine—137
Lacoste, Gus—59
Lacoste, Leopold—49
Lady of Lourdes Hospital—57
Lacasine, Attak. Chief—9
Lafayette "Advertiser"—65
Lafayette Airport—91
Lafayette Boundaries—57
Lafayette Census Records—61, 237
Lafayette, City Statistics—250, 251
Lafayette, Charter—84
Lafayette, Company B, Nat'l Guard—155
Lafayette House—51
Lafayette Motors—33
Lafayette Museum—46
Lafayette Parish, Evolution of—21, 27
Lafayette, Post Office—115
Lafayette, Post Masters—115
"Lafayette Progress"—119
Lafayette Public Library—63, 64
Lafayette Sanitarium—127
Lafayette Town House—178
Lafayette, Wholesale Gro. Co.—112
Lagniappe—135
Lake Catahoula—5
Land Grants, Early—216, 218
Landell, Herbert Stanford—201
Landmarks—48
Landry—15
Landry, P.—73
Landry, Eraste, 40, 57
Landry, Norbert—68
Landry, R. C.—66
Landry, W. B.—110
Langlois, Leroy—171
Lang Bernard—178
Laribeau, Rose Celeste, Alice—124
Lastrapes, T. and A.—108
Latiolais, Julie—198
Latiolais, Leon—142
Latter Day Saints—84
Law, Common—136
Law, Roman—136
Lawyers—138
LeBlanc—15
LeBlanc, Mrs. Luke—155
LeBlanc, J. Ozeme—69
LeBlanc, Verna—180
Les Brigands De Lafitte—178
"L'Echo De Vermilionville"—49, 53, 117
"Le Meridonal"—117
Le Rosen, W. A.—93, 118
Le Rosen, Mrs. W. A.—171
Lesley, Mrs. George P.—179
Lesley, Dr. William W.—123, 125
Les Vingt Quatre—46
Levy Bros.—118
Levy, Lazarus—83
Levy, Vic—60
Levy, Willie—60

Lewis, Dr. Ernest—124
Littel, Mary—119
Little Manchac—26
Live Oak Society—203
Lisbony, Auguste—209
Locke, Emelie—185
Logan, Burl—180
Longfellow—3
Long, Gov. Huey P.—90
Louisiana Ceded to Spain—12
Louisiana Public Utilities—62, 63
Louvier, Joseph—66, 143
Lutheran Church—84

M

Magnolia Plantation—193
Maison, Francais Acadienne—55
Malagarie, J. B.—73, 74
Manitou—7
Mansfield, Battle—183
Marr, Josephine—185
Marguilliers, Board of—79, 80
Marion's Restaurant—61
Martonne—126
Martin—15
Martin, André—16, 24
Martin, André Valerien—193
Martin, A. M.—26
Martin, Mrs. C. W's. Store—59
Martin, Clayton—33
Martin, E. E.—67
Martin, E. H.—88
Martin, Elia—49
Martin, F. X.—25, 186
Martin, G. A.—60, 134, 146, 175
Martin, Louis Stanley—146
Martin, Philip—97
Martin, Robert—98
Martin, Valery—77
Martin, Victor—66
Masse—146
Masonic Lodge, Charter Members—168
Matas, Dr.—124
Mayors, Early Lafayette—37
Mayors, List of Lafayette—244
Mayne, Alice—150
MacIntyre—159
McBride, Andrew A.—118
McBride, Thomas—94
McCaskill, Daniel—93
McCarthy, Gertrude—203
McClure, G. L.—109
McCullough, Hilda Elizabeth—178
McDaniel, Isaure—175
McElligot, Joanne—178
McEnery, John—65
McFaddin, Mr. and Mrs. T. A.—82
McFaddin's Grocery—60
McNaspy, C. J., Jr.—164
M. de Belle Isle—10
Megret, Rev. Antoine Desiré—77, 79, 80, 81, 84, 116, 127
Melancon, Marcel—72
Melchoir, Mrs.—96
Meriman, John—24
Mermentau River—3
Merchant's Gro. Co.—112
Methodist Episcopal Church—81
Mielly, H. V.—156
Militia, Attakapas—218, 226
Militia, Opelousas—220, 226
Milton, Town of—74
Mikado—104
Miller, Diane—178
Miller, Albert—178
Mills, Mrs. Eppie—51

— 259 —

Mills, W. G.—47
Mills, W. P.—51
Mississippi Bubble—147
Missonier—Veuve—139
Mobley, Coach Ray—155
Montgomery, Samuel James—60, 208
Montgomery, Thad & Elizabeth—84
Montet—74
Monnier, Auguste—37
Monnier, Henry—41
Monquis, Harris—43
Morgan, Mrs. A. A., Jr.—156
Morphy, A.—186
Morse, Delia—9
Moss, A. J.—109
Moss, Bros. and Co.—59
Moss, Frank—111
Moss, N. P., Dr.—38, 109, 111
Moss Pharmacy—60
Moss, Wilfred Capt.—155
Mouton, A. M. Thomas—140
Mouton, Antoine Emile—26, 39, 44, 77, 123
Mouton, Gen. Alfred—43, 44, 124, 133, 135, 143
Mouton, J. Alfred, Jr.—180
Mouton, Ashton—54
Mouton, Governor Alexandre—25, 39, 42, 43, 44, 46, 53, 55, 56, 57, 77, 83, 88, 124, 133, 135, 143, 153, 163, 193
Mouton, Alexandre, Grandson—39, 123, 199
Mouton, Anastasie—196
Mouton, Brothers—93
Mouton, Césaire—36, 44
Mouton, Charles—24, 98
Mouton, Madame Charles—43, —51
Mouton, Rev. Charles Burton—205
Mouton, Charles Homer—19, 45, 66, 140, 199
Mouton, Charlotte Odeide—39, 43
Mouton, Charles Olivier—26, 109, 171
Mouton, Cidalise—195
Mouton, Dan. J.—155
Mouton, J. Edmond—68, 139
Mouton, E. E.—66, 67
Mouton, Eraste—43, 49, 52, 53, 117, 143
Mouton, Euphemie—51
Mouton, Felix—155
Mouton, F. V.—156, 201
Mouton, Guillaume—94
Mouton, Helen Muriel—201
Mouton, Homer—118
Mouton, Jean—16, 29, 32, 72, 76, 115, 137, 139
Mouton, Jean Sosthene—45, 207
Mouton, Jerome—118
Mouton, Dr. J. Franklin—125, 127
Mouton, John O.—26, 37, 59, 108
Mouton, Mrs. John O.—59
Mouton, Joseph E.—49
Mouton, Josephine Eugenie—126
Mouton, Judge Julien—26, 110
Mouton, Lucile Meredith—201
Mouton, Dr. Marc. M.—159
Mouton, Marin—16, 72
Mouton, Mathilde—142
Mouton, Judge O. C.—49, 111, 141
Mouton, Onezime—169
Mouton, Philip—118

Mouton, Capt. Robert—146, 154
Mouton, Roche—72
Mouton, Salvador—12
Mouton, Sidney & Sosthene—146
Mouton, William—44, 49, 143
Mt. Carmel Convent—79, 94
Mudd, Dr. Francis Stirling—46
Mumme, Theodore—123
Municipal Ticket, 1899—26
Murphy, Morgan—119
Myrtle Plantation—122

N

Nazarene, Church of—84
Neverville—14
Neveu, Mayor Alphonse—37
Neveu, Cahe—108
Nevil, James & Mary—214
New Orleans—12, 13
Neyland, Inez—164
Nicholls, Gen. Francis T.—70, 141
Nicholson, James W.—46
Nickerson, Bella—178
Nickerson, John Cameron—46, 55, 156
Norton, Leslie—164
Nova Scotia—4, 12, 13
N. P. Moss School—98

O

Oakbourne—193
Oak Ave—42
Ogden, Capt. Charles Wesley—201
"Old Gerac House"—49
"Old Moss House"—52
"Old Swimming Hole"—52
Olivier, Aurelian—70, 135
Olivier, Emerite—199
Olivier, Daniel J.—178
Olivier, N. D.—178
Opelousas, Early Settlers—213
Opelousas Militia—220, 226
Opelousas, Records of Old Poste—213
O'Reilly, Gov.—2, 8, 12, 14
Organizations, Civic & Fraternal—225
Ortego, Don Joachim—214
Ostrich, Emmanuel—178
Overton, John H.—88

P

Packard, G. B.—70
Parochial Schools, Laf.—95
Patin, C. T.—66, 68
Patin, Laurent—93
Parent, F. P.—67
Parker, Gov.—156
Parkerson, C. M.—107, 111
Parkerson, J. G.—83, 109
Parkerson, S. R.—109, 111, 141
Parkerson, W. S.—141
Paxton, Ben. Porter—47, 81
Paxton & Templeton—137
Paxton, Sam. W.—52
Paxton, Sam. N.—47
Peck, Charles—72
Peck, Wilson—154
Pellerin, Laurent—93
Pellerin, Domartin—93
People's Cotton Oil Co.—107
Perry's Bridge—80
Perry, Capt. Robert—142
Persac—55
Petty, G. B.—109
"Pictorial"—119
Pierro Baptiste—149
Pin Hook Bridge—27, 39
Plaquemine—13
Plonsky—83

Police Jury, First Meeting—24, 116
Porter, Capt. Shadrach—24, 142
Postal Telegraph—120
Prejean, Dr. Louis—125, 127
Presbyterian Church—81
Primeaux, Percy—177
Protestant Cemetery—42
Prudhomme, A. W.—112
Public Library—63
Purchasers of Vermilionville Lots—63

Q

Queen Penelope—118
Quota Club—178

R

Racca Hotel—59
Rainbolt, W. K.—110
Ramsey, Mr. & Mrs. John—47
Randolph, Beverly—202
Raney, Dr.—124
Reaux, John J.—70
Reconstruction Leaders—66
Red Cross—154
Rees, David—26
Reeves, E.—108
Reeves, Joe—180
Reves, William—24
Rein, Pancross—143
Reon, Armojean—9
Revillon, Joaquim—88, 94, 108
Revillon, Jules—51
Revillon, L. Philibert—67
Ribetty, Jacques—33
Richard—15
Richard, Ancelet—77, 108
Richard, Vesta—164
Rickey, Horace—178
Rigues, M. F.—66
Robicheau—15
Robinson, E. K.—82
Roguet, Father—79
Rogan, F. A.—82, 93
Romero, Daisy—177
Roman, Gov.—107
Roman, System of Law—136
Rosalie Plantation—201
Rosenfield, Morris—61, 83
Rosk, F. J.—73
Rousseau—15
Rousseau, Zelia—46
Rotary, Members Charter—172
Roy, Desiré—73
Roy, Dorothy—180
Roy, J. J.—73
Roy, J. Maxime—46, 110, 112, 118
Roy Lucille—180
Roy, P. B.—68, 108, 109, 111
Roy, Mr. and Mrs. V. L.—82
Royville—73

S

Sabine—89
Salles, Charles Camille—48
Salles, G. C.—37
Salles, Dr. H. C.—52
Salles, Dr. H. O.—126
Salles, Miss Josette—48
Salles, Dr. Paul—125, 126
Salvation Army—84
San Domingo—13
Satterfield, Isaac H.—47
Saucier, Harry—180
Saucier, Dr. Merrick E.—125
Schmulen, Gus.—59
School Superintendents—247, 248
Schwartz, D. S.—110
Scott, G. P.—74
Scott Village—74

Scranton, Dr. G. W.—123
Scranton, Dr. G. W. P. S.—124
Secession Convention—20, 143
Sellers, Camille—66
Segura, Josephine—150
Shaw, Matthew—82
Sheriff's List—246
Simon, James D.—180
Simon, Joe—178
Smedes—15
Singleton, Lela—125
Sister du Carmel & Rose—94
Sisters of the Holy Family—151
Smith, Webb—180
Societies, Social and Fraternal—168
Sonnier, Dr. Lee J.—128
Soulier, E. E.—155, 178
Soulier, Mrs. Emile—118
Soule, Pierre—125
Southern Bell Telephone Co.—120
Southern Chemurgic Conference—112
Southwestern La. Inst. Grad. of 1903—251
Southwestern Louisiana Inst.—99
Souvay, Father C. M.—80
Spain—14
Stephens, Edwin Lewis—XI, 99, 202
Stephens, Gideon—81
St. Charles College—93, 94
St. John The Baptist—64, 77
St. Jean's Church, Early Records—225, 237
St. John's Cemetery—77
St. John's College—49
St. John's Hospital—128
St. Joseph's Academy—53, 95
Saint Julien, Aurelian—133
Saint Julien, Gustave—66, 73
Saint Julien, J. G., Mayor—165
Saint Julien, Madame Caddy—86
Saint Julien, Major—136
Saint Julien, Lucien—70
Saint Julien, Paul—80
St. Landry Parish—3
St. Louis Cathedral—124
St. Martin Church, Early Records—226, 227
St. Martinville—14, 22

St. Martin Parish—3, 5, 23
St. Pierre—72
Swanton, Author—7
Swayze, C. L.—108

T

Taylor, Gen. Richard—143
Têche Courier—117
Territory, Orleans of—22
Teurlings, W. J., Rev. Mons—78
Theriot, Nancy Jo—178
Thibaudau, Oliver—15
Thibodeaux, Mrs. Ben.—118
Thomas, Chas—118
Thomas, George—120
Tilden, Samuel T.—71
Tolson, Dr. Fred R.—125
Torian, Walter—108
Torian, William B.—208
Torrance, Benj. B.—82
Torrance, Mr. and Mrs. John D.—82
Trahan—15
Trahan, Haydee—124
Trahan, Dr. J. D.—123, 124
Trahan, Dr. Raoul Anatole—124
Trahan, Stella—124
Trappey, B. F. and Sons—111
Troubadours—178

U

Union Bank of La.—116
United Gas Co.—63

V

Vander Cruyssen, H. A.—118
Vermilionville Academy — 53, 83
Vermilion Bay—3
Vermilion Bayou—3
Vermilionville Becomes Lafayette—37
Vermilionville Before Civil War—57
Vermilionville Incorporated—33
Vermilion Parish—23
Vermilion White League Club—67
Verot—15
Verdine, Teet & Eliza—9
Vergor, Gov. 14

Vigilance Committees — 131, 132
Vigliero, Rev. Chancellor John 155
Vigneaux—15
Voorhies, Bennett J.—110
Voorhies, Cornelius—47, 56
Voorhies, Edward C.—141
Voorhies, E. G.—26, 110
Voorhies, Family of—195
Voorhies, Judge Felix—12, 131
Voorhies, Marcel J.—157
Voorhies, P. J.—157
Voorhies, Dr. R. D.—106, 125, 128
Von Tresco, G.—106

W

Wallace—15
Wallis Home—122
Wallis, Hugh—122
Walnut Grove Plantation—39, 144
Ware, E. O.—207
Warmoth, Gov. Henry C.—65
War Casualties—248, 250
War 1812, Veterans—142
Wartelle, Felix, Indian—9
Wartelle, Victorine—9
Webb—15
Webre—156
Weeks Bay—3
Western Union—119
White, Gov. E. D.—87
White, James—216
White League—65
White, L. E.—46
White League Clubs, List—65
Whitfield, Rosabelle—164
Whittington, John S.—86, 109
Wickliffe, C.—14
Wickliffe, Gov. Robert C.—135
Wilbourn, John—24
Williams, Delphine—9
Williams, Thelma—180
Williams, W. H.—149
Wiltz, Louis A.—70
Wise, Joseph—83
Women's Club—171
Works Progress Admr.—62

Y

Yandle's Soda Fountain—60
Young, A. L.—83
Young, Roy O.—107
Youngsville—73

www.ingramcontent.com/pod-product-compliance
Lightning Source LLC
Chambersburg PA
CBHW021833220426
43663CB00005B/230